PRAISE FOR *LET*

Sarnia Hoyt's memoir is ab[...]
anyone who has lost a mother to mental illness, this book is important.
For anyone who has loved a caretaker as a parent, this book will touch
their heart. For anyone who has lived their formative years in the dark,
separated from the truth of a family crisis, this book sheds light, especially as it opens up the restrictive, controlling mores of the 1940s and
1950s, and puts Hoyt's memoir in meaningful perspective.

—**Mary R. Morgan, LMSW**
author of When Grief Calls Forth the Healing

A delicately written memoir of a daughter whose mother was there, but
not there, and her nanny, who was. Poignant and haunting, the narrative
reveals the unnecessary suffering inflicted on the daughter by the secrecy
surrounding her mother's mental illness and lobotomy, and the lifeline
given her freely by Mady which sustained her.

—**Linda Bird Francke**
*author of The Ambivalence of Abortion,
Growing Up Divorced, and The Gender Wars in the Military*

Sarnia Hoyt skillfully brings to life the strength of her emotional bond
with Mady, the Norwegian nanny who raised her with Nordic sensibility.
Hoyt's love for this other country is natural; she is accepted into Mady's
extended family as "Mady's girl."

—**Aili Waris Flint**
Senior Lecturer in Finnish, Emerita, Columbia University

Sarnia Hoyt had a mother who could not mother. Her memoir movingly
describes her lifelong quest to understand the mother she lost and finally
to embrace the mother she found through letters and medical records.
All the while she attached to the woman who mothered her throughout
her childhood. This tale of two mothers is a love story.

—**Abigail Trafford**
author of My Time, Crazy Time and As Time Goes By

Letters from My Mothers
A Daughter's Memoir

Letters from My Mothers
A Daughter's Memoir

Sarnia Hayes Hoyt

ISBN: Paperback: 978-0-692-11475-9

Edited by Jo Ann Miller

Cover and interior page design by Jeff Brandenburg

Photographs copyright Sarnia Hayes Hoyt

Published by Sarnia Hayes Hoyt

sarnia.hoyt@gmail.com

First printing: 2018

Printed in the United States of America   20181117

For
Didi, Owen, Alex, Sylvia and Marie
and
To the memory of Mady

Canst thou not minister to a mind diseased,
Pluck from the memory a rooted sorrow
Raze out the written troubles of the brain
And with some sweet oblivious antidote
Cleanse the stuff'd bosom of that perilous stuff
Which weighs upon the heart?

WILLIAM SHAKESPEARE
ACT V, SCENE 3 MACBETH

Contents

Acknowledgments

I wish to thank the family members and friends who have generously donated time to read portions of this manuscript. Without their support and encouragement these pages might never have been written. They are Rosalie Byard, Mary Ann Casey, Deborah Condon, Edith K. Davis, the late Richard Eder, Nancy N. Faesy, Ailie Waris Flint, Linda Bird Francke, Edward A. (Ned) Hoyt, Jonathan W. Hoyt, the late Amos M. (Bud) Kidder III, Susan B. Lee, Rosemary MacLeod, R.N., Mary R. Morgan, Nancy Penrose, Beth Rabinove LCSW, the late Whitney K. Robbins, Bonnie Tinsley, Abigail Trafford, Jill Walsh, Jill Walsh, Gertrude Wilmers, and members of the memoir class led by Mindy Lewis, at New York City's West Side YMCA.

I owe an enormous debt of gratitude to members of Mady's family in Norway. They are Anne Kari Axelsen and the late Peder Mortensen in Kristiansand and Magnhild Foreid and Liv and Sigurd Simonsen in Sögne. They offered me valuable information and delicious hospitality. Most important, they opened their hearts to me.

My visits to New Haven, Connecticut, and Watch Hill, Rhode Island, were made possible by Dr. William Sledge and Jane Kellogg, to whom I offer my thanks.

Carolyn Waters, Head Librarian at the New York Society Library, led me to the vast resources available at the New York Public Library and the federal archives on Varick Street. Without her help I would never have been able to track Mady's arrival in America in 1927, find her name on the *Stavangerfjord* passenger list, or read her naturalization documents.

Melanie Daglian in New York and Cameron Barr in Washington D.C. gave me new and deeper insights into the Christian Science faith.

I am grateful to Betsy Smith, whose lecture on mental health at the Cosmopolitan Club in New York opened my mind to stigma's crushing impact.

My late cousin, Kathleen Niergarth Adams, of Lachine, Michigan, provided useful information about my father's early life in Ontario and Michigan.

Technical difficulties with communications between the West and East coasts have been resolved cheerfully by Jason Dare, in San Francisco.

I am indebted to Jeff Brandenburg and Mark Woodworth for their patience, editing, and design help and to Peter Dunckel for his mastery of restoration photography.

Dr. Linda Lewis at the Neurological Institute at New York-Presbyterian contributed her indispensable interpretation of the medical records from Yale University and Grace-New Haven Community Hospital.

Certain names have been changed to protect the living, and any factual errors are my responsibility alone.

Readers may wonder how I could write the scenes from my parents' courtship, or the dialogue from my father's interviews with the medical staff at Yale-New Haven Hospital. I had to give myself permission to imagine what I couldn't prove.

This book would not have been completed without the collaborative help I received from my editor in New York, Jo Ann Miller.

Finally, my husband, Edward L. Hoyt, gave me valuable feedback and steady emotional support throughout the years it took to complete this work.

Sarnia Hayes Hoyt
San Francisco

Prologue
The Norwegian Flag

On sunny days the red, white, and blue Norwegian flag flies above our breezy deck in Maine. I have no Viking blood and I speak only a few words of Norwegian, but down deep I am Norwegian-American. In one of my favorite photos, taken in 2011, I am standing next to a four-fingered troll statue among the fjords of Norway's western coast. There is a reason for my allegiance to the Norwegian flag and my affection for Norway—and it has nothing to do with my ancestry.

Indeed, through my mother, Margaret Kidder, I was born an eleventh-generation American, whose ancestors fought the British at Lexington. My father, Alexander Hayes, grew up in Ontario, Canada, the youngest grandson of Irish immigrants fleeing Ireland during the potato famine. More than anything else he wanted to be an American, so he worked his way through Cornell University, became an American citizen during World War I, and then found work in the finance industry. At age forty-five, thoroughly assimilated, he married Margaret, the woman he loved. My mother came from a well-to-do American family, and she fulfilled his fondest dream. With all the pride and devotion of an arriviste, my father had studio portraits taken of Margaret and me when I was a few months old and again when I was six.

Our family also included Edward Roberts, my mother's English stepfather, who had been confined during the war to his home in Lancashire, England. He had retired early as a cotton broker in the English Midlands. As the widower of my mother's mother, who died in 1921, he was the lifetime beneficiary of a trust my grandmother had set up in her will. Free at last to travel again in 1946, he took the long transatlantic flight to New York City. While his health permitted, Granddad continued to cross the ocean frequently—sailing first class on Cunard liners. For weeks at a time, when he wasn't traveling, he stayed at the Hotel Westbury, a block from our apartment in New York. He complained about the food and service everywhere he went, but he often enjoyed an afternoon cup of tea with my mother. He doted on her and brought her scarves, leather goods, and jewelry from London. When he came to dinner he wore a three-piece suit and dribbled soup on his vest.

In our diversity we were an odd family. But the most unusual thing about us—what set us apart from other families—was the fact that I had a third parent. Mady was a Norwegian nanny who hovered in the background around visitors but who was always front and center in my life. Taking the place of Margaret, whose mysterious illnesses prevented her from functioning as a real mother during my early years, Mady became the mother I was attached to—the woman I loved.

Her name was Petra Mortensen but I called her Mady, a contraction of "Mama" and "Daddy." Trained in Norway as a practical nurse, she came to live in the bedroom next to mine when I was ten months old. I remember she had made a needlepoint pillow for her bed with the word "Norge" stitched on it, and in the corner there was the colorful Norwegian flag. During the Christmas season, as is the Scandinavian custom, she and I lit candles in our rooms and talked about the reindeer from Lapland, which Mady promised would bring Santa to New York. She stayed on after I left for boarding school in 1953, and she became my mother's nurse until my mother's death, when I was in college. Then Mady retired to live in the Weehawken, New Jersey, house she shared with her sister.

Although our home had many photographs of my mother and me, there were only a few of me with Mady. My father, more than a little xenophobic, considered my beloved nanny lower class, mainly because of her unassimilated foreignness—she had little formal

I took this picture of Mady at the Central Park Mall in September, 1951.

education, wore old-fashioned clothes, and spoke with an accent. Yet I bonded with her because she was energetic, loving, and fun—unlike my mercurial mother who, despite her accomplishments as a linguist and a pianist, was passive, cool, and distant. I found my conflicting loyalties disturbing. Mady was my *real* mother even though that idea, far-fetched and illicit, spawned feelings of shame and guilt in me.

Until my late twenties I knew very little about my mother's childhood. She rarely talked about it. My father had told me that my grandfather William ("Will") Magee Kidder had died suddenly when my mother was a toddler. But this meant little to me when I was a child. It was only after my marriage, when I collected the Kidder family memorabilia from storage, that I began to learn about my mother's early life.

The memorabilia included scrapbooks and photograph albums. Rummaging through them in my eagerness to uncover the mysteries that surrounded my mother, I was surprised one day to discover that her father's sudden death, in May 1902, was reported on the financial pages of all the major domestic and European newspapers. I had not known the details of his death, nor had I realized he was such an important figure in the business world. My mother had cut out and labeled each article and pasted them into her scrapbook. At the time of his death she was three years old. He was thirty-seven.

One newspaper account offered more detail than the rest. William Kidder, it said, had packed up his household—his wife, three children, and the servants—and embarked from Hoboken for Liverpool on the ocean liner *Majestic*, heading to Europe for a family holiday. Before leaving he had complained of a sore throat and by the time the ship arrived in Liverpool he was desperately ill with quinsy, a deadly throat inflammation. He was transferred to a hospital in Manchester, where he died a day later. His widow, my grandmother Emily Bliss Kidder, and her three children accompanied his body on the sad voyage back to America. There is speculation in the family that his faith in spiritual healing may have denied him medical care.

Until my grandmother married her English husband, Edward Roberts, in 1910, my mother and her two older brothers grew up fatherless. Their mother, unable to manage her grief so as to be available to her children, left much of the parenting to governesses and other servants. Following the example of her Kidder in-laws, who had joined Mary Baker Eddy's Mother Church in Boston in 1900, my grandmother devoted herself to Christian Science. At age six my mother started Sunday school in the new faith. As long as her mother was alive she attended Christian Science services in Englewood, New Jersey, where the family lived, but after her mother's death she left the church.

My grandfather, the only son of Amos and Lucy Kidder, left his little family well provided for after his death. His father was the founder, in 1865, of the Wall Street brokerage house A. M. Kidder, which had underwritten the shares of a new soap company, Procter & Gamble.

From then on the company and its shareholders prospered. In the 1890s my grandparents built a large white house, called Burncroft, at the northern boundary of Englewood, New Jersey, across the Hudson River from New York City.

Literally "field house by a stream," in a Scottish dialect, Burncroft had thirty-six rooms, with the whole third floor reserved for the servants. It was surrounded by wide lawns, trees to climb, vegetable and flower gardens, a clay tennis court, and a stream that meandered through the property.

During the first three decades of the last century, Englewood had rural charm. The Hudson River was a deep, wide moat and the cliffs of the Palisades, on its western shore, made a thousand-foot wall protecting the northern valley from urban invaders. In the village, horse-drawn carriages delivered ice, milk, coal, laundry, and other household necessities to the large houses. In winter, children went sledding and skiing down the long western slope of the Palisades, and in summer the giant hardwood trees shaded the wraparound porches and turrets of the Victorian mansions. The Kidders, my mother's family, escaped the summer heat during a month by the sea in Kennebunkport, Maine.

Burncroft, in Englewood, New Jersey, was the house where my mother and her two brothers grew up. It had thirty-six rooms and the third floor was reserved for the servants.

In 1931, however, everything changed. The George Washington Bridge was completed, breaching the Palisade fortress that had once protected the northern valley. From then on, more people and cars began flowing across the bridge from New York City into Bergen County. Eventually it would also bring developers to subdivide the properties and tear down many of the large houses. An apartment building replaced Burncroft in 1960.

My mother's father, Will Kidder, married Emily Bliss in 1888. Their first child, born in 1892, was Amos Mansfield, called Mans. Then came Delos Bliss, or Dee, born two years later. And finally my mother, Margaret Emily, arrived in 1898. She was nicknamed Sippy, a child's version of the word "sister." Many people called her Peg or Meggo. My grandfather had attended Amherst College, class of 1885, but he left before graduation in order to develop the bond market in his father's investment banking firm.

Although my mother shared very little about her early life with me, she talked about Burncroft, the house she loved. She had fun there with her two brothers, especially Delos, her favorite. Mansfield became the socialite—outgoing and charming but extravagant— while Delos, handsome, athletic, and popular with women, chose the quieter life of a dairy farmer. As an only child growing up attending an all-girls private school, I had little contact with boys. In contrast, my mother was a tomboy: She played games with her brothers and their friends. She loved sports and the outdoors—they played baseball and croquet and built dams across the stream. On rainy days when they couldn't play outdoors they roller skated and played pool in the basement at Burncroft.

But tennis was always the family's game. All three Kidder children became good players and participated in tournaments. This was hardly surprising, for they grew up watching their athletic Aunt Ethel Bliss Platt, one of their mother's younger sisters, who was a nationally ranked tennis player. In 1906 Aunt Ethel and her partner, wearing long white dresses, won the national women's doubles championship.

As I grew older, I began to hear more about the Bliss girls, my grandmother and her five younger sisters. My grandmother, Emily, was the eldest of the seven girls—Gracie, fifth in the birth order, died as an infant. They grew up in a Victorian mansion called Stonegarth, across the road from Burncroft. They were well known in Englewood for their beauty and musical talent.

By the time I was born, in 1938, all the Bliss women except the two youngest, Ethel and Alma, had died. The Aunt Alma I remember had glacier-white wavy hair and smoked Philip Morris cigarettes, occasionally picking bits of tobacco off her teeth. Her husband, Alex Amend, called her "Skinny," which she was not.

Even though all but one of the Bliss sisters married, four of the five married sisters had no children. My grandmother was the only one to give birth. The Bliss heritage is preserved within the modern Kidder family, where many of my female cousins have chosen "Bliss" as a middle name. One cousin uses "Bliss" as a given name, and another calls her software business Bliss Consulting. I have a granddaughter named Sylvia Bliss Suzanne Hoyt.

I never knew my grandmother Emily, who died long before I was born, but I remember the sepia photograph of her and my mother seated together and holding hands. My grandmother, with a pearl necklace and a confident expression, has her right arm around her shy teenage daughter, who is wearing a soft middy blouse. How lucky Margaret was, I thought, to have such a protector—a mother so

The Bliss girls. From left to right, Emily, Susan, Laura, Bertha, Ethel and Alma. Emily was my grandmother (1866–1921) but I knew only Ethel (1881–1971) and Alma (1885–1971). Emily was the only daughter in the family to give birth.

self-assured and handsome. Her English husband, Granddad Roberts, once told me that Emily was "a fine figure of a woman."

Three of the six Bliss sisters died in their fifties. My grandmother died in 1921 at fifty-five. She followed Aunt Laura and Aunt Susan, who had both died in 1916. Because they were all Christian Scientists, the causes of their deaths were never disclosed, but there is the linger-

My mother and grandmother, Englewood. By the time of this portrait, around 1914, my widowed grandmother had married her second husband, Edward Roberts, an Englishman.

ing suspicion in the family that they were cancers. I often heard that my grandmother Emily's sons, my uncles Mansfield and Delos, were outraged that she never sought proper medical care.

With my grandmother's death, Burncroft passed into the hands of her three children. Uncle Mansfield, the eldest, who had joined his late father's firm on Wall Street, bought out his brother Delos's and his sister's shares, and moved in, together with his second wife, Gladys, and his two children by his late first wife, Lucy Hortense. When my mother moved out of Burncroft after her mother's death, she spent several months at Aunt Ethel's grand Italianate mansion, Ambercroft, before she moved into her own apartment. Throughout her twenties and early thirties, she traveled widely in Europe, America, and around the Mediterranean basin. When she was home in Englewood she did volunteer work and continued her language studies in New York.

At the time of my parents' marriage, in 1934, my mother was thirty-five years old. Both her parents were deceased, and if my father hadn't proposed marriage, she might have become what people then called unmarried women, an "old maid" or a "spinster." While the family may at first have wondered about my mother's choice of a husband, they welcomed the business acumen he brought into my mother's rarefied world as he managed his customers' financial port-folios. He tried hard to get along with her relatives, even her stuffy Presbyterian uncle, Ned Bulkley, who wanted to forbid alcohol at their wedding reception. My father managed to persuade him to serve champagne.

The marriage ceremony took place in the living room of Aunt Ethel's home on Booth Avenue, in Englewood. Uncle Mansfield gave my mother away. Aunt Ethel stood out among all the Bliss sisters. In 1899, at the age of nineteen, she married a brilliant Princeton graduate, Dan Fellows Platt, and together, with no children of their own, they built a large Italian Renaissance Revival mansion inspired by a Sienese palazzo. It was surrounded by spacious lawns, trees, and carefully tended gardens. I remember it smelled sweet because Aunt Ethel kept large pots of orange and jasmine plants in her conservatory off the living room. And as their summer buying sprees to Italy continued every year until the outbreak of World War I, their home became a museum for Uncle Dan's growing collection of Early Italian works of art.

Encouraged by her scholarly husband, Aunt Ethel studied botany, philosophy, literature, and astronomy and became fluent in Italian and French. The Platts' wide social circle included art historians in Europe and America, museum people in New York, other collectors, and Princeton friends.

In May, 1938, Uncle Dan died suddenly of a heart attack at the age of sixty-five. By then Ethel and Alma, the two youngest sisters, were the only survivors of the Bliss family. During the war Aunt Ethel, a widow in her sixties, continued to live at Ambercroft, where I spent several weeks during the summer of 1945, when I was six years old. Then, at the end of the war, higher taxes forced her to break up her husband's art collection. She sold many important pieces to museums in Detroit, Cleveland, and Washington, D.C., with most of the remainder going to the Art Museum of Princeton University.

In the late 1940s Aunt Ethel built a more modest French provincial style house and, beginning in my mid-teens, I often visited her there. She created a meadow behind the house with wildflowers, native grasses, and an organic vegetable garden. A sundial mounted on a pillar on her terrace cast shadows marking the equinoxes and solstices, and a multifaceted crystal paperweight caught the sun's rays, making the light spectrum dance around the ceiling of her living room.

Aunt Ethel had an inquiring mind and could carry on a lively conversation well into old age. On holidays we gathered in her living room for cocktails before we drove to the Knickerbocker Country Club in Tenafly, my father's golf club, for lunch. There Hector, the long-time maître d', made a fuss over Aunt Ethel. He addressed her as "Lady Platt," which made her laugh in the charming, bells-pealing way she had. Her gracious style sharply contrasted with my mother's awkwardness.

My father, one might have said then, came from the other side of the tracks. He was born in 1889 and was raised, until he was twelve years old, in the village of Springfield, Ontario, by parents with Scots-Irish and Irish antecedents. They were Protestants. His father, Henry Hayes, was a skilled barrel maker and an alcoholic. His mother, born Samantha Babcock, was an accomplished quilter. My father was named Tillison Alexander, after his uncle Tillison Babcock, but when he arrived at Cornell in 1910 he reversed his names because he thought Alexander sounded distinguished. And to a man who prided himself on his penmanship, the name Alexander was more fun to write than Till, which, he pointed out, is all straight lines. He liked the fact that he shared the name Alexander with his father's successful brother, Alexander Newland Hayes, who practiced medicine in Sarnia, Ontario, a city near the Michigan border at Port Huron.

My father was the seventh of eight children. Most of them died young, my cousin Kathleen, the family historian, told me, because their father's drinking deprived his children of food and medicines. They supplemented their limited diet with discarded orange peels. My grandmother Samantha boarded teachers and took in the neighbors' laundry. Nina, the oldest daughter, migrated to northern Michigan, where she met her husband, Jacob Niergarth, and raised seven children. I saw my grandmother Samantha only once, when she came to Englewood to celebrate my first birthday.

"Why do you name the child Sarnia?" Samantha asked in a letter to my parents.

"It's an odd name," they would have said. "She will stand out."

"Why don't you call her Roberta? Or Alexandra? They are a little different but not so very odd. I'm afraid that after a while she won't like Sarnia."

"I believe she will grow to like it," my parents must have said.

And so I was named for a city.

My grandmother's accurate prophecy impresses me. She was right. There indeed came a time when I wanted to exchange Sarnia for something less odd.

When my father arrived in Michigan by train from Canada in 1901 he had traveled 250 miles north to live with his sister Nina Hayes Niergarth and her large family. He found work as a much-valued clerk at their general store near the white pine lumber camps, in Long Rapids, Michigan. He worked hard and was able to further his education at Ferris Institute, in Grand Rapids, and gain entrance to Cornell in 1910. In his final college year he worked as business manager of the *Cornell Daily Sun*, the only paid position on the paper. In a college photograph he looked handsome, with his full head of dark hair parted on one side, his regular features, bright blue eyes, and perfectly straight teeth. He graduated with a degree in mechanical engineering in 1914 and then enlisted in the U.S. Army Signal Corps. He became a naturalized American citizen at Kelly Field, Texas, in 1918.

After several jobs in the oil fields and selling encyclopedias, my father traveled east to Wall Street and joined several other bachelors, old college friends, who rented a house in Englewood, New Jersey. In January, 1929, he took a position as a broker with the firm that eventually became Smith, Barney.

~

Mady's early arrival during my first year and her steady caregiving inevitably excluded my mother. Mady and I bonded and played our own version of *Upstairs, Downstairs*. Beginning with my mother's diabetes diagnosis in 1941, and other mysterious illnesses that emerged later, my mother excused herself from a maternal role in my childhood. I have few memories of her. In these circumstances she became redundant, yielding her place to Mady, my psychological mother. That both Mady and my mother continued to live under the same roof much of the time was an unusual circumstance and, for me, a confusing one.

This arrangement, which grew out of necessity, may have been hardest for Mady. As its principal player, she was, in effect, selling her love for me to my father, a desperate family manager who wanted control.

But love plays by its own rules, and he could never have predicted how things would turn out in our family.

Chapter 1

From Englewood
to Manhattan

*F*or years I've tried to understand how my family—with two mothers and a father old enough to be a grandfather—made me who I am. With no siblings to join me in sorting out the mysteries of my family life, and with adults unwilling or unable to explain things, I struggled to make sense of the confusion.

One of my earliest memories, from 1943, was of my father moving us out of Englewood, New Jersey, where my mother had been born and raised, and into an eight-room apartment at the corner of Sixty-eighth Street and Madison Avenue in New York City. I was almost five years old and had never lived in the city, much less in what seemed like cramped space compared to our three-story home in Englewood.

Built in 1911, ours was one of the first apartment buildings designed for families who were tired of managing large townhouses and who wanted something more "modern." When we moved into the city, the postwar building boom had not yet happened, and it was still possible to see the Empire State Building and the RCA tower atop Rockefeller Center from our wide living room window on the sixth floor.

Another reason for the move, my father said, was that wartime gasoline rationing made living in the suburbs difficult. And I believed him, because he showed me how he turned off the ignition so that his Cadillac could coast down the yellow brick surface of Englewood's Palisade Avenue and save fuel. It didn't occur to me then to point out that my friends were also driven around Englewood in cars but they didn't have to move into the city. Their families still used gasoline to bring them to my house to play. His explanation didn't make any sense. Why were we the only ones displaced by fuel rationing?

Years later I would realize that our move had a specific purpose quite different from gas rationing or convenience. My father never said as much to me, but looking back I know he desperately wanted to improve my mother's health. She had been diagnosed with diabetes two years earlier, and we had actually moved to the city to find more medical help. My father expected that once she got well—that is, once she and her doctors learned how to manage her illness so that she had fewer insulin reactions—he would take us back to the country, where he could breathe fresh air, chop wood for the fireplace, and take long walks on the Palisades with our Welsh terrier, Denbigh Dan.

After we moved into Manhattan I began to hear the words "diabetes" and "diabetic." I'd probably heard them before, but now I was old enough to associate the words with the large gram scale on the kitchen counter and the test tubes filled with urine samples. My mother had become insulin-dependent in 1941 at a time when the disease was harder to manage than it is now. It was impossible then to measure blood sugar directly from a blood sample—it had to be done indirectly by testing the urine, which was less reliable. My father hired a nurse to take care of my mother while he was at the office, and one of the nurse's responsibilities was to do the urine tests so that the cook could weigh my mother's corresponding food portions on the scale. As the bright colors appeared in the test tubes full of urine, I liked watching the nurse match up the changing color with a color wheel.

I never saw signs of my mother's illness when we lived in Englewood, and I have only two memories of her there. She took my picture with Denbigh Dan in front of the flower bed. I had wanted to pick some pansies but she told me not to. Another time, I was in the kitchen and she was there too. I wanted some celery sticks, my favorite snack, but she didn't know what they were. I remember crying in frustration.

Back then I wasn't at all sure why we had to move, but I knew I felt bereft. Manhattan had none of the things I loved in Englewood— regular play dates with my friends Barrie and Tommy, the flower beds planted with tulips and pansies, the blue morning glories that climbed a trellis to my second-floor bedroom window, and the warm, damp fragrance of the sandbox. Instead, it gave me the Madison Avenue shops without dolls or toys in the windows, noisy buses, hard side-walks, and gated playgrounds in Central Park. My father also decided that city life was no place for our scrappy terrier. Denbigh Dan had to stay behind in Englewood with new owners.

These upheavals troubled me. And Mady told me that my mother didn't want to leave Englewood, either. My parents might have had arguments about this decision, but I never heard them. I never heard them argue about anything. I suspect my mother simply gave in.

She was probably upset, too, when I spent much of our first winter in New York sick in bed. One after the other, I had measles, mumps, chicken pox, and strep throat. Finally, in May, 1944, I had my tonsils out; Mady took care of all contacts with the doctor. My mother had signed me up for kindergarten in a brownstone a block away from our apartment, but I was rarely there. I recall one school performance when I impersonated the last daisy on stage right, and another time when I refused to climb the long, steep staircase to the second floor. After kindergarten, in 1944, I entered the first grade at the Hewitt School, an all-girls private school on East Seventy-ninth Street. I remained a student there for nine years.

I loved school and my teachers. My mother had selected Hewitt from among the many girls' schools in New York, and I have always wondered why she chose this one. Perhaps she liked the new headmistress, Charlotte Comfort, who was taking over from the founder, "Miss

Hew," as the school acquired credentials to prepare girls for college. She may have even met Miss Hewitt, an Englishwoman who believed that Shakespeare was an adequate curriculum for any girl's education and that math and science were optional. As the step-daughter of an Englishman, my mother must have felt at home with Miss Hew. In any event she didn't think I should be pushed too hard.

After I got settled at Hewitt, with new friends, I began to like living in New York. And soon enough the resilient child in me began to love going to Central Park with Mady. For years my favorite destination was the Mother Goose playground. We entered the Park at Sixty-ninth Street and Fifth Avenue. I would roller skate ahead of Mady, splashing through puddles, then go up a slight incline past a magnolia tree to the tall sculpture of a kind-faced Mother Goose in a conical hat and a billowing cape. Flying astride a large goose, she beckoned me to the oversize swings, the seesaws, and the jungle gym.

The jungle gym was my special joy. Made of cold metal poles stacked in four-foot squares with a turret on top, it offered a way to climb high, get a commanding view, and terrify Mady. I would hang upside down from the highest bars, with my underwear showing. Then I would make my way down and, sitting on a lower bar, I would swoon backward, braced securely with my feet tucked under another pole.

During these maneuvers Mady kept her eyes fastened on me. There was no rubber surface under the jungle gym or the swings to soften a fall.

"That's enough," she would call out. "Come down now." After all, I was somebody else's child, and her responsibility.

By the time we moved into Manhattan, I was deeply attached to Mady. I hardly ever saw my mother—I wasn't allowed in her bedroom when she was there, and my friends and I couldn't play in the living room if she was resting because her bedroom was right next to the living room. For years my supper was served on a tray in Mady's room, so I didn't see my parents at dinner. Much later I learned from my father that when I was small I refused to get in the car if my mother was already seated in it. My father wanted to keep my mother and me apart, and he succeeded.

I did know, though, that in June, 1945, my mother, her nurse, Miss Forve, and I were sent to live with Aunt Ethel in Englewood during Mady's three-week vacation. My father commuted from there to work. Aunt Ethel had probably suggested this visit so that I could go to the day camp at the Elisabeth Morrow School. But shortly after we arrived my mother became very excited; she started talking all the time, her words spilling rapidly out of her. I didn't always understand what she was saying.

One night I was awakened by the wailing of sirens from an ambulance in the porte cochère. I was terrified. Mady was on vacation in Vermont, so I couldn't run to her for comfort. Miss Forve, with her red hair and buxom figure, was a virtual stranger to me. Two men rushed into my parents' bedroom with a rolling cot, loaded my mother onto it, and, followed by my father, put her in the ambulance and drove her and my father off to the hospital. I was six and a half, old enough to understand that she had somehow taken ill, but I had no idea what was wrong. No one explained anything to me.

I stayed on at Aunt Ethel's with Miss Forve; my father visited most evenings after work. He shagged baseballs to me on the lawn as locusts hissed in the tall trees that surrounded the house. No one explained why I was staying with Aunt Ethel or what was going on with my mother or why Miss Forve, and not Mady, was taking care of me. I didn't know where Mady *was*; no one explained her absence. I remember crying, being scolded and spanked, and hating the day camp I was sent to every morning. Soon, though, Mady returned from her holiday and we all went back to New York, while my mother stayed in the hospital.

Nearly seven decades would pass before I could unravel the mysteries of that miserable summer and of the months that followed. But then I only knew that my six-year-old world had turned upside-down and that the person I needed most was not there. A reprieve of sorts came when Mady reappeared and my father drove her and me to a seaside inn in Pine Orchard, Connecticut. Neither he nor Mady spoke about my mother—what was wrong with her, where she was—and I was so relieved to have Mady back that I didn't ask.

In Connecticut, on Long Island Sound, I waded out into the water much too far to suit Mady, and one day at dinner I discovered the sweet-sour taste of cranberry juice. At the end of the war, on August 14th, a fire truck took all the children for a ride to celebrate V-J Day, which marked the end of World War II. Always shy, I was too scared to go on the ride because I didn't know the other children and the siren was too loud. Perhaps it reminded me of the siren I had heard when my mother was taken away from Aunt Ethel's home.

In May 1945—just before the terrible night of the ambulance and my mother's disappearance—my father arranged for a photographer to take a black-and-white formal picture of our little family. Looking at it now, I see that it offers no hint of trouble, but I remember this was the time when my mother was reaching a frantic crescendo of religiosity. She would play "Onward Christian Soldiers" over and over on the piano in the front hall. And she would come into my room at night and talk to me about the Bible. She wanted me to memorize the names of the books of the Old Testament. I only got as far as First and Second Kings. She also urged me to follow the Golden Rule, "Love thy neighbor as thyself." Most of the time I didn't know what she was talking about, but these little chats at bedtime were so new, suggesting such urgency, that I paid attention. For a while we read Psalms 23 and 100 together, and they still remind me of her.

My mother was also determined that I be baptized. Being unchurched was no way to live, she thought, and my father went along with her wishes. A pastor from the Fifth Avenue Presbyterian Church was invited to baptize me at home, and my godmother, my mother's cousin K. Kelly, traveled from Baltimore for the occasion.

The 1945 picture, in its five-inch circular frame, is a serious, unemotional portrait of a family trying to look perfect. We are not engaged with each other—we all look in the same direction away from the camera. My father wears a three-piece business suit with a dark

With my mother and father in 1945. This portrait was taken by the Misses Selby in New York when I was six years old.

tie; my mother has on a brown dress and jacket with pink lapels and a matching corsage. She is also wearing a rope of pearls. Hatless, with her hair pulled back in the fashionable 1940s style, she looks pretty.

Seated between my parents, I am being adorable in my best short-sleeved party dress, a filmy pink frock embroidered at the waist with pale blue thread. My hair is neatly parted and had been carefully curled with Mady's homemade rag curlers. My cheerful smile reveals no tooth gaps in my mouth—they have been airbrushed into obscurity.

I don't know what was going on in my father's mind as he turned his head to the left, following the photographer's instructions. He was fifty-five years old that year, and his hair was thinning on the crown of his head. He desperately wanted my mother to get well again, to be the woman he had fallen in love with. And he wanted her to find fulfillment in motherhood. At that time he was still full of hope, even as he shouldered a heavy burden.

As the years went on, with my father focused on earning his living and taking care of my mother, I depended more and more on Mady's love and attention. I snuggled in her bed on cold winter mornings, listening with her to the news, Arthur Godfrey, or *Fibber McGee and Molly.* She talked to me about the famous Norwegian figure skater Sonja Henie, the trolls, the "three billy goats gruff," and the strange, brown goat cheese (*gjetost*), which she bought at a special deli in Brooklyn. She braided my pigtails, name-taped my clothes, and mended my dolls' clothes. And she telephoned the doctor when my temperature shot up to 103 degrees.

Sometimes we had fierce arguments. Finding the right clothes for cold weather became our winter battleground. She was often chilled and couldn't accept that active children stay warm. There were days when she was never satisfied unless I was wearing the nasty brown leather leggings that zipped up from ankle to thigh or the woolen undershorts she called snuggers. Spring brought a welcome respite from these battles.

But most of the time I depended on her. She, never my mother, was my main confidante. And she gave me encouragement, and reassurance.

"My feet are too big," "I'm too fat," or "I wish I had blonde hair." I would stand in front of the mirror at the sink in the bathroom we shared, scrutinizing the beauty problems I saw.

"But don't you see? You're fine just the way you are," Mady said from her bed, where she was reading the paper.

"Louise invited the Heiss girls to the ice show, and not me. Why didn't she invite me, too?"

"Oh, my, but you're so sensitive."

When I quarreled with my friends, she advised me to turn the other cheek and try to get along with everybody. And on the touchiest, most awkward subject Mady leaned on her Lutheran upbringing. "I don't love my mother," I told her one day.

"Please don't say that. Every child loves her mother."

"But it's true, I don't."

"God will punish you."

I didn't believe her. How could God know?

"I love *you*," I said.

"I know, darling. I know you do." And we left it there.

Even though I studied my mother whenever I saw her, I couldn't have a relationship with her—I felt I had to treat her carefully because of her illness. When I was younger, and she was out of the house, I liked to play on my parents' twin beds and do somersaults between them. Sometimes I would sneak into their room when no one was in there and explore my mother's chest of drawers—Venus hairnets for brunettes, amber beads, multicolored glass bangles, scarves, silk stockings, and lacy lingerie. I had never seen her in a frilly nightgown or fancy underwear, so I concluded that she must have had a different kind of life somewhere else—away from my father and me. And this was puzzling. Where was this other life going on?

Except for the brief period when she tried to teach me about the Bible, my mother rarely came into my bedroom, a dark space with one window looking out on a courtyard. It was the room of an only girl-child, with salmon pink furniture, and it was always tidy. My dolls, stuffed animals, and books sat undisturbed by the brothers or sisters I had longed for but had given up all hope of having. When we first left New Jersey and moved into Manhattan, I learned about the Foundling Hospital on East Sixty-eighth Street. I suggested then, to no avail, that a younger sister might be "found" there. With no siblings to play with, I turned to books.

For a long time, I read the Oz books and had trouble finding all the different books in the series. Mady never contacted a public library, so we limited ourselves to books in print at two local bookstores. I loved Nancy Drew, the Bobbsey twins, and the Enid Blyton Adventure series. But the Oz books, and *Ozma* in particular, occupied a central place in my imagination. For a time Princess Ozma was all I thought about. I kept wishing I could find the peach pit that would transform my life and usher me into a different world.

Even though my mother played no part in my daily life, I felt her presence, especially in the dining room, where her bridal portrait hung on the wall behind my chair. A fashionable 1930s hat, with a veil, was perched at a jaunty angle, covering part of her forehead. A long, single-strand pearl necklace rested on the loose-fitting bodice of a pleated long-sleeved dress, and on her left shoulder someone had pinned a triple orchid corsage.

My mother in her wedding finery, Englewood, 1934. Her dress was a pale beige-pink, not white. I still have its matching purse.

This was not a classic bridal gown, with a cascade of lace framing her face. It was a pink-beige cocktail dress. And there was something remote in her facial expression. Her subdued fashion choice may have been a gesture to the hard economic times she and my father were living through—they were married in 1934, when America was still struggling through the Great Depression. A lavish wedding party would have been inappropriate when so many people were out of work. Later I wondered whether her informal attire suggested ambivalence about the important step she was about to take. Her outfit was not what one might have expected of a woman in my mother's social position, marrying for the first time at thirty-five. Try as he might, the studio photographer never captured a flirtatious bride for future generations to speculate about. What I saw in that portrait was an enigma.

Once my mother became diabetic, insulin and mealtimes organized her life. In addition to her twice-daily injections, she also required a rigid diet of carefully weighed portions. The nurses monitoring her body chemistry tried to make sure she ate all the food on her plate. With practically no physical exercise other than walking in the park, she wasn't hungry, but if she didn't eat enough she ran the risk of insulin reactions. She would need sugar immediately to offset the insulin, or she would lapse into a coma.

One day, when I was a teenager, the nurse went out to do an errand and left me alone with my mother. I saw her eyes glaze over and heard her speech begin to slur. After a couple of minutes she began to slide off her chair onto the carpet. Her dress hiked up around her hips, showing her garters and bare thighs above her nylon stockings. I ran to the kitchen and poured orange juice. The nurse returned in time to hold my mother's head while I put the glass to her lips. She struggled to take tiny sips, and soon the juice worked its magic. Within minutes my mother returned to consciousness as if she were waking from a nap.

In the dining room at lunchtime, when my father was at the office, my mother would spend an hour eating the hot meal the cook had prepared, while I ate my soup and tuna fish sandwich in ten minutes flat. She would shove foods around on her plate with her spoon, sprinkling peas on top of her mashed potato, then move them back to their original position next to her lamb chop. At the same time she would speak so slowly that I would struggle to pay attention. It was often a monologue about the private lives of her favorite TV celebrities—Liberace, Dorothy Kilgallen, and Lucille Ball. Or about one of their programs. Or about someone I'd never heard of. Then, with a toothy grin, she would recount the details of the person's performance with exhausting accuracy.

Shortly before my twelfth birthday, when I was away at summer camp, my mother was moved to a hospital in New Haven. She stayed there until the following spring, and during this period only my father visited her. He took the train from Grand Central after work, returning to the apartment after I had gone to bed. On the days of these visits, Mady and I prepared our favorite meals, like chicken fricassée, and ate in the formal dining room.

After her months in New Haven my mother was transferred to Tenafly, New Jersey. After this move to Tenafly, television began to dominate family life. The living room of the two-story modern house on Oak Street that my father rented was furnished with two easy chairs, a sofa, and a black-and-white twenty-three-inch Zenith. I stayed indoors with my mother while my father played golf at his club. When she turned on the TV we both laughed at Lucille Ball and her predicaments, especially the moment when bread rising in the kitchen pinned her to the wall. But most of the time I dreaded these visits.

My mother and the TV set returned to Manhattan during the summer of 1953, and the TV acquired a central place in our living room. When my mother was home it was almost always turned on. Except for *What's My Line?* with Bennett Cerf, I didn't like most of her programs.

When I was a teenager, home from boarding school for the holidays, my classmates often ate at Hamburger Heaven while I stayed home. During those excruciating meals with my mother, I often wished I could join them. At the restaurant, only a few blocks away, I could have sat with my friends at the wooden counter and salivated with them over the chocolate cakes and lemon meringues displayed on pedestal platters. Instead, I would keep my mother company, with an eye on the ship's clock on the wall. When could I get up and leave the dining room, politely? While my mother droned on I would cross my legs one way, then the other. I would play with the linen place mat, curling and uncurling its corners. I didn't want to hurt her feelings, but sometimes I wondered if she had any feelings to hurt. If she did, she didn't reveal them. She never scolded me. She never got mad. And she never hugged. If I nagged her about fixing herself up, she wouldn't even argue. "Yeth, Puthy Kat," she would say. Finally, after a brief debate with my conscience while she went on talking, I would push back my chair, get up, and leave her alone with her plate of cold food.

One day, when I was enduring one of those endless lunches, I turned around in my chair to look again at her bridal portrait. Twenty years after her wedding in 1934, I could see only the slightest resemblance to her present appearance. Something besides the normal aging process had taken place. She would often spend half the day in her bathrobe without any lipstick, her dark hair as unkempt as the head of a mop, her chest slouched over the table. There was definitely something wrong, and it was not just the diabetes, even though my father used that diagnosis to explain everything.

"Couldn't we take care of Mommy?" I asked my father one day. "Does there always have to be a nurse here?"

"Yes," he said. "The nurses help her to follow her doctors' orders. One day I hope Mommy will be well enough so we can let the nurse go. And then we can move back to the country."

"Why doesn't she follow the doctors' orders?" I asked him.

"She doesn't like doctors," he said. "But she still has to pay attention to what they say."

This was baffling. I had seen the long list of doctors and their phone numbers next to the telephone in the front hall. If she didn't like doctors, why did she have so many?

Whatever it was that kept nurses on the family's payroll, I knew it was a secret that would never be revealed. Sometimes I heard whispers between Mady and the cook—Agnes the Norwegian who was a friend of Mady's, Marie the Swede who got into my father's gin, or Leila the Finn who made delicious biscuits.

"There's something wrong with Mrs. Hayes," they would mutter.

"She's crazy," said Agnes. "I found a stale loaf of bread on the floor of her closet."

The nurses talked about my mother, too.

"She sits in her room all day, doing nothing," I overheard the nurse Marie Clark saying to the cook. Clarkie's penciled eyebrows fascinated me. What had happened to the hair that was supposed to be there?

A Canadian like my father, she was my favorite. We read the Sunday comics together and played double solitaire.

Over the years of living with our family Mady also knew my mother's habits and preferences. She, too, had opinions and, unlike my father, she would share them with me. "It was the change of life," she said. I had no idea what she was talking about.

What was the "it" everyone referred to? No one explained. As a teenager I could only ponder the change that had occurred in my mother between 1934 and 1954. The main difference between then and now, it seemed, was that I had come into the picture. Was there something about me—or motherhood—that had wreaked havoc on my mother?

I didn't dwell on the secrets. I was too worried about my mother's behavior. She would embarrass me with her uninhibited, tactless remarks. One day as she sat hunched over the phone in our front hall, with her legs spread-eagled, she engaged my new boyfriend from Andover in conversation.

"Where do you live?" she asked him as she cradled the receiver.

When he answered, she said, "Why would anybody live in Hackensack? It's an awful place."

I never saw him again.

Another time, a college friend from Ohio, Barbara Apple, came to spend the night with me, sleeping on the daybed in my room. My mother stood at the foot of that bed, with Barbara in it.

"What kind of name is Apple?" she wanted to know. "Are you a pie or a tart?"

Barbara laughed. She was a psych major and she sensed immediately that there was something wrong with my mother. But despite her tactlessness my mother had many fans among my friends. She wrote letters to my roommates when we were at school. And she never rushed off to a meeting or a tennis game the way their own mothers did. She was always available and laughed easily. When Whitney and I and another friend, Nancy, graduated from boarding school, my mother had three large bath towels monogrammed with our initials and the date, June 6, 1956.

"Now you can dry your tears about leaving this school," she told us.

The slightest evidence of normal behavior prompted me to imagine an acceptable mother—a normal mother: someone who had none of my mother's glaring defects. I wanted to see her as part of the circle of class mothers at my school, which included Kathy's mother, a former Hollywood actress with a deep voice, and a pretty strawberry-blonde woman who modeled matching dresses with her daughter, my friend Debbie, for Ipana toothpaste. I thought that if my mother tried, and I helped, she could become a good-looking mom, someone I would want to show off.

There were times when my mother talked about the toughest questions of the modern world. War. Peace. Guilt. Redemption. God. Walter Lippmann's latest column on foreign affairs in the *Herald Tribune*. Sin and corruption. But her volatile nature always took these topics to extremes. During the winter of her intense religiosity, just before my baptism, she took detailed notes on the leaflet during the sermons at the Fifth Avenue Presbyterian Church and worried out loud about the postwar world order. When she spoke, as she often did, about "loving thy neighbor as thyself," I wondered if she was referring to our nearest neighbor across the hall, a Jewish doctor. It seemed to me that my parents didn't have any contact with him except when my mother needed emergency care in the middle of the night. When Jews became the topic of conversation at the dinner table, which was not often, my father would explain that he almost lost the job of business manager at the *Cornell Daily Sun* to a Jewish student. His competitor for the job tried to cheat him, he said. Then my mother would laugh about how many Jewish psychiatrists had offices in our neighborhood.

"They should call it Psychiatric Square," she said.

My mother was a mass of contradictions. In spite of her bizarre behavior and frequently unkempt appearance, she was widely traveled and well informed. In her younger days she had met interesting people and always sat at the Captain's table when she crossed the Atlantic. I knew this because Cunard White Star stickers, with a large initial "K" for Kidder, covered the old brown leather monogrammed suitcase I had found stored in a closet. Captain Rostron, the *Carpathia* captain who had rescued *Titanic* survivors, was her favorite. In her late twenties she had lived for a while in Geneva and attended sessions at the League of Nations. Her French and Spanish expressions, tossed around mid-sentence, placed her among educated, cosmopolitan people who had gone to the right schools and kept up with world events. She purchased French leather gloves for her beautiful hands, which I studied as we sat together on the living room couch. They were the same hands that shuffled decks of cards with a vigorous snap and navigated the piano keyboard, playing a Rachmaninoff prelude with ease. Her large fingernails had a perfect oval shape, which she kept filed with emery boards and lacquered with "Quiet Pink." This was all part of her mystique.

In my fantasies I envisioned my mother as a sustaining member of the New York Junior League. There she would teach English to recent immigrants, lunch with friends, and on the way home stop at a hair salon to have a shampoo and a massage. I imagined the things we might do—play four hands at the piano, speak French, and challenge each other in a set of tennis. We might even take a trip together.

These were all fantasies. None of them ever came true.

In addition to harboring fantasies, I was plagued with worries. I suffered from frequent headaches, which Mady treated with aspirin and a cold compress. Sometimes the headaches were so intense they made me sick to my stomach. Mady would always hold my head in the bathroom. By the time I was six I had become preoccupied with heads, my own and others'.

One day I played with my favorite doll, Diana. She was about two feet high, with yellow hair and bangs, and she lived with me, wearing the dresses Mady and I made for her. I was holding her on my lap when suddenly her head separated from her body and fell to the floor. I screamed while Mady tried to comfort me, and to convince me that

Diana's "beheading" wasn't my fault. But I had seen everything with my own eyes. I knew better. I was powerful and I had done this terrible thing. Diana looked so awful without her head. I had made her lose her mind. Maybe I had done the same thing to my mother and that was why she kept her distance from me.

Not long after Diana's beheading, I heard about a girl my age who fell in the playground and had a concussion. I pictured blood oozing from a crack in her head. Mady heard about the accident from one of the nannies at the playground, but she refused to give me details. A few years later, in history class, I learned about the singular feature of the French Revolution during the Reign of Terror. The guillotine quickly separated the heads of aristocrats and revolutionaries from their bodies when they knelt down on a platform in the Place de la Concorde. This was how *they* lost *their* minds. My mother had lost hers differently, but how or why remained a mystery to me. I spent a lot of time worrying about heads.

About that time, I decided to focus on French history; I was already a good French student. In college I majored in history and minored in French. In middle school I continued to study hard, often staying up late to finish my assignments and memorize irregular French verbs. My homework had to look perfect. Cross-outs were evidence that I wasn't smart enough and needed to work harder. I would rewrite a whole page even if there were only one mistake on it. I developed obsessive preferences about the kind of paper and ink I would use.

My father noticed how studious I was, and he began to worry that I was overdoing it. But I loved school, where I could shine as a star student. Besides reading, going to the movies with Mady, roller-skating in Central Park with my friends, knitting, and practicing the piano, there wasn't much else to do except homework. Sometimes friends invited me for the weekend to their vacation houses in Connecticut, on Long Island, or in upstate New York, but I still spent a lot of time alone.

My father insisted that my studiousness wasn't normal. By this time, I was in eighth grade, well past happier days in elementary school when my father would allow me to pour the cream into his breakfast coffee. "You're the cream in my coffee," he would croon as I mixed the cream with a silver spoon. Now I was becoming stubborn and difficult.

"You spend too much time studying," he would say. "I don't want you to be a bookworm. You have so many advantages, you know. There are other things…"

"But I have homework. And exams. I can't just drop everything," I said.

"Remember Aunt Mary," he said. "She's a good dancer, light on her feet." She was the model he always held up for me to aspire to.

"So?" I said, my temper rising, "You want me to be a social butterfly?"

"No," he assured me. But he made it clear that he didn't want a grind, either. He was starting to think I'd be better off going away to boarding school in the tenth grade, so that my study hours would be limited and I'd have to spend more time playing sports and doing other activities.

Now that many of my friends were leaving Hewitt to study abroad, or moving out of New York, I was getting used to the idea that after ninth grade I would leave, too.

Chapter 2

Mady and Me

$\mathcal{B}$efore I went away to boarding school in the tenth grade, I spent nine years at the all-girls Hewitt School in Manhattan, not far from my home. Of the eighteen girls in my class, I was one of the few who entered in first grade and stayed through the ninth. Many of my classmates had parents in the arts. Vicky Brandt's mother and father owned a literary agency; Debbie Condon's father, Richard, wrote the bestselling *The Manchurian Candidate;* and Liza's father, Howard Dietz, was a celebrated lyricist who, Liza said, sang his songs in the shower. Judy Garland named her daughter after Liza.

One of my closest friends was Katharine Reed, who joined the school in fourth grade. Kathy was pretty, and when we were young she wore her shoulder- length dark hair in ringlets, which I envied. Like me, she was an only child, but her life seemed better than mine: For one thing, she had a cocker spaniel. More important, Kathy's parents, Mary and Kurtis Reed, spent time with us, unlike my parents. They took us to the Ballets Russes de Monte Carlo and to Broadway musicals like *Paint Your Wagon* and *Miss Liberty.* They had a blue convertible, and Kathy and I liked riding to Westchester with the top down for a steak dinner at the family's favorite restaurant.

Mr. Reed, a short, portly man with a big smile and a thick German accent, liked to tease me. Sometimes he called me Helen Hayes, but more often he and his wife called me Sonja Henie, which thrilled me. How did Mr. Reed know that in my dreams I was the blond Norwegian ice skater who had won her first medal in 1928 when she was only fifteen? Did he think of this just because *Sonja* and *Sarnia* sounded similar? Or because our names had the same initials? I hoped he thought there were other similarities—that I could move on the ice with grace. That one day I, too, would be a champion skater. In fact, I belonged to the Junior Skating Club, and I wanted to learn how to do an Axel jump, making one complete revolution and a half in the air between takeoff and landing. Mr. Reed inspired my dreams of becoming a skating star.

Kathy didn't ice skate. She wanted to be an actress, like her mother, a petite woman with short dark hair, a deep voice, and a beautiful face. Kathy and I liked to learn the lyrics to songs from movies and Broadway musicals, so we would go to the Liberty Music Store, a block away from my apartment on Madison Avenue, find an empty listening booth, and play records, making notes.

Along with Kathy's parents we made up rhymes based on the foreign-sounding names of musicians and conductors like Leopold Stokowski, Arturo Toscanini, and Dimitri Mitropoulos. "Skafapoulos Mitropoulos is conducting this afternoon," Mary Reed would call out to us from the kitchen. In the car we played memory games, naming all the musicians we could think of in alphabetical order. At home on weekends the Reeds played classical music on long-playing records, a stark contrast to what went on at my home. My father once bought three records—Ravel's "Bolero," Beethoven's Fifth Symphony, and Gershwin's "Rhapsody in Blue"—to start a small collection. We played all three, and I loved them, but Dad thought he had spent too much money. Maybe he also thought my mother wouldn't like "Bolero," with its insistent sexual beat. He returned the Ravel record to the music store.

It wasn't until I was an adult that I learned the Reeds' full story.

Mary Reed had been born a Russian Jew, and Kurtis came from a cultivated Jewish family named Reifenberg in Berlin. He had an import-export business and met Mary on one of his trips to California. After a successful career on stage and screen as Mary Doran, in the MGM Studios, Mary abandoned the theater when she married Kurtis and moved with him to Germany. Soon, however, they had to seek refuge from the Nazi threat by moving to London, where Kathy was born in 1938. According to her birth certificate she was named Kay P. Reifenberg. They were fortunate that before the Blitz began, they were able to move to safety in New York, where Kathy started school.

One day I was invited to the Reeds' for supper. Kathy's grandmother, who had emigrated with the family from Europe, prepared the meal, and on my plate was a most delicious twice-baked potato flavored with sour cream. The next night at home I raved about this marvelous dinner.

"It was so yummy. Can we add sour cream when we have mashed potatoes?"

"But that's Jewish cooking," Mady said, her eyebrows knitted together in disapproval. "Only Jews use a lot of sour cream."

This was the first time Mady, the Scandinavian immigrant, had expressed her opinion about Jewish refugees. From then on, she couldn't say anything positive about Kathy.

"She copies your homework!"

"We were doing it together," I insisted. "That's what the teacher said we could do."

"*Nei*, I don't think so. Kathy lets you do all the work and then she copies it."

I shrugged. I wondered what Mady had against Kathy. And Jews, for that matter.

"That's typical of those people," Mady added.

I didn't believe her, and I didn't say anything to Kathy.

Mady, unlike my mother, knew all my friends because she was the one who picked me up at other girls' homes or dropped me off for play dates. She knew my friend Louise's mother, Mrs. Santry, and she was impressed by Louise's grand apartment on Seventy-first Street. She knew I had learned to ride a two-wheeler in Louise's enormous bedroom.

No matter what she said, or thought, I loved Mady and her smiling face. When I climbed into her warm four-poster bed on cold winter mornings, we would snuggle together. Sometimes on freezing days she warmed up my school clothes on the hot radiator in the bathroom. She washed and ironed my dresses, cooked my favorite hamburger dinners on the cook's day off, nursed me when I was sick, and read to me even after I could read by myself. When I was tired or upset I could lean into her soft breast and get a warm hug or a soothing backrub. Her breath smelled of coffee as she braided my hair into two pigtails before school.

"*Mitt söte barn*," she would say as she held me tight. "My sweet child."

Mady and I played Canasta, Parcheesi, and checkers. She helped me stir the batter for cookies and brownies and taught me how to knit sweaters and make clothes for my dolls. On my birthday, and at Christmas, she found just the right presents. Later, in my teens, there were gifts with cards signed by my mother, but I was sure that Mady had done the shopping and made the selections. She had found the fourteen-carat gold ballerina charm for my bracelet and ordered the five-year diary with my name on the cover. And she was always the person who helped plan my birthday parties, chartering the bus and chaperoning the whole class to the Ice Capades.

"Mady" was not her real name. According to the American passport she was issued when she became a naturalized citizen in 1936, she was Petra Charlotte Mortensen, born in Sögne, near Kristiansand, on Norway's southern coast. She never married. She had emigrated to America in 1927 to help her widowed sister in Norway support her six children. For ten years the McGraw family—of the McGraw-Hill publishing empire—employed her to take care of their son, Jimmy. Then in 1939, after a long summer vacation in Norway, she moved into my parents' house in Englewood, New Jersey, to become my nanny. I was an infant then, with no memory of the two nurses who had preceded her nor of her arrival at the end of September. The following spring, in April 1940, Hitler's army invaded and occupied Norway, making it impossible for Mady to return home until the end of the war.

Norway's—and Mady's—misfortune was my good luck. During those early years she rarely left me. But even though I spent most of my time with Mady, I knew more about my parents' background than I knew about hers. She would never tell me her age—that was for her to know and for me to guess, she said. Only much later did I learn that she was born in 1893, which meant that in those early years as my nanny she was in her late forties and early fifties.

Around my seventh birthday, long after we had moved into Manhattan, I stopped calling Mady "Nana" or "Miss Mortensen" and started addressing her as "Mady." I pronounced the first syllable to rhyme with "Pa." I didn't like the name Morty, a shortened version of her family's name. And I didn't want to go on calling her anything formal like "Miss Mortensen" or so generic as "Nana," as my father did. I wanted to give her a special name that felt right. Much later, when I was an adult, I realized that "Mady" combined the first syllable of Mama and the second syllable of Daddy: *Ma-dy*.

When I was in seventh and eighth grades, Mady and I would visit my orthodontist once a month on Saturdays. My eye teeth stuck out and my lower teeth were all bunched together. Mady and I would get up early and stand at the bus stop at Madison Avenue and Sixty-eighth Street, waiting for the Number 4 bus, which made every stop in Manhattan for more than a hundred blocks. At the terminal at West 178th Street, we boarded another bus that took us across the river. We were headed to Engle Street, in Englewood, and the office of the orthodontist, Dr. Drews. Counting the time we stood waiting for our buses, the trip could take up to two hours each way. Mady usually had her knitting bag—she was always working on sweaters or mittens—and I brought homework as well as comic books or a Nancy Drew mystery. The trip was still an ordeal.

One cool spring morning when I had an appointment with Dr. Drews, Mady and I were invited to Aunt Ethel's house in Englewood for lunch. We would walk there after my appointment. She lived up the hill on Cedar Street, a long walk from Dr. Drews's office. Mady knew Aunt Ethel from the time when we lived in Englewood, and I knew she found her patrician manners overbearing.

I didn't like Aunt Ethel any more than Mady did. I was afraid that if I spoke she would think I was talking back to her, or that my fear of her would show. She was tall, thin, and fussy, and she hardly ever smiled. Except for Kirsti, her Finnish housekeeper, Aunt Ethel lived alone with her books, her garden, and her telescope, so that on clear nights she could observe the planets and the Milky Way.

At Christmastime when I was young I noticed that Aunt Ethel never gave presents or had a proper tree with glittery balls and tinsel. Instead, she had a pink poinsettia plant. A large portrait of a kneeling angel hung over the fireplace and two-dimensional Virgin Marys with halos around their heads covered her walls in heavy gilded frames. The artists didn't seem to know how to paint lifelike figures. Some of the Virgins had the infant Jesus on their laps; others just sat with their heads bowed. I could never figure out why Aunt Ethel had so many paintings of this mother and child when she had no children of her own.

Before we left Dr. Drews's office, Mady inspected my hands and fingernails. She made me go to the rest room to wash off some ink smudges on my right hand.

"Aunt Ethel will want to see clean hands," Mady said.

"I wish we could go home," I said. "I don't want to go to her house for lunch."

"We won't be there long. And when we get home I'll make you a nice supper."

"But my mouth hurts. The wires are really tight this time."

In the bathroom I discovered I had just gotten my period—I'd been menstruating since the middle of seventh grade. I told Mady, which turned out to be the wrong thing to do.

On our way to Aunt Ethel's house we walked up the tree-named streets, past large brown shingled houses with wrap-around porches, tall hedges, and wide lawns. Elms and oaks, just beginning to leaf out, made a lacy filter for the sunlight.

Our shoes crunched the gravel of the driveway that led up to Aunt Ethel's white-washed brick house. She greeted us at the front door, shaking Mady's hand and giving me a kiss.

"Welcome," she said. "But before you take off your coats, please go admire my daffodils over there, under the pines. Aren't they lovely?"

Aunt Ethel annoyed me the way she always pointed to her meadow and the garden, with bold little flowers claiming her attention. During wartime, when we moved into the city and when Central Park was neglected, I had to abandon flowers and shrubs. How could I love them again? I knew Aunt Ethel would ask me to name the plants on either side of her flagstone walk, and I would fail her test. I was a city child. I didn't know a rose from a daisy.

Mady had already taken her coat off, so she had to put it back on, and in the process she dropped her knitting bag, rolling the large ball of yarn into the flower bed, near Aunt Ethel's feet.

"Watch out, Mrs. Platt," Mady cried. "Let me pick up the yarn before you take another step on the terrace."

But it was too late. Aunt Ethel tripped on the ball of yarn and stumbled against a potted evergreen next to the front door.

"Let me help you, Mrs. Platt," Mady said.

Aunt Ethel stood up straight but she was shaken.

"I think you should put away your knitting, Miss Mortensen."

"Oh, I'm so sorry."

"Now, come in. Kirsti has prepared a nice lunch for us."

She instructed us to hang up our coats in the hall closet and then she ushered us into her living room, where a small dining table near the window was set for lunch. A telescope on a tripod near another window pointed at the sky.

"Don't you want to wash your hands, Sarnia?" Aunt Ethel said.

"That's a good idea," Mady said, nodding at me. "And maybe this is the time for you to take care of something else."

I shot Mady a look of horror as she pulled a sanitary napkin out of her knitting bag.

Aunt Ethel raised her eyebrows. "Has Sarnia already started to menstruate?" she asked.

I was mortified. Mady never explained my period and I was the first in my class to get it. In the beginning I thought I was dying. "You're too young to know what it is," Mady said. "I'll explain it when you're a little bit older."

But now the cat was out of the bag—the napkin had emerged—and here Mady and Aunt Ethel were discussing my big secret as if they were entitled to talk about my private life. I wanted to go home and call Kathy.

As I headed down the hall to the guest room I began to feel sick to my stomach. I made it to the bathroom, though, and there I sat down, trying to think about something besides how nauseated I was. And how mad I was at Mady. I must have stayed quite a while because Mady came and knocked on the door.

"Well? Are you coming?" she asked. "Aunt Ethel is waiting for us."

I sat, trying to stop feeling miserable. I could feel my heart pounding.

"Have you put on the napkin?"

"I'll do it right now."

Mady went back to the table and I followed. Kirsti had prepared fresh asparagus and soft-shelled crabs. Aunt Ethel explained I was supposed to eat the whole crab, shell and all.

"You're going to love these, Sarnia," she said. "Here, squeeze a little lemon on the crabs."

I love lemons. But this time the acid juice hurt my mouth where the dentist had poked around. I pushed the crabs aside and sat in my chair staring at my full plate while Mady and Aunt Ethel talked about me. Eventually I ate the asparagus but my soft-shelled crab went back to the kitchen, untouched.

In my late teens I grew closer to Aunt Ethel. When I took art history in college, I began to appreciate the medieval paintings and the Modigliani drawings on her walls. I respected her knowledge of botany, astronomy, and poetry. Sometimes, though, she threw me a curve ball. I remember one conversation that began with "Santayana. Have you read his study of Descartes?" But that day when Mady and I had lunch with Ethel sticks in my mind. We were never invited together again. And it wasn't just because I got sick and couldn't eat my lunch.

It turned out that my father had arranged that lunch for a reason. He had asked Aunt Ethel to meet with Mady to discuss my future. Becoming a parent for the first time at the age of forty-nine, he had always relied on my mother to navigate the socially correct circles of Englewood, where she had been born and raised. Now, in my mother's absence, he was turning to her patrician aunt for advice. Once he had consulted her about Persian rugs for our living and dining rooms. Now she was to advise my father about whether I should continue to live at home or go away to boarding school. If I stayed at home, could someone with Mady's limitations teach me what I needed to know?

Aunt Ethel must have found Mady wanting. She would have noticed Mady's weak command of English and her ignorance of the English names for common flowers and birds. Her failure to expand my horizons by taking me to the Metropolitan Museum of Art or the Frick Museum was another shortcoming. If Aunt Ethel had asked her about the Met, Mady would have said that she had never been there. And if she had, she would have been uncomfortable among the nude statues in the Graeco-Roman galleries.

If anyone had asked me about Mady when I was fourteen, I would not have mentioned her English. To me she spoke perfectly clearly as long as she wasn't speaking Norwegian. Instead I would have complained about what happened on a cold winter day at the end of December 1952, when she took me to the Caruso Salon, in midtown, to have my braids cut off.

For many years Mady had been my hairdresser—washing, drying, braiding, and occasionally trimming my hair. Then I learned to wash and braid my hair myself, sometimes looping each braid around and pinning it under the other with a barrette. Even though I was always "the girl with the braids"—they were an important part of my identity—I had decided to cut them off because they made me look like a third grader. At fourteen, with the body of a grown woman, I was interested in boys and I was going to dancing school. I wanted to look more sophisticated.

I had never been to the Caruso Salon and I didn't know how Mady found it. It was a smelly place with many older women getting shampoos and sets, haircuts, coloring, and permanents. When we arrived, some clients were seated under giant chrome helmet-dryers. As the youngest client, I felt out of place.

The hairdresser who cut off my braids gave them to me to take home in a plastic bag. Then, with instructions from Mady, he gave me a permanent wave.

"I don't want a permanent," I protested.

"But you have to do something," Mady said. "Your hair has some natural wave but it's not curly. It will be easier to manage this way."

Before my haircut, I had successfully resisted a number of her ideas. She opposed brassieres, but I knew I needed to wear one. She disapproved of makeup—women who painted their faces were headed down the wrong path in life, she said. But I insisted on wearing Tangee lipstick, which was clear when it went on my lips but gradually took on color. Mady also opposed smoking, alcohol, sunbathing, chewing gum, and candy. She never touched a drop of alcohol, although in her later years she often sipped sherry before lunch or dinner.

It turned out that Mady was right about many things, especially sunbathing and smoking, but she was wrong about the permanent. The operator left the chemical solution in my hair too long before applying the neutralizer. The result was a pageboy style with curls so tight I couldn't get a comb through them. I thought I looked ridiculous, nothing like what I'd imagined. I was self-conscious enough about the way my body was changing, and this haircut made things worse.

I cried quietly as the stylist fluffed my hair with his hands. "There," he said, looking at us both in the mirror, "isn't that prettier than those long pigtails?" I tried to smile, but tears were running down my cheeks. The following summer, just before tenth grade, I had most of what was left of the permanent wave cut off. From then on, I figured out a way to curl my hair in clippies at night so that I had a page boy.

My hair was short and curly when I traveled to Europe for the first time, in 1953, with my favorite teacher. Barbara McDonald had arrived at the Hewitt School in 1951 to teach American History, Latin, and Current Events. I was in the eighth grade. She was tall, slim, and pretty, with curly blond hair and blue eyes. She didn't have a brogue but she was thoroughly Scottish in her reserve. She often wore pleated tartan skirts to school. With her sense of humor and sparkling good looks, Barbara quickly became a favorite teacher.

The following year, Barbara taught ninth grade Current Events. Right after Christmas vacation, she announced that she would lead a group of students to Europe next summer, in 1953. She had spent her junior year abroad studying German in Zurich and she wanted to return to see the Swiss family she had lived with. She also wanted to work on her French. And I wanted to work on mine, too.

I was curious about seeing the Alps that Caesar had struggled across and the Eiffel Tower Kathy had visited when she went to Europe with her parents. I wanted to take this trip with Barbara and see what my mother had seen. After years of studying French, I could finally visit France and hear the language spoken.

My father liked my summer plans. They solved a problem for him—what to do with me while my mother was making the transition from Tenafly back to Manhattan. But before he would okay the plan he wanted my mother to meet my new chaperone. He decided to drive Mady, Barbara, and me to Tenafly, where we would have dinner at his golf club. And because this was an important family decision, Aunt Ethel was to join us.

I was nervous about the dinner plans, even though they had developed out of my own wishes. When we got into the car I realized I'd never sat so close to Barbara before—the space between us in the back seat was charged with my anxiety. I wondered what we would talk about as we headed up the West Side Highway to the George Washington Bridge. Barbara would learn much more about me at this dinner than I was comfortable sharing. She would certainly wonder about Mady, and why I needed to have a nanny. And why my mother was living separately from my father, as if they were divorced or separated. And then there was always the awful possibility that my mother would look unkempt and ask Barbara silly questions. But, I reminded myself, at least Aunt Ethel could be there to handle the awkward moments.

"Where are we going, Sarnia?" Barbara turned to me with a lipsticked smile. I noticed the crookedness of the front teeth in her lower jaw. Maybe she should visit Dr. Drews, I thought.

"Tenafly," I said.

It was a reasonable question to ask, but she looked puzzled.

"Next to Englewood. Across the bridge," I added.

"Do you have a house there? On weekends?"

I hesitated. I didn't like this conversation. How could I explain about my mother and her temporary home in Tenafly? The house I hated to visit. The situation was so strange and complicated.

"It's a rented house," I said finally. "My father couldn't find what he wanted in Englewood, so he picked this place in Tenafly." I tried changing the subject. "I've always wondered how 'Tenafly' got its name," I remarked.

There. Maybe I got things going in another direction. This was a kind of intellectual inquiry, and maybe Barbara, the history teacher, could figure out an answer.

"It's probably the English corruption of a Dutch name," Barbara said. "I think the Dutch settled this area. Very early, of course."

At last. We made it into the history of northern New Jersey, away from my mother.

"Oh, yes, and later George Washington came through with his troops."

"George Washington slept here—and there!" By this time Barbara and I were laughing.

Over dinner at the club I learned that Barbara expected at least two other students to come with us. What I didn't know until later was that I was the only Hewitt student to sign up for the whole trip. Once our group arrived in Southampton, the two other girls left us to visit their English relatives while Barbara and I continued traveling alone. My father felt it was so important to keep me away from home during the first few weeks after my mother's return to New York that he paid all of Barbara's expenses to Europe as well as mine.

I hated leaving Mady in New York, but I was so excited about sailing to Europe that once we left New York harbor I didn't think much about her.

Some of Mady's letters to me from that summer have survived:

June 20, 1953

I hope the Dramamine did work, so that you now can enjoy the trip. You were looking a bit pale and I am afraid you did not feel too well, neither did I. Always a little sad to part.

June 24

Thinking of you all day. Now you are halfway across the ocean and I hope you have lots of fun.... Mother and Mrs. Myer went shopping. I made chicken fricassee, junket and chocolate cake for dinner. Everybody happy. A goodnight kiss from Old Mady. Xxx I miss you very much. The house are not the same without you.

July 6

Great disappointment. No letter from Sarnia. I suppose you see and hear many new things that it is hard finding time for letter.... I am going on my vacation together with Lydia, a trip to Montreal. Love, Mady

Barbara and I docked in New York after a rough return voyage in early September. She was going to return to the classroom while I prepared to go away to Miss Porter's School.

"Please write after you get settled at school," Barbara said as we hugged each other. I would be leaving for boarding school in two weeks. "I want to hear how you get along."

I promised her I would write. And I kept my word. In my letters I told her about my new teachers and my roommates. I was behind in Latin, I wrote, but ahead in French. I was sorry not to have any vacation until December but I hoped to see her then.

Summer vacations always challenged my father to find a way for me to have a good time away from home. The 1953 voyage to Europe with Barbara gave me a good chance to use my French. And I think my father was pleased that I had fun. Now, new adventures awaited me as I packed my trunk to go away to school in Connecticut.

Chapter 3

The New Girl

The fall that I turned fifteen, I drove with my parents and Mady to Miss Porter's School in Farmington, Connecticut, where I was to start tenth grade. My mother had been a student there forty years earlier. This was not the first time I'd left home, so I wasn't afraid of being homesick. But going away to school was different from going away to camp. In boarding school I'd have a busy schedule outside the classroom. I'd have to play a team sport and join the glee club or the drama club. Would evening study hall be long enough that I could finish my homework before lights out?

I sat in the back seat next to Mady, both of us watching in tense silence as the new fall colors flew past the windows. Questions ran through my mind. Would I like my roommates? My teachers? I kept wondering if I'd made the right school choice. More than a year before, when I was in eighth grade, my father and I took a day trip to visit three schools. Our first stop was Miss Porter's. During my interview with Mr. Johnson, the headmaster, I kept looking at the solemn portrait of Sarah Porter, in a black dress with a white lace collar, which hung over the mantelpiece. What sort of a woman had founded this school for girls more than a century ago? And why was there now a man in charge of it? Still, I liked him and his friendly smile. He seemed interested in my life at Hewitt and my job as editor of the ninth-grade quarterly newspaper. And I liked the two smiling girls who showed me around the school. They wore heavy oxford shoes and they answered my questions as they pointed out the historic colonial houses converted into dormitories or classrooms on both sides of Main Street. They seemed happy at the school, so it was easy for me to think I would be, too.

Being my mother's legacy at Farmington was not foremost in my mind then, but later I thought it would be good to go to her school because it might encourage her to pay more attention to me.

Now, in 1953, driving to Connecticut more than a year later, I started to feel nervous as we saw road signs for Farmington. The school had informed us that I would have two roommates, and I thought three in one room was too many. Two could gang up on the third and make her life miserable. Thinking about this gave me a pain in the pit of my stomach. I didn't want to be that third girl. My experience had taught me I was different from other girls my age and an easy target. I had an unusual family, with two older mothers; I lived in a city apartment; I had no pets or brothers and sisters; we had no summer home to talk about; and I didn't do any team sports at a country club or a country day school. I had an odd name and except for two winters of weekly dancing classes, a shipboard romance with a boy from a public school, and flirting with dancing-school partners, I had very little experience with boys. They were curiosities who made me nervous and excited at the same time.

We arrived in Farmington on time. After my father parked the car on Main Street, we pulled my suitcases out of the trunk and climbed the stairs to my room on the second floor of Ward, a large white classical Greek-revival building that housed fifty girls. My name was listed on the door of my room, together with two other names: Mary Ann Bickford, from New Haven, Connecticut, and Whitney Kemble, from Wenham, Massachusetts.

"Wenham!" my mother exclaimed when she saw the sign. "That's where Grandma and Grandpa Kidder spent every summer."

This was news to me. I had never heard my mother talk about Wenham or her grandparents. On a school campus already familiar to her she seemed to come to life as she watched the other new girls milling around with their parents. For the first time I realized my mother knew how to behave. She looked presentable, too, in a navy blue suit and blue leather pumps that were probably uncomfortable— she always had shoe problems.

One of the windows of our corner room looked out on Main Street and the other window faced Main Building, next door. But even with two windows and cross ventilation this was a small space for three girls: there were three iron beds made up with pastel spreads, but there were only two desks and two bureaus. A third bureau, we discovered, was hidden in the clothes closet, but there was no third desk. Would I have to be the odd one who wouldn't get a desk? And if I didn't have one, wouldn't it be hard to do my homework? My worries were starting to pile up.

"Well," said Mady. "You're never going to be lonely!" It was typical of Mady to see the good side of any situation. I decided to try to stop worrying.

My steamer trunk, with its old European hotel stickers, had already arrived and stood outside in the hall. When she saw it, Mady dropped to her knees, unlocked the hasp, and started unpacking and putting away my clothes. I left the room and wandered up and down the hall-way, gazing at the names on other doors. Meanwhile, my father paced back and forth between the beds in my room while my mother made a half-hearted attempt to help Mady organize my clothes.

When I got back to my room I found that the Bickfords and the Kembles had arrived. They were studying the names on our door and chatting with my parents and with each other. There were introduc-tions all around, and my mother spoke about Wenham with Mrs. Kemble. I was relieved to see her carrying on an animated conversa-tion. Ever since she'd returned from Tenafly to live with us, she'd been passive and subdued, easier to be around. I noticed she had trouble making simple decisions, but she was also more cooperative when someone else came up with a plan. I often found myself wondering if something had happened to her in New Haven and then in Tenafly that had changed her personality. Neither my father nor Mady would talk about it. And now here she was conversing comfortably with the Bickfords and the Kembles.

While the parents were getting to know each other, I took a good look at my roommates. Mary Ann Bickford had short wavy dark hair, blue eyes, and interesting angular features. She was tall and athletic, with a deep, loud voice, and she impressed me immediately as someone who knew how to get attention. I was sure she would never be that "third girl" whom others would gang up on.

"Sarnia. What kind of a name is that?" Mary Ann asked.

"Who is that unpacking your trunk?" her mother wanted to know. "Is that your grandmother?"

"No," I said. "She's not my grandmother. She lives with me and my parents." I didn't know what else to say. I hated being seen as someone so different from everybody else—someone who still needed help like a child. Why else would Mady be providing it? She often told me I acted helpless. But I knew that the way to get her to take care of chores I didn't want to do was to act as if I was indeed helpless. Now I wanted to seem independent and grown up even though deep inside I felt nervous and unsure of myself around so many new people. I didn't want to be known as the girl with a nanny.

Mady went on putting things away. She explained that she was hanging up my skirts on special hangers in the closet and had put blouses and sweaters in the bureau drawers. She had even put Bruno, my dark brown teddy bear, on the bed by the window that Mary Ann had already claimed with her tennis racquet. I could see the situation was getting complicated, that it would be better for me and my room-mates to work things out for ourselves.

"Stop!" I said to Mady. "I'll do it."

Then I told my parents it was time for them to leave—to drive back to New York so I could begin my new life. I was so busy I hardly noticed that they left.

Later that afternoon Whitney and Mary Ann said they thought my name sounded Russian. They had watched Mady hunched over my trunk, and they thought I might be royalty with a personal servant. They had not expected to room with royal blood and they had no idea how to treat me.

"Are you a Russian princess?" Whitney asked me.

Me? Anastasia, the lost princess? What an idea!

Kiss my ring, I wanted to tell them. Then I thought, I don't want anything to do with Russia. The Russians want to knock us off the planet with their hydrogen bombs.

"No," I said, smiling. "I'm not a Russian princess. I'm not royalty." I hoped that would settle the matter.

Within a couple of weeks after school started I got a letter from Mady. She missed me:

My darling Sarnia,

We all have been so very anxious to hear from you. Well today the letter come, but not in time for Daddy and Mommie, they left this morning about 8:45, but I will hurry and get it in the mail right away and perhaps it will be waiting for them when they arrive in (Sea Island) Georgia. I will not ask you for a letter, because I know how busy you must be, but if you think of me and have a few moments, well you know how I love your letters.

Send a few word soon darling.

Affectionate,

Mady

Although we corresponded, I didn't see Mady or my parents until I went home for the winter holidays. There was no break in classes between September and Christmas. Farmington had a tradition of keeping us at school for new-girl initiation during the week just before Thanksgiving. During these four days old girls did not speak to us; they frowned and looked mean, as if we were a collective embarrassment to the school and should be expelled.

Before lunch on Thanksgiving Day there was the old girl–new girl field hockey match that the demoralized new-girl team usually lost. As we sat down to eat our first course of the Thanksgiving meal, the dining hall was silent except for the ominous clinking of spoons on our bowls of canned fruit cup.

Then suddenly it was over. With great fanfare the old girls jumped up from their seats and rushed over to the new girls they had hazed for four days. There was hugging and screaming and laughter and tears. Afterward, Mary Ann, Whitney, and I decided this initiation was an unfortunate tradition that brought out sadistic qualities in some girls, upsetting many others. It turned out that we were not the only ones who felt that way; soon after we graduated the custom was discontinued.

By Christmas vacation, when I went home on the train, so much had happened it was impossible to share all of it with my three parents. I had begun to separate from them and form new friendships.

As I studied the other girls and learned their names, I began to see the school differently. I was happy to have left Hewitt, where the older girls chewed gum, cinched their waists with elastic belts, wore lipstick and heels, and met boys on the sidewalk after classes. Here, the girls seemed younger, more polite and cheerful. Everyone had a favorite stuffed animal on her bed and wore a crazy hat when it rained. New girls held the heavy outside doors for old girls. "Hi, hi," they would say with big grins. They didn't wear uniforms or lipstick and didn't dress as if they were going out on a date.

In the 1950s there were rules about having a Saturday afternoon date with a boy on school grounds. Mrs. Johnson, the headmaster's wife, would put the boy's name on a list, and precisely at 2 p.m., with lipstick carefully applied and a little powder dusting her cheeks, the girl would meet her caller at the headmaster's house. For two hours she could escort him around the Gundy Loop and other prescribed village paths, and by 4:30 they would return to the headmaster's house for tea and cookies. Then, promptly at 5:30, he would leave.

Would I ever have boys call on me on a Saturday afternoon? I hoped so. But before that, I wanted to meet more girls my own age, to make new friends. Looking around at them during daily prayers and announcements, I admired them. Many girls in my class and ahead of me were pretty. Most of them dressed neatly according to the unofficial dress code, which Mady and I had misinterpreted when we bought new clothes and packed my trunk. I didn't know that the "long-sleeved shirt and sweater" suggested in the school guidelines really meant a Brooks Brothers button-down men's pastel long-sleeved shirt with a Shetland long-sleeved pullover or cardigan. The red and green plaid polo coat Mady and I had picked out at Bloomingdale's was all wrong. No one wore anything except a camel's hair polo coat, preferably with a boy's striped school scarf in the colors of Groton, Brooks, Harvard, or Yale. The girls wore knee socks, plaid skirts, and heavy lace-up shoes called Abercrombies. Many were athletes who had played field hockey, basketball, and tennis at their country day schools.

I tried to imagine what the girls' homes and families were like. And after visiting one of my new friends, Nancy Niles, and meeting her parents and her brothers, I was amazed at the differences between their home and mine. Nancy said she liked to visit me in New York because our cook squeezed fresh orange juice for breakfast; I liked going to see her in the country. In the winter we could ice skate on the frozen pond behind her house.

One summer I visited Mary Ann's family at their summer home on Saranac Lake, in the Adirondacks. My mother was eager to know everything about my visit with the Bickfords, because when she was growing up she had visited her cousins, the Bulkleys, at their camp on Lake Placid, not far from Saranac. I took an all-day train trip to the Saranac Inn post office, and the Bickfords' caretaker came over by boat to pick me up and take me to Pine Rock Camp.

From the moment I saw the boathouse, with its long dock and the large log-cabin-style building above it, I knew Pine Rock Camp was the most marvelous place I'd ever seen. Mary Ann and her two younger sisters slept dormitory style in a big loft on the second floor of the boathouse, and there was an extra bed for me. Her two younger brothers slept in the big house, near their parents. A large brass bell summoned us to the meals, prepared by a cook named Lenz, who baked cookies every day. There was a tennis court, canoes, rowboats, and a motorboat to take us water skiing.

I had never water-skied before. When Mr. Bickford arrived in the Bethlehem Steel company plane for the weekend, he slipped into the power boat, fitted me out with a well-worn pair of water skis, and whisked me around in front of the camp, calling out instructions about how to stand up on the water. Mary Ann was already expert.

My visits to Mary Ann and Nancy and my experience at Farmington showed me family life that was very different from mine. I had trouble finding words for what was happening, but I knew I was eager to become a person who fitted into this world, with friends like these smiling girls. I, too, wanted to have an attractive boyfriend from a correct school like Groton, St. Mark's, or Exeter, and I wanted him to call on me and have tea and cookies at the headmaster's house on a Saturday afternoon.

During my three years at Farmington, my mother reentered my life. Our school had brought her out of the shadows into a more active maternal role. I began to understand the importance of attending the same school as my mother during my first semester, when the legacy students were photographed together in front of a white picket fence. We were identified as the daughters, granddaughters, cousins, or nieces of "Ancients," the term they used for Farmington graduates. At first it seemed silly to me. But after a while I felt reassured. It confirmed my place in this new world as my mother's daughter.

Each term my parents drove up to Farmington to take my room-mates and me out for lunch. Mady stayed home in New York. I had always wanted a nice-looking mother, just like my friends' mothers, and my mother had begun to pay more attention to her clothes and her hair. My hopes for her were being realized. My friends had no idea about my mother's history; by this time her behavior and appearance seemed more normal, and she endeared herself to them by writing them letters. Yearning for mail from home and from prep-school boys, my friends gave my mother high marks.

What interested her most was my complexion. My roommates and I were embarrassed about having pimples, and my mother found a little white plastic tube with a black stopper that was supposed to remove blackheads. Whitney called it "the pimple popper," and we all took turns using it. My mother continued to win over my friends.

At home she was concerned about my health. She would make appointments with doctors for me, but she never accompanied me. And she would write little reminders on "Don't Forget" pads, giving me the names, addresses, and phone numbers of a doctor's or dentist's office. "Leave early," a note would say. "Don't forget to thank the doctor for squeezing you into his busy schedule!"

Then there were the instructions about personal hygiene.

"After bathing take time to dry between your toes—to prevent athlete's foot."

"Don't forget to use your dental retainer at night."

"Wash your face at night with Phisohex [an antibacterial soap in a green plastic bottle] to prevent pimples."

In the middle of all her fussing about personal care, there might be a quote from an inspirational speaker. Cleanliness and godliness were high on her list; Norman Vincent Peale and Billy Graham were her favorites. She often ended her letters with "Read your Bible!" or with quotes from Mary Baker Eddy in *Science and Health with a Key to the Scriptures*, the bible of Christian Science.

Depending on my mood, I found my mother's new persona either interesting or irritating. Sometimes she was an uninvited guest, someone I had to put up with and be nice to. She had missed her chance to establish a close relationship with me—I already had intimacy with Mady. But to humor her, I listened and enjoyed watching her contacts with my friends.

As I approached my eighteenth birthday, in 1956, and my freshman year at Vassar, my mother got caught up in the old-fashioned ritual of presenting me to society. I was making my debut just as she had in 1916, in Englewood. Coming out was a common practice then for many girls in New York and New England private schools. The Plaza, the Pierre, or the Waldorf Astoria hotels were the setting for large charity balls held during the winter and spring school vacations. Girls invited boys to be their escorts, and additional boys on the organizers' lists joined the stag lines so they could cut in and give girls a nonstop whirl on the dance floor. Dance orchestras led by Meyer Davis or Lester Lanin added to the festivities, which could go on until one or two in the morning. If a girl's parents could afford the fees, the long white dresses, and the gloves, they had the satisfaction of knowing they were making a tax-deductible contribution to a reputable charity while nurturing their daughter's social prospects at a marriageable age.

My mother couldn't stop talking to her out-of-town relatives about my adventures on the dance floor—the color of my dress, where I dined before the dance, and whom I danced with. After years of neglect it was as if she was discovering me for the first time. And she was getting a vicarious thrill from my social life. For my father, too, my coming-out year was proof that he had achieved his goal of helping my mother recover her health and giving our family the appearance of normalcy. It was as if the emperor had new clothes and they fit perfectly.

For me, coming out meant a more active social life in New York. Isolated from boys at all-girls schools and now heading to a women's college (Vassar did not admit men until 1969), with no teenage cousins or family friends who had children my age, coming out gave me the opportunity to meet young men. It also allowed me to continue seeing my friends, some of them women in my college class, over the holidays. When I wasn't at a dance I could be on a date with a boy I'd met at a dance the night before.

I met Sam Brown at a coming-out party. He was a wrestler and a hiker from New Hampshire, and a sophomore at Yale headed to medical school. Known to many of his friends as Uncle Sam, he had a wise, avuncular manner and a deep resonant voice; it was fun to kiss him and be kissed back. I would linger anxiously near the phone at home or at college, waiting for him to call and say he was coming up to see me. He agreed to be one of my two escorts at the Junior League Ball, to be held on the Wednesday evening before Thanksgiving.

I was excited that Sam would accompany me, but my excitement didn't last long. We were having a beer in New Haven before the November Yale–Dartmouth game when Sam shifted uncomfortably in his chair and said he had something to tell me. I leaned forward expectantly. He stared into his beer and confessed that he was in love with his roommate's sister, Nancy, and he said she was coming to the Junior League Ball as a guest of one of her friends from another college. I hated this idea and I was heartbroken that Sam was in love with another woman.

My brief romance with Sam was over. But later that same month, I met a man like none other I had ever known—or would know again. Johnny Apple's real name was Raymond Walter Apple, Jr., but everyone called him Johnny. His younger sister, Barbara, was a new friend and classmate at Vassar who lived down the hall from me. Early in December she and her brother planned a blind double-date with Fritz, a friend of Johnny's. We four went out for dinner at The Stone Chimney, one of the many red-and-white-checked tablecloth eateries in Poughkeepsie that catered to the college crowd, and Johnny ordered his favorite gin martini on the rocks. Immediately I could feel the connection between us.

Johnny and I had many more dates over the next year. Brilliant, funny, literate, and outrageous, he was larger than life. Large in body too—but he was not at all embarrassed about his physical bulk. He had a deep cleft in his chin and a short, dark crew cut. He collected friends and ideas the way other people collect recipes or pennies. He loved surprising me with gifts: perfume—Shalimar was his favorite—costume jewelry, special delivery letters, and sudden appearances. In his letters he played with words on the page as if they were his favorite toys.

When I first met him, Johnny lived in New York and worked as a reporter for the *Wall Street Journal*. He had flunked out of Princeton because he had spent too much time working on the campus newspaper, *The Daily Princetonian*, before Alger Hiss, the alleged Communist spy, was scheduled to speak at the university. When the college administration wanted to cancel Hiss's talk, Johnny wrote passionate editorials about free speech and the First Amendment.

In his early twenties, Johnny knew what he wanted. The family grocery business—and his father—awaited his return to Akron, Ohio,

With Johnny Apple, the New York Infirmary Ball, the Waldorf Astoria Hotel, December, 1956

where he had grown up, but he had other plans. He wanted to write for *The New York Times*. He wanted to be the next James Reston, the much-respected foreign affairs columnist. And his ambitions came true. He had a distinguished and colorful career at *The Times* for more than forty years, as an associate editor, chief correspondent, and Washington Bureau Chief. He was also known for his food articles, and he published several well-received books about travel and food.

Shortly after our first couple of dates I was overwhelmed to receive a love letter.

> *The best expression that I can give to the way I felt on Saturday night as I left Grand Central Station is on the record player right now. It's Toscanini's record of Siegfried's Rhine Journey from "Götter-dämmerung": you first hear strings building in volume and intensity; then, of a sudden, there's a beautiful crescendo from the trumpets and other brass — it sounds like a complete expression of human joy. That's the way I felt; that's the way I feel. I hope perhaps you sense a little of the same thing; for it's a wondrous emotion when you feel so exulted that you think you may at any moment burst right through your skin.... It was the best night I ever remember having spent with anyone, anywhere.*

A month later he wrote: "It all adds up, I guess, to the fact that I am very very much in love with a very very wonderful woman—you."

I was thrilled about being with him, but I worried about sustaining this relationship and keeping up with my coursework. Johnny agreed that I should study on Friday nights and Saturday mornings, and he would arrive on campus late Saturday and stay over at a local motel until Sunday.

Johnny also taught me how to enjoy the city. He reveled in

everything New York offered. Brancusi at MoMA. Mike Nichols and Elaine May at the Village Vanguard. Eugene O'Neill on Broadway. On New Year's Day we attended a matinee of *New Faces of 1956*, in which the sultry Eartha Kitt made her debut, and in the evening we saw the hit revival of *The Iceman Cometh*, with Jason Robards. We listened to Brahms and Beethoven in his apartment—I was so glad to be with someone who liked classical music as much as I did. We kissed and we talked. Politics. History. Family.

And food. Johnny loved to eat. We would go out to dinner to places he knew, usually on Ninth Avenue, that could prepare best what he felt like having for dinner. German specialties like *Wiener schnitzel* and *sauerbraten* were among his favorites. He charmed my parents into taking us to Le Pavillon, one of New York's top French restaurants at the time.

Above all, Johnny made people laugh. My mother enjoyed him. Even my father, who took a dim view of journalists because he thought they drank too much, found him amusing. But as much as they liked Johnny, my parents worried. Why was I returning home at 3 a.m.?, they wondered. What was I doing?

They intervened, as they almost always did, with letters to Pough-keepsie, in my mother's elegant handwriting:

> *Will you bear with me while I give you some advice?*
> *We would be so pleased if you could take us into*
> *your confidence more, and talk things over....*

Rereading my mother's letters now, I see how good they were, how difficult they probably were for her to draft, and how sad that this genuine display of maternal concern and affection about my dates with Johnny came so late in my mother's life and in our relationship. She became her best self, able somehow to put herself in my place and see things from my perspective. But by this time I was separating for good, unwilling to acknowledge advice. My parents didn't actually use the scary word "marriage." But their fear that I would run off with Johnny was clear from their letters. As for me, marriage was far from my thoughts. I was having too much fun. The Apple affair ended not because of my parents' letters, but because Johnny was drafted into the army. By the fall of 1957 his letters were postmarked Fort Knox, Kentucky, and then Camp George G. Meade, outside Washington, D.C.

My romance with Johnny ended for other reasons, too. In the army he began to see other women. And I began to feel that he was too domineering and powerful a personality for me. But despite his ego he left me a stronger person than I had been before. I had begun to stand up to my parents about all sorts of things—including reading a steamy novel like *Peyton Place* even though they had hidden their own copy. And to Johnny, in large part, I owe my commitment to writing, which he encouraged. He helped me with some of my English papers. And he urged me to write for the *Vassar Chronicle*, the campus weekly.

Shortly after my mother wrote her "advice" letter to me, she entered Columbia Presbyterian Hospital for what I was told was "minor surgery." But during the operation she had a cardiac arrest and stayed in the hospital from February until May of my freshman year. By the time she came home she was so weak that she grew breathless walking up the slight incline on Madison Avenue to our apartment building. Her health was never the same again.

Chapter 4

Sudden Departures

Sophomore year I continued studying French in a course on French geography and history. It prepared me for the following summer, 1958, when I traveled with nine other college students to Bordeaux as part of the European program of the Vermont-based organization The Experiment in International Living.

On the application form I had asked for a large French family that spoke no English. The Couprys were all I'd hoped for. Henry and Genevieve Coupry had eight children, five of whom were still living at home. Annie, a Russian-speaking Communist, was usually available to accompany me on sightseeing excursions. Charlie, in his early twenties, had just returned from a six-month stay in French Equatorial Africa, and he had many artifacts to show me. It was exciting to ride with him on the back of his Lambretta scooter. Chantal, a pre-med student, and Claude, the two sisters closest to my age, nicknamed me Lulu and embroidered a "pocket" for my dinner napkin with their jokes about America's space program and its rocket launches from Cape Canaveral. "Cap Carnaval," they called it.

Mealtimes, seated next to Monsieur, who liked to help himself to my *vin ordinaire*, were my favorite events of the day. I can still taste the potato purée flavored with nutmeg and the fresh peaches marinated in red wine. I had never eaten such fresh fruits and vegetables as those at the Coupry table. I resolved that someday I'd learn to cook the French way and that my meals would not depend on the meat and potatoes my father loved. I knew that when the homestay was over I'd miss my culinary treats, but, more important, I had grown so fond of this family that it was hard to say good-bye. In our Christmas cards, decades later, I am still their American "Lulu."

Back in New York, with only three days to prepare to return to Vassar, I barely noticed that my mother's health, which had declined after her cardiac arrest during my freshman year, was worsening. One morning, out of breath, she wandered into my bedroom and sat down in my easy chair. I was surprised—she rarely came into my room—and I didn't encourage conversation because I was caught up in my own thoughts. I showed her pictures of all the Couprys and bottle labels from my favorite wines. She looked at the photographs, the expression on her face barely changing, and then with some effort she got up from her chair and left.

In October, several weeks after I'd returned to campus, I received a letter from my mother. It was written and postmarked five days after the event she described.

Dearest "Puthy Kat"—

On Saturday Daddy and I went to his favorite steak joint for dinner. We were home at nine-thirty and after he read the paper he turned on the 11 o'clock news. Meanwhile, I was in bed. Just then Mady came limping in followed later by three policemen. She had been held up by two colored boys and in the struggle she landed flat on the sidewalk just outside the drug store on Madison Avenue. She screamed and someone called the police. Then three men with her asked if she would come to the Station with them to try to identify two kids who had been caught.

She went reluctantly and was gone about an hour.
I did not see her but she got her pocket book back.
The colored boys were young — one sixteen, the
other twenty. The latter had just been released from
prison where he had spent three years! She spent a
sleepless night and was in pain. So Sunday Daddy
called Dr. Lyman who came about nine am. They
took her to Roosevelt Hospital for X-ray pictures and
care. She has a partial fracture of the hip and will be
recuperating for several weeks! So that is our latest
news. Nice town we live in.

I was so appalled that I put the letter down. Mady had had a terrible accident and my mother hadn't bothered to call to tell me about it right away. Why not? She revealed no emotion whatsoever about Mady's situation. Didn't she have feelings about this?

I immediately called Mady at her apartment in Weehawken. Even now I can remember her number: UNion 3-1637. I burst into tears when I heard her voice.

"I just heard what happened," I said between sobs. "How *are* you?" She was getting a little better each day, she told me, and didn't have a lot of pain. She was so glad to hear from me.

"I'm going to be fine," she added. "Please don't worry."

We talked about my courses and my parents, and then we hung up. I went on reading my mother's letter. In the next paragraph she discussed new upholstery for the sofa and a couple of chairs in the living room. Then she concluded:

We are looking for a new nurse to fill in while Mady
is hors de combat. I interviewed a very nice Swiss
woman this morning who I believe is available. I will
know more about her tomorrow morning when I get a
reference from her last employer.

Mady's role in my teenage life was never clearly defined, especially after she became my mother's nurse in 1953. By the time I went away to boarding school that year, I knew I no longer needed a nanny. But I wanted to maintain regular contact with Mady—and tell her about my boyfriends. Even though I was no longer going out with Johnny, she liked to tease me about him. "Apple" she called him. And I hoped she would continue living in the bedroom next to mine. This was where the photograph of her parents hung on the wall, where her Norwegian Bible stood next to an English dictionary on her desk, and where a faded color photograph of me as a girl, together with the ceramic bud vase I had made for her, sat on top of her chest of drawers. I had some close confidantes among my school and college friends but no one as close as Mady. She was the person who knew me best.

During the five years I had been away at school and college, my mother wrote me frequent letters. She usually commented on her favorite TV shows and the quiz show scandals she was following in the papers. In her beautiful handwriting she filled up the pages with news about my father's golf games, referring to him with nicknames that varied with the stocks or bonds he was buying for his customers: Pipeline Hayes, Mr. Lily Tulip Cup. Rereading my mother's letter, I was amazed to see that she said so little about Mady's injury. My mother had another perspective. Did she think of Mady as a rapacious Viking who had plundered her daughter?

Her letter concluded with "Please forgive my dilatory habit. But letter writing is not easy. As always affectionately, Mom." Her comment should have caused alarm bells to go off in my head. Letter writing was always easy for my mother. If she was having trouble writing, there was something wrong.

My mother wrote me again during the last week of October. She was looking forward to a Hayes family visitor from Canada. Buried in the fifth out of nine paragraphs was the following:

...It was good of you to write to Mortensen. I am sure she appreciated it. She may not come back here at all. That is the way it looks now. She is trying to get used to crutches which is some job....

Not come back here? *What?* This was the bombshell I wasn't expecting. For my mother, it seemed, changing nurses was less important than the visit from one of my father's distant relatives. She assumed that writing to Mady was a chore for me. And referring to Mady as "Mortensen" was a not-so-subtle put-down.

I was upset. But I didn't linger long over the big news and these innuendos—the following day's reading assignment and my long history paper were on my mind. My mother had never been a source of comfort, and I knew this wouldn't change. So, when I came home for Thanksgiving, I took a bus to New Jersey to visit Mady. The air was chilly and a brisk wind stirred up dried leaves on the ground as I walked through the working-class neighborhood of Weehawken's first-generation immigrants, past the narrow houses toward 158 Nesbit Street. Mady's yellow-brick building was on a dead-end street lined with sycamore trees. She occupied the ground-floor apartment; her sister Tomine had the upper one.

As I rang the doorbell, I was anxious—and also curious to see her home for the first time. I had never been with Mady outside the world she shared with me. As she opened the door, leaning on her crutches, I could see a living room comfortably though modestly furnished—a sofa, a coffee table, lamps, and a small dining table on one wall. Above the table was a painting of a red wooden house at the edge of a luminous indigo-blue bay, with evergreens in the background. Norway.

Now, more than a month after her accident, she got around indoors with the help of her crutches and a cane, and she was happy to see me. It was nice I hadn't forgotten "Old Mady," she said. She served tea and we chatted pleasantly. "You ought to spend as much time as you can with your parents," she urged. I had the feeling she was pushing me away, toward them. Why were we talking about my parents when I had come here to talk about *her*, to reassure myself that she was getting better?

I hated seeing her so handicapped. She had always helped me, and now I was helping her, letting her use my arm to pull herself up from her chair. I placed the teacups and teapot on the coffee table and poured the tea, while she leaned on her cane.

At Christmas, when I took the train back to New York, I saw Mady again but not where I expected. When I opened the door to my apartment I encountered the Swiss nurse, who told me that my mother had just been admitted to Harkness Pavilion, at Columbia Presbyterian Hospital. The nurse was packing a suitcase to take up to her. There was no sign of Mady. Agnes, the cook, was trying her best to create a sense of normality. "What would you like for dinner, Sarnia?" she asked.

Dinner? Where was my father? Where was Mady? And what had happened to my mother?

"Thank you, Agnes," I said. "I don't feel hungry just now."

I ran to the telephone and tried to reach my father at the office, but he had already left for the day. His secretary told me he had rushed my mother to the hospital around lunchtime. She was complaining of chest pains.

I was shaken. Why hadn't my father given me some warning the day before that my mother was getting worse? And why was the Swiss woman and not Mady nursing her? Was her heart failing? As usual, he didn't help me understand what was happening, and the nurse couldn't tell me anything.

Over the next week I visited my mother at the hospital every day. I brought her favorite African violets. I also saw some of my old school friends and went to a couple of holiday parties. But each night I lay awake for a long time before falling asleep.

On Christmas Day my father and I drove up to the hospital for a turkey dinner served on trays in my mother's room. She dozed on her bed, seemingly unaware that we were there. Then, just before sunset, we left and drove across the bridge to Aunt Ethel's house in Englewood. There we removed our coats and gathered in front of the living room fireplace.

After some rough spots when I was young, I had come to love Aunt Ethel. As a childless widow she had taken a special interest in my mother and me. On this forlorn Christmas Day she put on a festive air and asked, with her plaintive voice, "Isn't anyone going to make martinis?"

My father heard his cue and mixed the drinks in a shaker. But he was not in a holiday mood.

"What are we going to do if Margaret dies? And if she dies, where is she going to be buried?" he asked Aunt Ethel.

I was shocked. My hands were ice cold with fear. I was sitting in an armchair sipping tomato juice and I almost dropped my glass. What was he talking about? For as long as I'd known her, my mother had been sick. For half of my freshman year she was in the hospital recovering from the cardiac arrest she had suffered during minor surgery for some gynecological problem I knew nothing about. I was sure she wasn't going to die. She wasn't old enough—she'd just had her sixtieth birthday. I figured that even now, when she seemed sicker than usual, she would rally and go on being chronically ill.

My father persisted. "Is there any room in the Bliss family plot? She was so fond of her Grandma Bliss." He was talking about Aunt Ethel's mother, who was my mother's grandmother.

Aunt Ethel told my father there was a double space in the Bliss family plot, next to my mother's maternal grandparents. My mother could be buried there, she said, and there would be room for him too, when the time came.

Aunt Ethel took a long sip of her martini. "I'll call Brookside Cemetery tomorrow."

"Room for two caskets, side by side, would be best," my father said, as if he were ordering up a meal from room service.

Early in the morning three days later I woke up to the sound of the telephone ringing in the hall outside my bedroom. I ran toward the phone, but Dad, with his thin gray hair still tousled from a restless sleep, got there first and picked up the receiver. I heard his voice break as he repeated the message and thanked Dr. Atchley for calling.

My mother. I knew right away.

My father's blue eyes caught mine as he slowly put down the receiver and repeated the doctor's words: "Heart stopped—nothing more to be done—the end was peaceful."

The instant I understood what had happened, part of my brain registered an unacceptable thought: What a relief. I didn't say this to my father, but if I had he might have remembered that a year earlier I told him I hoped he would survive my mother. She was in the hospital then and he'd looked startled. Had I read his mind? It was impossible to feel heartbroken about her death. This was good news mixed with bad.

I trembled as my father and I held each other and walked into the living room. We sat down on the sofa, pulling each other close, and cried. He smelled musky and his moustache scratched my cheek. His tears came in huge chokes, together with long, loud howls of pain. His wailing went on for several minutes as he held me against his chest. In this, our most intimate moment together, I put my head on his shoulder. I was crying partly because he was sobbing, for I had never seen him cry before. But I knew I was crying for myself too, as the enormity of what had just happened began to sink in.

My mother. Dead.

For a moment I distanced myself from the scene, watching us both from the safety of numbness across the room. Too much was happening at once. My hands were freezing, and my breathing came in short spurts. Agnes heard us and came into the living room.

"I feel so bad," she said.

Memories—snapshots—linger in my mind from those cold days at the end of December, when the ground froze and time stood still. I saw my mother lying in her casket at the Englewood Funeral Home. She was wearing a blue-gray silk dress I had found in her closet, and her lips were tinted with Quiet Pink. Her face looked transformed and beautiful, much younger than her sixty years. I hesitated to walk over to her coffin and the banks of fresh floral funeral sprays that surrounded it, but Aunt Ethel, who was standing next to me, took my hand in hers and leaned over to kiss my mother's cheek.

"Oh, Margaret," she said in her quietest voice. Aunt Ethel was seventeen years old when my mother was born to her eldest sister. My mother always loved to play tennis and croquet with her aunt and appreciated being included in her activities.

I touched my mother's face and it felt soft.

My mother's funeral took place at eleven o'clock in the morning on New Year's Eve at the First Presbyterian Church in Englewood.

It was a cold, sunny day. I sat in the front pew between my father and Aunt Ethel. The church was crowded, but almost all the faces were unfamiliar. My parents had lived in Englewood for many years, and my father had kept up with their old friends there after we moved into Manhattan. Their friends knew that my father had taken good care of my mother, and they wanted to show their support.

From my seat in the front pew I kept turning around to look for Mady. I hadn't seen her since Thanksgiving. She had told me on the phone before the service that her nephew, Oskar, would drive her in his car, but I couldn't see her. I thought she should sit in the front of the church with my father and me. Where *was* she? At the end of the service I dashed out the side door without my coat to look for her—it took me a while, because people I didn't know, who seemed to know me, stopped me to express their condolences. When I finally ran down to Palisade Avenue I saw Mady seated on the passenger side of Oskar's car, waving to me. She had been at the service, she told me, in the back of the church. She had seen me in the front pew. I felt tears gather in my throat and well up in my eyes. Why hadn't she come forward to sit with me? I reached out to touch her arm.

Mady patted my hand away. "Take care of your father," she said. "He needs you now."

"I want you to come to the luncheon at Aunt Ethel's house," I said. "Daddy's relatives will be there, too."

"That's all right, darling," she said. "We never expected to get an invitation. We have to go now."

"What? No invitation?" I was furious. I took her hand. "Please," I said, "for me."

She shook her head. The car was double-parked and holding up traffic, so Oskar had to move. Awkwardly, I leaned into the car, kissed Mady's cheek, and told her I'd call her the next day.

The family gathered for lunch at Aunt Ethel's house before the burial. I had never seen members of my mother's and father's families together, and I wondered how they would get along. Whenever we went out to lunch at my father's golf club, I had noticed how formal Aunt Ethel could be.

The guests milled around Aunt Ethel's living room. There were my father's relatives from Alpena, the small town in the northern part of Michigan where I had spent two summers living with Aunt Nina. My father always said his nieces and nephews were "the salt of the earth." There was my chatty cousin Kathleen Adams, the postmistress in the village outside Alpena, and Jean Niergarth, the nurse at the Alpena General Hospital. My cousin Don Niergarth, a banker from Flint, was there, too. I had good memories of being with them in Michigan when I was twelve and thirteen. But here in Englewood they seemed unsure of themselves.

As hors d'oeuvres were passed, Aunt Ethel and my father ordered martinis, which the Michigan cousins declined. "Just Coke or soda water," they said.

"Oh, come on," said my father. "I'll make them weak. Lots of ice."

With logs blazing in the fireplace and poinsettia plants blooming on a couple of tables, the room felt warm and cozy on this frigid, sad day. I sipped a glass of Aunt Ethel's cream sherry and began to feel better. Lunch came, and then the waitress asked about coffee. I could have spent the rest of the afternoon at Aunt Ethel's, but my father looked at his watch and said it was time to go. The hearse was parked down the street and the other funeral cars were due to come to pick us up.

I dreaded going to Brookside Cemetery—I'd never been to a burial before. I couldn't figure out how they were going to lower the casket into the ground if the top layer was frozen. But as we followed the hearse from Aunt Ethel's house and parked near the Bliss plot, I could see a mound of earth covered with a tarpaulin and some men in black standing near it. The coffin was already positioned over a deep rectangular hole.

The minister from the church read a passage about ashes to ashes and dust to dust, but I found it hard to concentrate. Finally we recited the Lord's Prayer, and then it was over. As we turned to leave I thought how odd it was that we were going home without my mother. She would be all alone in her casket on this cold New Year's Eve. I shivered and fought back tears.

At home in the dark, empty apartment, we hung up our coats, turned on the lights, and sat down in the living room. It smelled of my father's Barking Dog tobacco. And loneliness.

"It's just you and me, kid," he said as he reached for his briar pipe. "The two of us alone in the world. We have to stick together."

My father and I sat quietly on the couch. He was packing the bowl of his pipe with tobacco. This was the moment he chose to give me advice about mourning. His own experience had taught him, he said, that the passage of time would help. I'd get over my sadness and I'd feel better. "Staying busy with your studies is a good thing." Then he said, "Now is the time for you to show what you are made of." He probably meant I should be strong. Not weak. Because he had already made it clear over the years that he didn't want to see tears, I assumed that "strength" meant no tears. Crying wouldn't bring Mommy back.

I knew my feelings were different from his. He was mourning my mother, but I had a double loss. Both my mother and Mady were gone. And when I cried, which I did in the privacy of my room, it was hard to tell which loss troubled me more. I was afraid that what had happened to my mother could also happen to me.

One morning, several days after the funeral, I stood in front of the mirror in the bathroom Mady and I had shared for fifteen years.

I had cried myself to sleep the night before and I wanted to see if my eyes looked red. I turned on the mirror light for a closer look. When I was younger I used to stand here, or sit on the edge of the sink, and complain to Mady about my blemishes. She would always say I looked fine, they would soon go away. She always found positive things to say. Now, as I covered my lips with Tangee, I noticed a new ache that felt like pins shooting through my stomach.

Mady was not coming back.

But I couldn't hold this thought in my mind very long. It was as if Mady was still standing beside me, warming my school clothes on top of the bathroom radiator on cold winter mornings. Hers was the shape I saw as she leaned over the sink, rinsing her teeth and soaking her false teeth at night. In the mornings I didn't even knock on the door of her bedroom; I just opened it, ran to her four-poster bed, and slipped under the covers with her. She would take my cold hands in hers and blow on them with her warm breath, making a funny noise that made me giggle.

That was long ago. Her photographs, her Bible, her bud vase—even the special glass she used for soaking her false teeth—were already gone. My mother's death meant that after nineteen years Mady's job with our family was over. While my father was mourning my mother, I was mourning Mady.

Before I returned to school I decided to visit Mady in Weehawken. Once again, I took a bus from the Port Authority and walked the few blocks to Mady's apartment.

"Come in, come in, get out of the cold," she said as she opened the door. "Let's have a nice hot cup of soup." I found a hook for my coat near the door and gave her a big hug. She had a kind look on her face and eagerness in her eyes. She felt soft and fragile.

"I'm getting along," she said. "I have no pain, thank goodness. But I have to ask Tomine upstairs for a little help. Once in a while."

She gave me the eyes-glancing-at-the-ceiling look that I understood. The two sisters had never been close, even though they had shared this house for decades. But she loved Tomine's four children, now grown.

"I feel so bad about your mother," she said, her voice quavering. I could see a tear form in the corner of one eye. She took a deep breath and looked away. "Good health is so important."

There were two places to sit at the table, one on the sofa and one on a wooden chair. The table, covered with a white cloth, had been set for lunch. Open-faced sandwiches with ham, sliced egg, and cucumber were arranged on a large plate. Mady asked me to serve the soup into bowls warming on the stove.

"I wanted to make you some cookies for dessert. I'm sorry I couldn't manage it this time. And I couldn't do much about Christmas either! Next time you come, I'll have some cookies."

"That's all right. Next time I come home from college you'll meet me at The Three Crowns," I said. "People say it's the best Scandinavian restaurant in New York. And then we can go to *Around the World in 80 Days*. By that time, you'll be off your crutches."

"Mmm," she said.

"Have you ever had the *smorgasbord* there? They have lots of herring and smoked salmon."

I might as well have suggested that we fly to California. My plan seemed preposterous—and so expensive. Mady kept a tight grip on nickels and dimes.

But I persisted. I knew I could almost always get her to see things my way. She finally agreed to accept my invitation for the end of the month.

After we finished lunch, I washed the dishes, over Mady's protests, and made us coffee. Finally, I looked at my watch and stood up to reach for my coat.

"You know something?" I said, looking straight at her as I buttoned up, "I don't miss my mother. It's a relief she's gone."

Mady looked at me and frowned. "Don't say that, honey. The mother is most important. God will punish you for saying that."

I didn't believe her. Besides, how could God know what I felt or thought?

On the last night of Christmas vacation, my father took me to dinner at Christ Cella, his favorite steak place. I wanted to console him, as Mady had suggested. I would listen to whatever he wanted to talk about. We were now free to have dinner whenever we felt hungry, without having to watch the clock and dine exactly a half hour after the insulin shot. We could even go out for dinner if we felt like it. We were now a tiny family of two, and already things were different.

At the restaurant, I looked across the table at my father. Now in his late sixties, he was handsome in his Italian suit, and he smelled good with Old Spice after-shave lotion on his face. It was nice to go out to dinner with a man who didn't agonize about the prices on the menu. There was a time when he had steered me to cheaper cuts, not the most expensive steak, but now that he had fewer expenses, with my mother's nurse or Mady off the payroll, and his inheritance from my mother's estate, my father felt more prosperous. I could order anything I wanted. With the waiter hovering over us, my father ordered his martini on the stem. I followed his lead and ordered one too.

When the drinks arrived, I started to tell him about my sadness, that I had hoped to spend more time with my mother after I graduated. I thought I could learn something about her childhood and what it was like to grow up in that thirty-six-room house, Burncroft, in Englewood—the place I recalled only dimly. We could have talked about important things, not about her TV programs. I might have even gotten answers to the questions I'd thought about lately: Why had she seemed so much better between 1953 and 1957? And why did she have to have surgery during my freshman year?

"But now it's too late," I said. "She's gone. I'll never know."

My father nodded and looked thoughtful as I spoke. He seemed to understand what I was saying. But then, instead of talking about my mother, reminiscing about their good times together, or addressing my questions, he changed the subject. He wanted to talk about my mother's will. The lawyer. Estate taxes. The cost basis of her portfolio.

It was good she died when she did, he said, at the end of the year. The timing was perfect from the income tax perspective. He expected to be busy in the coming months doing paperwork.

"And by the way," he added, "I've already ordered a headstone for her grave. A pale granite. Space for two names. It will look nice."

I didn't know what to say. "I'm sure she would have liked that"? Or "What a good idea"? He was treating me like a grown-up, talking about grown-up things, but I didn't feel grown up. The conversation made me yawn. Yawning made my eyes water, and I dabbed at them with my napkin. Last week my father was sobbing about my mother's death, and now he was talking about money. Was he embarrassed that he had wept in front of me, showing me his softer side? Was this how adults talked about grief? Was he actually grieving—or was he experiencing some of the same relief I felt?

With all this money talk, my mind wandered. Mentally I put myself back on campus, where death didn't exist. The place where I was going to be immersed in teacher conferences, evening lectures, weekend dates, and studying for exams.

I decided to change the subject again and tell my father about my summer plans. For years he had been the choreographer of my vacations, arranging for me to go to camp, to visit Aunt Nina in Michigan, or for Mady and me to go together to the beach for part of the summer. The past summer I had arranged the trip to France myself. Now, once again, I was making my own plans.

"I've applied for the Washington Summer Internship," I told him. "I'll find out if I got in by January fifteenth."

My father took a sip of his drink.

"For six weeks," I went on, "I'll be working for a Congressman, helping the office with constituents' correspondence and seeing how Congressional committees work. And then if all goes well I'll stay on with a paid job in August and share a house in Georgetown with some other interns."

My father was silent for a moment.

"No," he said. "I want you to come home after the internship is over and we'll take a trip somewhere."

He sounded bossy but I was also intrigued. He and I had made short automobile trips together, as far as Vermont, Michigan, and Virginia. Always without my mother. Now I figured he wanted to take a longer trip—something he'd never been able to do during my mother's lifetime. What would that be like? And where would we go?

Chapter 5

Alma Mater

$\mathcal{I}$ was pleased that my father wanted to take me on a trip during the summer after my junior year, but I told him I'd made summer plans of my own. I hoped to be accepted as a Washington intern on Capitol Hill. Still, I wanted to know what he had in mind.

I was concerned about him. His brave comments about staying busy and letting the passage of time do the healing seemed like wishful thinking. Maybe joining him on a trip would help him feel better. I thought about this as we drove up the Taconic Parkway toward Poughkeepsie after Christmas vacation. He was quiet, seemingly lost in thought about living alone in the apartment with no one to come home to at the end of a long day.

I broke the silence. "Dad, you said you want to take a trip with me. Where do you want to go?"

"Let's go west," he said. "I've never seen the Canadian Rockies."

Canada? His native land! What a good idea, I thought. Except for one short flight from New York to Buffalo, my father had never been in an airplane. This would be an adventure for him. Perhaps for me, too. What if I divided up the summer? I suggested this to Dad, and as we approached the turnoff to Poughkeepsie we agreed that if I was accepted I would go to Washington for the six-week internship right after exams in June. Then in August he and I would fly to Denver to see my old Vassar roommate and take a puddle-jumper through Wyoming, Montana, and Alberta. He had always wanted to play the golf courses outside Calgary, at the Banff Springs Hotel and Chateau Lake Louise.

Thick Hudson Valley fog had settled over the landscape when my father and I drove through Taylor Gate onto the Vassar campus. My dorm, a brooding dark stone building called Raymond, towered over skeletal trees and evergreens on the quad. The austerity of the scene echoed my mood, but I knew I'd feel better when I saw my friends again.

As we pulled up at the curb in front of Raymond to unload my bags, I saw Tania, an attractive, athletic girl, a year ahead of me, who had lived across the hall during freshman year. She was standing in the parking lot next to her dark green VW bug, removing skis and poles from the rack.

"How was the skiing?" I called out.

Tania waved. She came over and said hello to my father in the driver's seat. "Very icy at Stowe," she said, wrinkling her nose. "But at least I'm in one piece. And it was fun. How 'bout you?"

I shrugged. I wondered if she could read any sorrow on my face.

I didn't know how to answer Tania. Should I tell her myself, or let her find out about my mother through the campus grapevine?

My room on the third floor of Raymond looked comforting—as if nothing had changed over the holidays. The aqua café curtains hung the same way as they had in December. And yet everything was different. I could feel the room's emptiness. My roommate, Devon Adams, had come back to school from vacation but after exams she planned to return to Colorado for good. Down the hall my good friend Barbara Apple was also leaving Vassar, transferring to the University of Michigan. I was happy to see my friends again, and now I had to try to imagine dorm life in the future without them.

I told Devon and Barbara about my mother and they both gave me hugs.

Over dinner in the dorm that evening, Devon and Barbara spoke to Hazel Grossman, our dorm president. The next evening Hazel held a meeting in the dining room for all Raymond students. Before making her announcements, she asked everyone to be considerate of me in the coming weeks because of my mother's death. Setting a tone of kindness and compassion, Hazel relieved me of having to make repeated explanations. After her announcements, I realized there would be no shame in asking two of my professors for extensions on my papers. I was in people's thoughts and I now knew they would understand.

If anyone had asked me to be honest about my mother, I would have said she was an albatross—someone who could attract unwelcome, stigmatizing attention. I recalled the time the year before when my parents and Mady arrived late to observe a history class. All the seats in the classroom were taken. I had to get up and find three extra chairs for them from another classroom and I was embarrassed by the disruption. Later the same day, my mother had an insulin reaction in the dining room, which drew even more embarrassing attention. I didn't want to say anything about my mother.

Her death had taken me by surprise, and I didn't know what to think. But I did know I'd lost the future I'd imagined for my mother and me after college. We had unfinished business. I had a dream that one day we would spend more time together. Perhaps we'd laugh at each other as we walked on a beach or a mountain trail. She had a sense of humor even though we didn't always laugh at the same things. Our future was going to be better than the past. But now the door into that future had closed. She was gone.

As Devon and I finished our papers and studied for exams, I dreaded her departure. I was used to her. She smoked expensive-looking Du Maurier filter cigarettes packed in flat red boxes, and as she sprawled on her bed studying Spanish, I enjoyed her secondhand smoke. With her dark blond pageboy and cat-like eyes she might have passed for Lauren Bacall.

While she talked to her Princeton boyfriend on the phone I tried to keep my mind on political science, French literature, history, and economics. But I couldn't stop thinking about my mother and the sudden upheaval at home. One night before Devon left for Colorado, I started to cry as I lay in bed with the lights out. She heard me, got up, and gave me a hug.

"Tell me how it happened," she said gently.

I was still sobbing, my whole body shaking so violently I couldn't talk. I could barely breathe and my chest ached.

"It's okay," she said. "We've got all night. Take your time." She offered me one of her cigarettes.

As I lit up, I couldn't stop shaking. Finally, I was able to say something. "Well, you knew about Mady's accident last fall?" I took a long drag on the cigarette. "So Mady was still recovering when I came home for Christmas," I went on. And then I described how I encountered a new nurse packing my mother's clothes to take to her in the hospital. Through my sobs I told Devon about the early-morning call from the doctor a few days after Christmas.

"I really had thought she was going to be okay—eventually. And then that phone call. I couldn't believe it. And now Mady isn't coming back because there's no job for her."

Devon put her arms around me. "Sounds like a lot for you to handle. First Mady's accident, then your mom's death."

"Yes." I started to cry even more. The pain in my chest was excruciating.

"And. Now. You're. Leaving," I said between sobs as I crushed the cigarette in the ashtray.

"I know," Devon said. "My timing is pretty lousy, isn't it?" And she hugged me again.

Devon seemed to understand. She was giving me the green light to talk and I felt a little better.

"I don't know what's the saddest thing," I said to her. "Was it my mother's death or the fact that Mady had moved out of the apartment?

They're both gone now—except for the furniture and the carpet, Mady's bedroom is empty. It's just my father and me now."

"Wait a minute," said Devon. "Mady was your mother's nurse, right? She didn't have that much to do with you, did she? Wasn't she called in after your mother's operation during freshman year?"

I stared at Devon through my tears. I didn't know what to say. I realized there was a whole story no one knew about. My friends, even my roommate, never knew Mady. She filled a secret corner of my life. No one understood my deep connection to her. And to talk about it meant trying to deal with questions I had no answers for. Why was I so close to Mady? And why did my mother need her? If my mother's main problem had always been diabetes, why had she required so much nursing? I didn't know how to talk about Mady's importance. I just knew that I missed her.

Sobbing again, I told Devon about our visits to the hospital to see my mother. I couldn't stop thinking about her last few days.

"Wouldn't a good daughter have stayed with her mother at the hospital when she saw how sick she was?" I asked her. "Yet my father and I went home every night, hoping that the nurses could make her comfortable. But we could see they were short-handed because it was Christmas."

Devon and I talked until midnight and then turned off the lights. I thanked her for being there, even though I knew she didn't really understand about Mady.

"I'm going to miss you," I said.

In the darkness of our room my mind kept reviewing the events of my mother's last few days. As I handed in my papers and took my five exams, I tried to forget self-punishing thoughts and questions about guilt. With a sense of relief I tidied up my room, did my laundry, packed my suitcase, and caught a late morning train from Poughkeepsie back to New York.

As soon as I arrived at the apartment I called Mady and we arranged our lunch date at The Three Crowns for the next day. I was happy to learn that she was completely recovered from her accident. At the restaurant we piled our plates high with smoked fish; pickled beets; Swedish meatballs; *gjetost*, the brown Norwegian goat cheese; and crispbread. After lunch we walked a few blocks to the movie theater where *Around the World in 80 Days* was playing.

During our outing I became aware of a shift in our relationship. Before, Mady had authority over the wallet. Now there was a question about money. Who was going to pay for lunch and the movie? Since I had invited her, I thought it was up to me. But she had more means and independence than I did, especially now that she had a new job as the companion to an elderly woman. I was still my father's dependent and Mady was no longer his employee. But I insisted she was my guest, even though she didn't seem comfortable watching me spend my allowance on her. We both struggled to understand our new situation.

I could sense that Mady was remembering our outings when she was the nanny and I was her charge, when our relationship had clarity. As we came out of the theater, she turned to me. "You were such a cute little girl," she said with a wistful look on her face. "Why did you have to grow up?"

I laughed.

Mady seemed to be holding her feelings for me in check. I think she knew how much she mattered to me, and she wanted me to grow up, to become independent of her for my sake. But eight months later, in September 1959, after I'd gone back to college for senior year, she wrote me a long letter. She had been away visiting Norwegian friends in Vermont, she said, and had come back to her empty apartment in Weehawken. She spoke of a get-together we had just before I left for school.

> It was so nice to have a few days together with you before you left for college. I have to try to get used to living alone. I still feel you are my girl. I suppose I always will feel that way, just cannot stop loving you.

She wrote this letter on the anniversary of the day she started working for my parents, September 25, 1939. We had known each other for twenty years.

She closed with this:

> *This is not much of a letter, but just to let you know I think of you, always. Keep happy and send me a few words, if you have time. I don't expect them long and appreciate it very much.*
>
> *Loads of love, Old Mady.*

Was this her goodbye? I cried when I read those words. I was struggling to grow up, take care of myself, and feel independent. But back in the middle of junior year, with Mady gone and my mother dead only a few months, that struggle was just beginning.

After exams, during the midterm break in New York, my father and I had dinner together one night at home. Agnes cooked. She was a stocky Norwegian grandmother, with freckles and a warm smile. She broiled steaks the way my father liked them and she made a chocolate soufflé for me.

That was the same night, over martinis in the living room, that my father told me I'd have to get over Mady, that I wasn't a baby and I didn't need a nanny any more. He also spoke of me showing what I was "made of." I didn't understand. Did he mean I should be a Hayes, not a Kidder? That I should be strong, not weak?

I wasn't at all sure who or what I was. All I knew then was that I wanted to finish college and become a teacher. What would I be like if I were "weak?" And if I told people about Mady, and what she meant to me, was that weakness? Talking about Mady always triggered tears and brought up questions about my mother.

Why do you have a mother *and* a nanny, people asked, especially when you're old enough to be served alcohol and drive a car? It was the question I couldn't answer.

I knew my father's life would be different without my mother. I hoped he could get away for a while and play golf in South Carolina. It would do him good. At home it was nice to have his undivided attention, without my mother to worry him. But there were times when I felt uncomfortable with my father. One weekend late in February, when I was home visiting, we drove out to Englewood to see Aunt Ethel. As we left her house, he called me "Margaret," my mother's name. He also fondled my hair and the collar of my coat.

"I'm not Margaret," I said. "I'm Sarnia. You know that."

"All right, all right. But you don't have to use that tone of voice. You sound vicious."

Vicious? Was I? I didn't want to be. Did he hear something in my voice I didn't intend? I wondered what it would be like to go on a trip together if he felt like this. But how could he confuse me and my mother?

At restaurants I disliked his touch on my shoulder as he pushed me forward to catch up with the maître d' escorting us to our table. And with little warning, only a quick knock on the door, he would enter my bedroom in the morning to wake me. He wanted to kiss me goodbye, he said, before he left for golf or the office. I thought he should knock first and wait for me to say "Come in."

Over the years I had often been my father's companion, a substitute for my mother. When I was in grade school he would take me to the annual father-daughter dinner at the University Club—but he never took my mother there on other occasions. I also accompanied him on his springtime golfing vacations in Virginia, leaving my mother behind in New York with a nurse. She was rarely included on those trips even though we always visited her favorite brother and his wife, my Uncle Delos and Aunt Mary. As if to make up for abandoning her, my father telephoned my mother every night. I began to understand that these trips were his vacation away from her and her diabetic routines, a short break from always listening for an insulin reaction in the bed next to his. Although he was committed to taking care of her, she was no longer his emotional anchor.

But now, having my father all to myself, without my mother to distract him, felt different. How was I going to comfort him and also still keep him at a distance? I liked the feeling of being needed—it felt better than being the burden I thought I was before. I felt drawn to him in a new way.

~

One day, during the second half of my freshman year, I had felt my father's burden acutely when we were sitting alone in the living room of the apartment. At the time my mother was in the hospital, recovering from her cardiac arrest. The doctors had opened up her chest and massaged her heart to get it going again.

"I hope Mom dies before you do. Then you'll have a chance to travel and enjoy some freedom," I said.

I couldn't believe these words had come out of my mouth. But they were honest. I felt my cheeks reddening, my heart speeding up.

My father was seated across the room in the wing chair. His usual deadpan facial expression changed as he leaned forward with a look of interest. But he said nothing, and I'm not sure what he heard. Was he as tired as I was of caring for the sick? Tired of living in an infirmary?

When I headed back to school after the junior year midterm break, I hated leaving Daddy alone. I knew he would miss me. As soon as I returned to campus I made an appointment to see the academic dean, Marion Tait, to talk about a possible transfer to Barnard. I wanted to live at home so I could keep my father company. Many other students I knew were also leaving Vassar to finish their degree at other institutions. Some were getting married, planning to join their new husbands in another city or on an army base. Others felt imprisoned in a Poughkeepsie nunnery, too far from men and all the excitement in New York.

I had never met Dean Tait. I had hardly even seen her except at ceremonies like Convocation. I knew she was tall and thin with a nose curved like a puffin's beak. Her second-floor office in Main was lined with books and files, and she had huge windows overlooking the giant Norway spruces around the Circle. I felt intimidated.

Dean Tait's off-putting manner didn't help. She hardly looked up as she asked why I had requested the appointment to see her.

"I would like to transfer to Barnard for senior year," I said, staring straight at her, my hands folded primly in my lap. "I'm sure they have an excellent history department."

She studied my transcript. "Tell me more."

I took a deep breath and raced through my story about my aging father's loneliness and my mother's recent death. Then I mentioned the fact that two of my good friends were leaving and transferring to other colleges.

"I know good grades are a requirement for a transfer," I added, "and I hope mine are good enough."

She flipped through my folder while I waited, my heart somewhere near my throat. Then she looked up. "I won't approve it."

I got up, thanked Dean Tait for her time, put on my coat, and walked back to my dorm. In our room Devon was sitting at her desk, waiting for her boyfriend to call.

"How did it go?" she asked.

"I'm going to stay here," I said. "Maybe that's the best solution. I don't really want to leave this campus."

But Devon did want to pack up and return to Colorado. And when I came back after the semester break I found I didn't miss her as much as I had expected—I liked having our two-room suite and the private telephone all to myself. For five years I'd shared small rooms, and now I was happy to have a single. I started keeping things in order. I put away my clothes in the chest of drawers instead of piling them on the floor. I made my bed every day. I changed my sheets once a week. I started reading current fiction as well as the daily newspaper. And I paid more attention to my appearance—matching my Shetland pullover sweaters with my plaid kilts and knee socks, and using fragrant Mary Chess lotion after a shower. If I looked good, I thought, maybe I'd feel better.

I supposed I was expected to acquire my own fortitude. Then I would be "strong" instead of "weak."

One afternoon early in the second semester I walked down the hall to visit Betsy Hamilton, Barbara Apple's old roommate. She had also grown up in New York and the dorm receptionist always confused us because we were the same height, with round faces and short dark hair.

"I'm going to see Dr. Nixon," she announced.

"Who's he?"

"He's the campus psychiatrist. You can go and talk to him and there's no charge."

It had never occurred to me to seek professional help. I didn't understand then that I needed a place to talk about my feelings with someone I trusted, and to be reassured that I wasn't crazy and that what I was going through was normal. Despite my doubts, I decided to follow Betsy's lead and make an appointment with Dr. Nixon. Maybe I would learn something new. Maybe he could help.

Dr. Nixon stood up and shook my hand as I walked in the door. Then he motioned me to a chair on the other side of his desk. A box of tissues was perched to my left. Did he expect me to cry? I wondered how to start talking to a stranger about my family. How could he possibly understand?

"What's going on?" Dr. Nixon asked. He took his glasses off and wiped them clean with a handkerchief while I sat for a moment of embarrassed silence, tapping my foot on the carpet.

I told him about my mother. Then I admitted that I was relieved my mother was gone but that now I worried about my father. He was all alone in New York, and I missed him, but I couldn't really talk openly with him. My father rarely talked about subjects that were important to me, so I was accustomed to not talking about my mother. As I spoke Dr. Nixon took notes on a legal pad.

"I have to use camouflage with him," I said. "I have to pretend I feel all right and that time is helping to lift the sadness. He doesn't want to see me cry." I never mentioned Mady.

Dr. Nixon listened and went on scribbling. Finally, after three sessions over the next three weeks, he said I was fine. I should "continue my camouflage." After my last meeting with him, I felt relieved to hear he didn't think I had serious problems and that I was "normal."

In February I started the research for my long history paper. Even though students had nicknamed him "D-plus Degler," Carl Degler was a popular young professor and everyone wanted to take his American cultural history course. Ever since I'd driven with friends through Salt Lake City and heard the Mormon Tabernacle Choir perform during the summer after freshman year, I'd been curious about nineteenth-century utopian or religious communities. From my reading, I learned that the early Mormons promoted polygamy as a stabilizing social institution because there were so many more women in the community than men. Some of these women were Scandinavians, the text said. I decided to write my paper on early Mormon society in Utah. Professor Degler praised my paper and gave me an A-.

In the years since then I have often wondered why I picked this particular subject. I had never met any Mormons and had no plans to visit Utah. I have concluded that my interest in Mormon society came from an unconscious source: I was drawn to the Mormons precisely because of polygamy and my deeply unconscious wish for my father to marry Mady, my third parent. I wished that even though he was married to my mother, my father would marry Mady, too, so she could be my other mother.

～

During the spring term of senior year my classmates were full of plans about what they would do after graduation—weddings, graduate school, job hunting, and finding an apartment in New York. I spoke with the director of the Vocational Bureau, who advised me to improve my typing and learn shorthand before going out on job interviews. In those days it was thought that educated young women would have a hard time getting a "foot in the door" without practical office skills. My father suggested that I work as an executive secretary in the financial industry. Despite my reservations about this, I asked him to set up my interview at his Wall Street firm. He arranged an appointment with the head of personnel for a Friday afternoon.

In deciding what train to take to Grand Central Station from Poughkeepsie, I didn't consider that the hour of the appointment wouldn't allow for any delays on the train. I couldn't get there with enough time to spare without cutting a class, which I didn't want to do. In the end, there was a delay, and I walked into the interview forty minutes late, full of apologies.

The director of personnel had gray hair and a serious manner. He pointed me to a chair next to his desk.

"After four years in college, whom do you admire most?" he asked.

I had to think. I wasn't expecting this question.

Finally, I said, "Plato and Aristotle."

"Why?"

"They both had big ideas about all aspects of the universe—they thought about everything, not just about money and profits."

The interviewer laughed. I was so accustomed to my father dismissing my ideas as "cock-eyed" or "bunk" that here, in his bailiwick, I was sure I was hearing the same reaction from this man. I left his office thinking I had ruined my chances of ever getting a job in Wall Street, but I didn't care. My career in finance ended before it had begun.

That evening at dinner my father scolded me for being late to the interview. I knew he was right, but I was still a long way then from thinking about punctuality as a cardinal virtue, and behaving accordingly. I told him that I thought a career on Wall Street was a bad idea. I was pretty sure that people like my father and his friends were not my kind of people, and I didn't want to have anything to do with finance or money. I wanted to teach, I said. And he said *that* was a bad idea. He didn't want a "bluestocking" for a daughter.

I left the dinner table in tears. Did my father have a point? Was teaching the wrong career for me? Were there other options I should explore?

We argued. And argued. Ever since Farmington, where my father questioned a history teacher's wisdom in assigning us *The Communist Manifesto* to read, he and I had disagreed about social issues and the New Deal. As a staunch Eisenhower Republican, he maintained that the business of America *was* business. But I supported a safety net for the needy and deficit spending to get a sluggish economy going again. I felt it was legitimate to take out a mortgage on a house and live in it while paying off a loan, but he would have none of that. All cash was the only way. We had often argued about politics along partisan lines and now we were in conflict about what I was going to do with my life. He was no longer the same person who had piggybacked me around the dining room table or who had washed dishes with me at the pantry sink. I had also changed.

While I was still living on Vassar's beautiful green campus, I had tried to focus on the future but it was all a blur. I didn't want to leave college. I loved the towering Norway pines, the neo-Gothic crenellated architecture, and the giant sycamore in front of the library. I loved being surrounded by friends. Vassar had been my home for four years and now I had to leave and find my way in the "real" world. But I didn't know what was "real" or even what "real" meant. I was scared. Teaching seemed the best way to continue doing what I had loved doing at Vassar—reading, learning, and talking with my friends.

I knew I was lucky I didn't have to find a job right away in order to eat or pay the rent. My father was willing to house me as long as I wanted to stay with him in the New York apartment. Except for babysitting with a family one summer I had never held a paying job. I rationalized that I didn't want to take a job away from someone who needed it more than I did. Besides, I now had the means to take care of myself because my mother's will had established a trust for my benefit. The income was enough to support me if I lived carefully.

I envied the few classmates I knew whose academic work led directly to graduate school. I wanted to stay busy doing something while I figured out my next move, but I was going around in circles, trying to decide what direction to take. For there were choices. It was true that many classmates were tying the knot and joining their future husbands in other cities or campuses, but Vassar had ideas for those of us who were still single. Middlebury College invited me to apply for a place in its M.A. program in French. Vassar's Alumnae Association offered a yearlong assignment as a traveling liaison between the college and Vassar clubs around the country. There was even a fellowship available at a Danish *hoch schule* that I was eligible for. If I'd known then how easy it is for Danish speakers to understand Norwegian, I might have considered it more seriously. I've always regretted not knowing Mady's language.

By the time I graduated from college in 1960 my father had started seeing Mary Case, a divorcée who lived five blocks from our apartment. Even though she was an old friend of my mother's, I had never met her. I was relieved that my father had a new companion and I was curious about her. I wondered if he would remarry.

I was lounging on the sofa under the living room air conditioner one hot evening in August when my father brought Mary Case back to the apartment. They had just finished dinner at a neighborhood restaurant. She was petite, with short blonde curly hair and a trim figure. She wore a good silk print dress and tasteful antique jewelry. I liked her and her sense of humor. My father said that he was happy to "run around with her." They often spent time at her weekend house in Norfolk, Connecticut, where they played golf. For several years, Mary Case served as a cheerful buffer between my father and me—we didn't argue in front of her. I enjoyed dining with my father whenever she joined us.

Although I wasn't sure what career path I was going to follow after graduation, I knew it was time to strike out on my own, to stop living under my father's roof. Our arguments had become heated, and they made me uncomfortable. Before graduation I'd gotten the idea of moving to another city and finding a roommate. Of the eight women I'd lived with during my senior year, six flashed new diamond engagement rings in a headlong rush to the altar. They were either already married or engaged to be married shortly after graduation. One was already pregnant. I was happy that one of my roommates, Susan Bradley, from Corning, New York, was still unattached and wanted to move to Cambridge, Massachusetts. She needed to find a place to live, so we agreed to share an apartment and split the rent.

As graduation approached, when there was little to do besides sell old furniture, return library books, and say goodbye to friends and favorite professors, I felt sad. I had accomplished my goal, becoming the first woman in my family to graduate from a four-year college. But having this degree didn't make me feel very different inside. I was still full of doubts and anxieties. And I worried about the future.

Chapter 6

Lost

$\mathcal{I}$n my father's mind, my move from New York to Cambridge, Massachusetts, six months after college graduation, was an act of rebellion. I didn't even have a job waiting there. I had only vague plans and a romantic notion about living in the heart of picturesque, historic New England.

Nothing pleased me more than the clock towers and low-rise red brick buildings around Harvard Yard. It didn't matter that I wasn't a Harvard student—knowing Harvard was there, with smart students walking around the cobble-stoned streets, was enough. I liked the ancient trees, the lazy curves of the Charles River, and the wide-open sky. And Cambridge was only a two-hour drive from my aunt and uncle, Mary and Delos Kidder, and their organic farm in southern New Hampshire. I would always be welcome there on weekends.

City living in the dirty, dark, noisy canyons of Manhattan had never appealed to me. New York was Mecca for people from other cities, but to me it was the place to leave. I wanted to escape commuting on buses and subways. In those days before central air conditioning I hated the summer heat and humidity, when I felt trapped inside a waffle iron turned on high. I couldn't imagine living in a New York apartment on my own or with a roommate.

Boston, on the other hand, had all my favorite things—beaches on the Cape and the North Shore, boats, access to the White Mountains, historic landmarks, and friends from college. Most important, by this time, it offered me the right distance from my father.

I knew he wanted me to stay in New York and work in a brokerage house. And he didn't confine his wishes to my future employment. No matter what I was doing, he exerted pressure on me as I tried to find my way among the facets of my life—jobs, men, friendships, and family duties. There was no other member of the Hayes family to distract him from his tight focus on me. In 1960, the year I graduated, he was seventy-one, past retirement age. Except he didn't want to retire. "I'll just keep on working," he would say doggedly, with a touch of pleasure in his voice. As long as his health lasted he wanted to continue working part time, sharing clients with a colleague, and traveling to the many places he had never seen. And until he and Mary Case became a couple and married, as he hoped, he needed a traveling companion.

He needed me.

Our two-week trip together to the Canadian Rockies during the summer before my senior year had been a success. We stopped at Denver, Jackson Hole, Bozeman, Glacier National Park, and Calgary on our way to the grand old hotels at Banff and Lake Louise. We avoided our usual conflicts by going our separate ways during the day—golf for him, tennis and swimming for me. One day I walked part of the beautiful Banff course and watched him drive, pitch, and putt his way to the eighteenth hole. Evenings over dinner I couldn't help noticing that the busboys and waitresses were all college students. I wished I was among them, my cohorts, rather than being waited on as a hotel guest. But, I told myself, soon enough I'd be on my own, facing problems I couldn't even imagine. I'd better enjoy this vacation while I could.

My father needed more than a traveling companion. Unspoken but equally potent in his mind was the hope—the assumption—that

I'd be available to care for him when the time came. He had nursed my mother and he had supported his parents and his older sister, my Aunt Nina, in their old age. Now it was his turn, and I know he expected me to pick up the family script and play my part.

But facing my father's mortality and recognizing that except for me he was all alone in the world was almost impossible for the recent graduate I was then. I was too full of questions, plans, and desires. I was perfectly willing to take whatever help he would give me, but I was not ready to be charitable and give much back. What did I owe him? I ignored his conclusions.

∾

On a steamy Friday afternoon in August, two months after graduation, I drove out of New York and headed to Boston. There I planned a rendezvous with my college friend Susan Bradley to look for an apartment in Cambridge that we could share, beginning in the fall. She already had a job lined up at the Boston Lying-in Hospital.

For the first time in my life I was alone in a car—traveling on my own timetable. I had studied the New York-to-Boston map and expected to arrive in Cambridge, Massachusetts, in time for supper. But somewhere east of Hartford I made a wrong turn and ended up on a single-lane road instead of the four-lane Massachusetts Turnpike. Signs pointed to small towns I'd never heard of. I'd been driving for four hours and it was getting dark. I looked at my hands on the wheel and saw they were shaking.

I was lost.

I pulled over at an Esso station and let the freckle-faced young attendant fill the tank and clean the windshield while I studied the map again. He pointed me toward a road that he assured me ran into the turnpike. I thanked him, turned on my headlights, and shifted into first.

When I finally arrived at the Cambridge motel where Susan and I had reserved a room it was past 9 p.m. Stiff and exhausted, I called my father to tell him I had arrived safely. I knew he was anxious—he had urged me to take the train. Susan was anxious too. In those days before cell phones there was no easy way for me to let her know I was delayed. I was much too nervous to stop on the road to make a phone call, which would have helped.

Susan and I hugged each other when I finally arrived at the motel office. I registered at the desk and she helped me carry my bag to our room. I remember how excited we were that night as we sat on our twin beds and talked about the new life we were embarking on. Susan was attractive, with long dark hair and the trim figure of an athlete. I knew we'd get along well, with our books and classical music. We would shop at Faneuil Hall and cook for our friends on weekends. Maybe I would meet someone I wanted to go out with and we could double-date. Susan was seeing Dick Lee, who was about to start his first year at Yale Medical School. Before long, my exhaustion caught up with me; I collapsed on the bed and fell asleep.

Over the weekend Susan and I looked at several two-bedroom apartments. The one we finally chose was on the third floor above a grocery store, two blocks from the Charles River. From the kitchen bay window we had a clear view of the clock tower on Harvard's Dunster House. As of the 15th of September the apartment was going to be available for a year while its current tenant, a Harvard professor, went on sabbatical with his family. The apartment was partially furnished and the rent, split two ways, was affordable. We were thrilled with our find.

Less thrilling—and far less certain—was the path into my future. Only a few months earlier I had stood proudly at the commencement ceremonies in the amphitheater behind the chemistry building. The college president shook my right hand and put a diploma in my left. I had accomplished my goal. But now what? Vassar had been my home for four years and I'd have to leave and enter another world. Yet I felt academia was where I belonged. What was my new goal?

Mady was no help. After my mother's death, she found a part-time job as an older woman's companion. It never occurred to me to discuss my future with Mady except to tell her I was planning to move to Cambridge. "You'll have to come up for a visit after I get settled," I told her. She had few opinions about my future. She wanted me to be happy but she couldn't advise me. Mady saw herself as part of the working class, people who had to work to earn a living in menial or routine jobs. I grew up hearing from her and the other help in our house that work was a burden, something unavoidable. And in Mady's case, her "work" had the nerve to grow up and move away.

In the meantime, though, moving back into my room at home, with my music, typewriter, books, and clothes, I found a little comfort in familiar surroundings. I parked my car in a local garage. My room was often hot and dark, but it was all mine—I didn't have to share it with anybody. I brought home the bicycle I had used on campus, and on good days I biked around Central Park.

After a peaceful week at home, I started to find it difficult to live with my father. He talked about the stocks and bonds he was recommending to clients—which didn't interest me at all—and he continued to offer unsolicited advice about what I should do, including trying to get a job on Wall Street. In the evenings I was always happy to have company at dinner to distract him from his laser focus on me. Sally, another still-single roommate from Vassar, was a frequent dinner guest. I liked seeing her because she steered the conversation away from touchy political subjects and what my father called my cock-eyed opinions—among them my new membership in the Democratic Party.

"Your friend is quite a talker," my father said after dinner one night when we were alone. This was not a compliment—I knew he didn't like women who talked a lot. But she appreciated him, especially the way he twinkled his blue eyes at her.

"She's domineering," he said. "Why don't you invite your other friend instead—the one who lives on Fifth Avenue?"

"Why Mary?" I asked. "You hardly know her."

"Well, she comes from a good family. They do things in a nice way."

I took a deep breath. I'd heard him praise Mary before, for all the wrong reasons.

"You don't understand Mary, Daddy. She was crazy in college—staying up all night to finish papers, sleeping all day, then driving off in her Mercedes to see her fiancé on weekends. It was impossible to get to know her."

But in my father's eyes Mary's family's wealth and connections trumped her peculiarities.

"Well, then, get to know her now. Or see one of her brothers. You knew one of them in dancing school, didn't you?"

I had had enough of his social climbing talk about my friends and working on Wall Street. Yet I was finding it easier to figure out what I didn't want to do than what I *did*. I envied people whose interests and aptitudes had emerged while they were still undergraduates. I had a few classmates who were headed to law school, to business school, or to graduate school in English or psychology. But I felt I had to look around before I could figure out my next step. I thought that without a *cum laude* or Phi Beta Kappa key I couldn't plan on a life in academia. So that left me with my original idea of becoming a teacher—working in an environment already familiar after sixteen years of schooling. Teaching would also allow me to work and learn during the school year, leaving summers and vacations free.

But what subject did I want to teach? I had studied French for a long time, but I had majored in history in college. Beginning French would be easy enough to teach but I worried it might become repetitive—I didn't consider the fact that every year I'd have different students. History or social studies might be harder and more challenging but I'd learn more.

By this time in June I had decided to take typing and shorthand at the Berkeley Secretarial School in New York. I hoped this would help me get what the vocational counselor at Vassar called "a foot in the door" of the job market. Then I'd have more to offer a potential employer. This was a typical experience for young women then, but my heart wasn't in it. I was annoyed that I had to go through the tedious process of acquiring these skills when I already had a bachelor's degree. It was one thing to increase my typing speed to sixty words a minute—I could always use typing—but learning Gregg shorthand squiggles so that I could take dictation made me feel I was operating on only three cylinders when I had eight.

To my surprise, though, I began to find secretarial school useful. Boring and repetitive as it was, I saw how valuable shorthand might be to transcribe a lecture—either for a boss or for myself.

One day in the middle of the summer, as I was pondering my options, my father came home from the office with an astonishing suggestion. How would I like to accompany him to Europe, leaving New York on September 7th? We would sail first class to Southampton on the *Queen Elizabeth* and return the same way on the *Queen Mary* from Cherbourg. He was able to reserve rooms at two good hotels his friends had recommended. He asked me to select a hotel for us in Geneva and another in Zermatt.

My father had never been to Europe, and he needed a French-speaking guide. I was excited to travel again, even though leaving New York so early in September meant I wouldn't finish my typing and shorthand course. And if I stayed in Europe for a month or more I would forget all the Gregg I had learned. But to postpone our departure to a later sailing of the *Queen Elizabeth* would mean cold and wet fall weather in Europe; September was the best month to travel. Finally, I said yes—if I forgot Gregg, so what? I would go to Cambridge a little later than originally planned, share the apartment with Susan, and find work that didn't require shorthand. When I called to tell her about the trip, Susan assured me that she'd save my place until I arrived later in the fall.

My father and I loved the Atlantic crossing. He took regular walks around the deck while I played squash and swam in the pool. Wrapped in a blanket, I lounged on a deck chair with a novel and picked up conversations with other passengers. Evenings we dined in the Veranda Grill, on the highest deck, where the head steward prepared my first Caesar salad, breaking the eggs and adding the anchovies, cheese, and croutons at our table.

"What's that?" I asked as he chopped up something that looked like garlic into the wooden bowl.

"Shallots," he said.

"What are they?"

"They're a kind of onion."

I had a lot to learn in the kitchen. And I certainly didn't know until he explained it that the salad originated with a chef named Caesar Cardini in Tijuana, Mexico, not with Julius in Rome.

From time to time my father would look up from his reading and announce, "This is a deluxe trip." Why did he keep repeating this? Did he think I didn't notice? Or was he just reassuring himself that after all these years of worry and hard work—he had been working since age twelve—he was finally enjoying his rewards. I wondered if he thought it wasn't quite as grand as he had expected.

Our London hotel, on Hyde Park, was close to many of the vestiges of empire my father wanted to see. I was pleased to photograph the moment when, dressed in a dark suit and a wide-brimmed straw hat, he stood reverently in front of Buckingham Palace, gazing at the balcony. The Changing of the Guard, Whitehall, Westminster Abbey, Big Ben and the Houses of Parliament, Kew Gardens, the British Museum, Tate Gallery, 10 Downing Street—he loved it all. One warm day he hired a car and driver to take us to Windsor Castle, to Oxford, and then on to the county seat of the dukes of Marlborough at Blenheim. In between the daytime tourist attractions there were theater, restaurants, concerts, and a couple of his friends who invited us for Sunday lunch at their club outside London.

We went on to France for six days. In Paris I contacted François, the eldest son in the Coupry family, and invited him to join my father and me for dinner. He spoke no English, my father spoke no French, so I sat between them and translated. Then we flew to Geneva, where we took the train around the lake and spent the next five days in the mountains. After two days of walking the scenic trails through the meadows and pastures above the village of Zermatt, my father grew impatient: There were no golf courses, he lamented. To make matters worse, dark clouds were moving in to hide the magnificent scenery.

By this time we had been traveling together for almost a month and I was getting restless, ready to travel on my own. By prior arrangement I flew to Vienna to travel with two friends in their rented VW. We planned to drive south from Vienna, to Venice, Ravenna, and then Florence and Rome. My father proceeded to Paris and his return passage to New York on the *Queen Mary*.

I saw no reason to rush back to New York. Soon enough, I thought, a job would cut vacations short. My father and I had traveled to cities that were already familiar. Now I wanted to explore new places. I wanted to see Italy.

Before I left New York, Aunt Ethel had briefed me on Florence. She wrote a letter of introduction for me to Nicky Mariano, companion and secretary to the distinguished Renaissance scholar Bernard Berenson, who had died the year before. She asked Ms. Mariano to allow us to visit his famous Villa I Tatti, in Settignano, outside Florence, which Harvard University would soon begin to use for its history of art program. I wanted to do this because in college I'd become interested in Italian painting through a year-long course—and I Tatti was filled with glorious Renaissance artworks.

At the villa I wanted to linger in front of the Giottos and Duccios as well as the Masaccios and Masolinos at the Uffizi Gallery. I was moved by the paintings, and grateful for the course that had prepared me to appreciate them.

From Florence my friends and I drove on to Assisi and then to Rome. Once we arrived in Rome we thought, why not leave the car there and fly to Athens? And once we arrived in Athens and had seen the Acropolis and Delphi we thought, why not continue to the Greek islands? And so the trip evolved and changed, making it difficult for our families to keep track of us. We boarded a cruise ship in Piraeus and sailed to Crete, Mykonos, Delos, Patmos, and Rhodes. Eventually after a detour to Lebanon I returned to Paris, and then, finally, I flew back to New York, in time for Thanksgiving.

~

Before his inauguration on January 21, 1961, President-elect John F. Kennedy came to Harvard for an Overseers' meeting, and all of Cambridge, it seemed, turned out on the snow-packed streets to welcome him. I was thrilled to be so close to "my" president, the one I had voted for in my first general election, and also to be living in the state that had first elected him to public office. My father disagreed, calling my choice of candidate yet another of my crazy ideas.

My father arrived from New York later in January to inspect my new life in Cambridge.

"This is not Park Avenue," he concluded.

He was not wrong. Our third-floor walkup in Cambridge turned out to be a firetrap, and Susan and I were lucky to escape safely after less than a year. But we were happy there and made friends with our Armenian landlord, Henry, who owned the grocery store on the ground floor. My father didn't like my favorite restaurant either—with its red and white checked tablecloths, candle wax dripping over empty wine bottles, and French ballads as background music. His complaints validated my new choices. I never minded our dingy, spartan surroundings. I was euphoric to be living on my own, away from New York, with a cheerful roommate who appreciated my tentative efforts to cook dinner. I bought an omelette pan, a soufflé dish, a couple of casseroles—and I experimented. We drank sherry before dinner, nibbled on wine cheddar, and invited friends over.

At the beginning of my job search I interviewed for two positions in Boston. The first, editing the Adams family papers at the Massachusetts Historical Society, seemed dry and academic—I wanted more contact with people. And I was sure a lot of typing would be required. The second, a secretarial position at Northeastern University, didn't meet my requirement that I work at a famous institution: I'd never heard of Northeastern. My third opportunity, at a bank, didn't tempt me either. I wanted to work in a school, around teachers and students, in a familiar setting.

As it happened, my old Farmington friend Whitney was moving to Newport to marry her naval officer fiancé, vacating her position as the apprentice in French at Shady Hill School's Teacher Training program. I decided to grab the opportunity to take over her job and learn how to teach French to seventh, eighth, and ninth graders. I'd learn through observation and practice teaching, and the apprenticeship would lead to good contacts in other schools.

At Shady Hill I reported to Frank Vincent, a veteran French teacher, and observed his work. I also observed history and English teachers, and joined regular seminars where faculty members and Harvard professors discussed the "new math" and the teaching of reading in the early grades. Over several months of daily observation I became familiar with the school's curriculum, teachers' resources outside the classroom, and theories of educational psychology.

A reserved, formal man, Mr. Vincent shared his classroom responsibilities reluctantly. He asked me to correct students' homework and classroom exercises, but I continued to pester him for teaching opportunities. Finally, after several delays, Mr. Vincent asked me to present the *passé composé* to the eighth grade. I would have to explain, in French, the uses of the auxiliary verbs *avoir* and *être* in constructing the past tense. I was nervous and excited about my chance to see what I could do. But just as I was getting my plans together my father called to tell me he was going into the hospital in New York for an operation to remove his prostate gland.

"Prostate? I've never heard of it. Where is it?" I asked him.

"That I cannot tell you, I'm sorry," he replied.

His reluctance meant I'd have to consult the dictionary. "It's serious and I'm worried," he went on. "If anything happens to me you'll find my Last Will and Testament in the safe by my bed. I'll show you when you come."

My heart sank. He'd never before alluded to his age and what would happen if he died. I was scared, and I knew I had to go to New York. The *passé composé* would have to wait.

Eventually I had a chance to teach another, shorter, verbs unit with the eighth graders, under Mr. Vincent's guidance. But the earlier interruption reminded me that family duties come first, and I was filled with resentment. Teaching French would have been a good choice for me, but I didn't see it that way when I was twenty-two. I was afraid to make a commitment. What if my father needed me again? I decided not to look for a full-time teaching position. Instead I signed up for a Master's degree in Education at Tufts that would certify me in Massachusetts and allow me to practice teaching history in the public schools. Graduate school would give me more flexibility, temporarily, than I would ever have under a teacher's contract.

By the end of the school year, in June 1961, during my first six months in Cambridge, I had started my new independent life, had made new friends, and had reconnected with some old ones. I wanted to stay there and pursue a career in teaching because I felt excited by what I had seen at Shady Hill. I figured I'd eventually decide whether to teach history or French, and at what level.

Susan had gotten engaged to Dick at Christmas and was going to marry him and move to New Haven in June. I'd miss our shared life but I had a new plan. I would live with three women from Connecticut College in a furnished apartment on Hammond Street. One of them had landed a job teaching second grade at Shady Hill, and another was an assistant in the art studio.

I didn't think it mattered much that I didn't have a paid job. For the time being, doubling up and saving money on rent stretched my income. And somewhere in the back of my mind floated the fear that my search for interesting work didn't matter either. Maybe such a thing didn't exist. Mady certainly didn't think so. How was it possible to like work so much that one could do it day after day? And what about the work itself? If I didn't get a good teaching job and wound up in an office, what would it be like to spend all day typing and taking dictation? I would feel trapped. At some point, though, wouldn't the right man come along? I would get married and bring my own ambitions in line with my husband's. These were my thoughts as I tried to sort out my alternatives and combat the depression that was occasionally invading my mind.

But what was taking me so long to find Mr. Right? After all, most of my friends were already married. And it wasn't that I hadn't met suitable men. If geography were not a factor, there were already two proposals waiting for an answer. Something was standing between me and marriage. At twenty-three I was poised to find out what that was.

Chapter 7

So Many Men

I'd been a bridesmaid too often. At one wedding I wept hot tears down the front of my crimson taffeta dress while the minister blessed the newlyweds. Every wedding, it seemed, meant saying good-bye to a woman friend as she moved to another city to start her new married life.

These losses made me wonder what was blocking my way to the altar. Was it my father and my questions about caring for him in his old age? Did I fear that after a few years a husband would become domineering, like him? Although I'd had relationships over the years with several men, I'd never been in love. What was holding me back? Was I too fussy?

On a perfect June day a month after graduation I sipped champagne at the Connecticut garden wedding reception of Peggy, a former classmate. Weeks earlier she had promised to introduce me to David, a graduate student in aeronautical engineering at MIT. "David's brilliant," she told me, "but he's not one of those engineering nerds without any social skills." I wanted to meet him.

As David and I clicked our glasses together to toast the bride and groom I noticed his thick bifocals, but whenever he pushed them up over his forehead to rub his deeply recessed eyes I saw a handsome, square-jawed face capped by wavy dark hair. He had a quick smile, a good sense of humor, and a gentle self-effacing manner. He played the cello and loved outdoor sports, especially sailing and skiing. I was glad he suggested that we get together after I arrived in Cambridge.

"You could come to the frat for dinner," he said.

"The what?"

"The fraternity. The Number Six Club," he explained.

I didn't know what he was talking about.

"It's the building on Memorial Drive overlooking the Charles, in Cambridge. Twenty of us live there, and it's very civilized. We always have guests for dinner on Wednesdays, and the food is good."

As soon as I was settled in the apartment I was sharing with Susan, I started going out with David. One long weekend we went skiing in New Hampshire. Later in the spring we visited his mother on Cape Cod. Sometimes we double-dated with Susan and her Yale medical student fiancé, Dick.

The Wednesday after our first date, I joined David for dinner at the frat. I'd expected a rowdy, drunken scene, like the ones at Yale fraternities and Princeton clubs, but here the "brothers" wore jackets and ties and sat around a large dining table with a white linen tablecloth and napkins. A waiter named Bud served a delicious meatloaf with mashed potatoes and gravy and a tart and flaky apple pie.

The next time I went to dinner with David at the Number Six Club I met several of his fraternity brothers. One of them, seated across the table, introduced himself as Ed. During the course of the conversation I told him where I had gone to college.

"I really like the Vassar campus," Ed said, smiling at me. "It's beautiful." And he was handsome.

"I didn't want to leave," I admitted. "But what could I do? I have the diploma. I couldn't stay." After that exchange I shifted my attention back to David.

Most of the time David and I were busy working—I was at Shady Hill during the day and taking an evening history course at Boston

University. I was teaching myself to cook and finding my way around Boston. After he got his Master's degree in June, David planned to spend the summer traveling in Europe, and then in September he would fly to California to start a Ph.D. program.

I never told David before he left for Europe that there was another man. It was a serious, long-distance romance with Arthur, an English diplomat. We had been introduced on a blind date by mutual friends in New York, in August 1960, and then we spent an evening listening to jazz in Greenwich Village. By the summer of 1961, when David was leaving MIT, Arthur and I had been corresponding for almost a year.

Before he left New York for London, in 1960, Arthur had sent me his temporary London address and telephone numbers. He hoped that we could meet again before his first Foreign Office assignment took him to Lebanon to learn Arabic. When my father and I visited London in 1960 Arthur invited us to dinner and the theater.

Arthur and I fell in love on our fourth date. We were going to a Proms concert at Royal Albert Hall, in London, on a Sunday afternoon, and I was running late. As Arthur and I hurried across Hyde Park from my hotel he lamented the late hour and the music we were missing. So I put my arm through his to comfort him and he took it, pressing me close. His first touch sent an electric charge through me. This had never happened before. I fell hard for this Englishman.

It was the same for Arthur. Sometime later he wrote:

> I know that in these last few days something wonderful, significant, and beautiful happened.... I shall always remember the girl who thought and felt like me, the girl who took my arm when, of all things, what I most wanted was that she should take my arm, the girl who kissed, not as part of the evening's entertainment, but as one who wanted to kiss, the girl who trusted and was strong and sincere.

When my father and I left New York in September of 1960 I never expected that I'd soon be in the grip of passions and desires I didn't know I had. How was I supposed to focus on Dad on his first trip to Europe, guiding him around London and Paris, and translating French, when all I could think about was Arthur and how much I wanted to kiss him? I was unfamiliar with such powerful feelings.

Arthur and I shared a love of piano music, literature, and European history. But after I returned to America and moved to Cambridge, all I had were my memories, a black-and-white framed photograph, and a stack of love letters from Lebanon, written on blue stationery and addressed to me with Arthur's loopy new Arabic version of "U.S.A." I missed his deep voice, his warm breath in my ear, his honey-colored chest hair peeking out above his collar, and his precise Oxford English. In my loneliness for Arthur, who was so far away, David was a welcome distraction.

Not that I wasn't conflicted. But I knew I wasn't willing to bide my time in America like a cloistered nun while Arthur spent fifteen months finishing his Arabic studies and starting his first two-year posting for the Foreign Office in another part of the Middle East. He would get a two-week home leave to England every eighteen months. My uncertainty was complicated by a preliminary taste of the Middle East, when I left my traveling companions, and flew on from Athens to spend nine days with Arthur in Beirut.

I had heard that Beirut was "the Paris of the Middle East," which raised the wrong expectations. There were luxurious high-rise waterfront hotels and beaches attracting wealthy tourists who water-skied in the Mediterranean and dined on fresh fish, fine wines, and typical Lebanese fare. As we sat at a bar having drinks with one of Arthur's old Oxford friends—with Big Ben tolling in the background during a BBC news broadcast—it was easy to imagine we were still in London.

But Beirut was very different from London. And it was certainly no Paris. This was my first look at the Third World, and the poverty, dust, and street chaos visible everywhere beyond the luxury hotels disturbed me. Arthur, slightly more acclimated to this foreign world, had his hands full making plans for our week together. At the same time he had to keep up with the intense pace of Arabic study in a mountain village more than an hour's drive by taxi from downtown Beirut. I spent several nights at a village inn near the school and took walks among the stone houses and fragrant gardens, which overlooked a vast expanse of blue.

During this visit I wondered whether Arthur and I had any future together. Could I live in this world? Village women, unveiled but swathed in black from head to toe, stared and laughed at my cotton shirt dress, sometimes pointing at my bare arms and legs and my camera. Men brushed against me on the streets of Beirut. I felt awkward and uncomfortable, knowing that my Western appearance offended them and that Western behavioral norms, like holding hands in public, were forbidden. Alone at night at the village inn I had headaches and insomnia, wishing I hadn't gotten myself into such a muddle. I had nightmares about drowning in the sea, unable to speak. I would wake up sweating and scared.

A few diversions—the American University of Beirut campus, an all-day excursion to the majestic Roman ruins at Baalbek in the Beka'a Valley, swimming in the Mediterranean, and dining in various restaurants—provided the only respite from the sense of being displaced. This was a world that made me wonder how I could give up America—and live a whole ocean away from family and friends. Arthur's career would tie both of us to a bureaucracy at the Foreign Office.

~

Before leaving Cambridge for travel in Europe and then study in California, David had suggested to Ed that he call me because I might get "lonely" during his absence. Not losing a beat, Ed invited me to a beach party in Nahant, a long rib chop of a peninsula floating in Boston Harbor. I didn't know any of his friends, and I figured I'd be a stranger at the party, so I declined. Besides, I couldn't put aside my feelings for Arthur. I was already involved with David and Arthur and I was reluctant to add a third man.

Later that summer Ed telephoned again. I invited him to lunch at my apartment. "I'd like to cook lunch for you," he said. It seemed odd that I would be the hostess and he the chef, but he seemed so enthusiastic that I agreed. As it turned out, he cooked us perfect ham and cheese omelettes—crusty outside, runny inside—and he brought with him an endive salad, a bottle of good red wine, and a loaf of French bread. We ate at the card table and sat on the folding metal chairs Susan had donated before she left to get married. As we talked over lunch, we realized that in the fall we would both be studying on the Tufts campus. I was excited about the Master's program in education that I'd enrolled in, and I was happy to have a friend on a new campus.

Ed told me he had studied chemical engineering at MIT, but by the time he enrolled in the Ph.D. program at MIT he was burned out. A few introductory courses in economics at Boston University encouraged him to switch from chemistry to economics at the Fletcher School of Law and Diplomacy, at Tufts University. Fletcher prepared students for U.S. government work or for the Foreign Service. Ed hoped to work in international economic development as well as teach economics at the college level.

Over lunch Ed told me about his childhood and sunburned adolescence in the Southwest—hiking, skiing, running rapids, and camping along the Colorado River. As twelve-year-olds he and his identical twin brother, Alfie, had chased turkeys through alfalfa fields on their parents' working ranch twenty miles north of Santa Fe.

Turkeys? I'd never seen a turkey outside a roasting pan. And I didn't know what alfalfa looked like.

"You're so exotic," I said. "Aren't turkeys the all-American bird? Or is that the bald eagle?"

"It has to be the eagle because turkeys are dumb."

This was not a topic I could take very far. I was used to men like David, products of the suburbs, who'd spent little time in rural

America. I'd also had little contact with the country or farming. All I knew was what my Aunt Mary and Uncle Delos had showed me in their organic vegetable garden in New Hampshire, where slugs ate their lettuce. I never wanted to do so much physical outdoor work or fight so many battles in order to eat.

I changed the subject. I told Ed about the identical twins I knew at boarding school who used to read each other's letters from boyfriends. I wanted to know more about Ed and his brother.

"So where is Alfie now?" I asked.

Ed was leaning back on his folding chair, making me nervous. He seemed too big for my small space.

"He's here in Cambridge. He went to Harvard when I went to MIT."

"What's it like being an identical twin?" I asked. Then I thought that was a silly question—the same one everyone probably asked.

"Most of the time we wanted to kill each other. Ma had to remove the rocks from our pockets."

I laughed. I'd always wanted a brother, and I'd never have thought of throwing a rock at him.

"And now?"

"Why don't the three of us go out for dinner? Then you can meet him."

During the remainder of that afternoon, as we finished our lunch and did the dishes together, I learned more. Besides his affection for cow-milking, alfalfa-raising, and turkey-herding, he loved city life. He enjoyed restaurants and didn't mind paying for a good meal. He had traveled in Europe and Mexico, he spoke Spanish, he could pilot a single engine plane, and he had already done his six-month military service in the Army's Chemical Corps. In New York, he told me, he enjoyed visiting members of his extended family—his two aunts and an older female cousin.

I learned more the following week, when Ed and Alfie, one twin on each arm, escorted me across Boston Common for dinner at the Locke-Ober Cafe. Ed had told me that Alfie—"Fred"—limped slightly from the polio he'd had in his teens, but I didn't see it. When I looked at them side by side I couldn't tell them apart: They were both athletically built—tall with dark wavy hair, aquiline noses, eyes a little too close together, and long narrow pigeon-toed feet. Soccer players, both. When they smiled I could see their teeth were perfectly straight. It was only while we were passing around the bread basket that Ed pointed out Alfie's fingernails, which curved like a spoon while Ed's lay flat as a knife. So long as Ed was wearing his glasses to read the menu, I could tell them apart. He looked like a studious owl.

During dinner they teased each other about mistaken identity pranks. They had the same voice, the same hand gestures and verbal tics, saying "ah" as they paused mid-sentence. Ed tried to convince me he once sat for a math exam at Harvard so that Alfie could pass the course. Another time someone approached him in Harvard Square, saying Ed owed him money. Ed said, "You've got the wrong guy. That's my twin brother." And the accuser said, "Oh, bullshit."

As I listened to the twins talk about Alfie's wedding plans, I noticed the difference between Alfie's cranky reserve and Ed's playful tone. I liked Ed's irreverence and his sense of humor. Although he'd been born in New York to a family with deep roots there, he loved the West.

Ed was attractive and I enjoyed his company. We had several more dates over the summer and I told him about my pending move to the apartment on Hammond Street. Before classes started, my lease ran out. I had to move my belongings—books, typewriter, pots and pans, dishes, and clothes—into the furnished apartment on the third floor of a yellow frame house on Hammond Street. I was going to share this three-bedroom space with three women. The small kitchen had hardly enough room for my things. I missed the view I'd enjoyed before of the picturesque clock tower—there were no views at all from the small third-story windows. Cambridge felt different now.

On moving day my car battery died just as I pulled up in front of the Hammond Street house. My emotional battery seemed to run out of juice too. I put my head in my hands and leaned on the steering wheel as angry tears poured down my cheeks. I was furious at my car and exhausted from the move. I had felt so upbeat living with Susan in Cambridge earlier in the year, but now, without my schedule at Shady Hill, and without David, I felt alone in the world. My mother was dead, Mady had a new job, my father was difficult, David had left MIT and flown to California, and the man I loved lived on the other side of the world. Things had changed too fast.

Despite my misery, I managed to unpack the car and move my boxes and two suitcases upstairs to the third floor of the house. Later I poured myself a glass of milk, ate a sandwich, and then collapsed into bed.

The next morning I had a hard time getting up. I wished I were anywhere except Cambridge on a holiday weekend. Most people had left town, and here I was, stuck with a car that wouldn't move. I'd have to walk to the gas station two blocks away on Massachusetts Avenue and they would have to send someone to recharge the car battery. Then I could finally do my errands before registration and classes started. When I left the house I noticed that there was a piece of paper stuck under the windshield wiper of my car.

Oh, no, not a parking ticket on top of everything else! I groaned.

I grabbed the paper and saw that it was a sealed envelope with a note inside.

"Hi," the note read in unfamiliar handwriting. "I don't have your new phone number—this is the only way to contact you for now. Would you like to go out to dinner with me this evening? If you've never been to Joyce Chen's it's a great restaurant. Here's my number. Call anytime if you need help." It was signed "Ed."

Did I dare tell him about my battery problem? No. I would be resourceful and handle it myself. Instead I called Ed and told him I'd like to have dinner with him. That night, sharing rice and chicken with cashew nuts in hoisin sauce with Ed, I felt grateful and cared for.

Over the next week my moods kept changing. One day I felt elated about my new program, eagerly anticipating the beginning of classes. Then I'd fall into a black depression, apprehensive about the future and feeling alone and unloved. Life seemed pointless.

It never occurred to me to wonder how much my depression had to do with losing Susan and Dick—my newlywed friends—or how the apparent loss of my relationship with Mady, or the memory of my mother, hovered over me. I was swimming in what looked like a calm ocean, unable to see the powerful undertow of the past. For my mother, marriage and motherhood had preceded her downward slide, and I wondered if there was any connection between these events and her strange behaviors later on. Indirectly my father had suggested as much: "Things were fine until you were born," he had said. Was I also doomed? Biological urges and social needs were pushing me toward the altar, while another force, equally strong, was holding me back.

Thanks to Ed, whom I started to see regularly, I began to feel better later in the fall. Some nights he came over from Fletcher after dinner with a gallon of Brigham's chocolate chip ice cream. Other times he would bring a chrysanthemum plant or cut flowers. My new room-mates welcomed his regular appearances: "Prince Edward," they called him. He helped me forget my doubts and questions. One Sunday, after we'd come back from a morning bike ride, he gave me an impromptu gift of a carved miniature tapir—a creature, he explained, that was "shy and nocturnal." I'd never heard of a tapir before and I found his interest in animals and their habits endearing.

On the Tufts campus, in Medford, I attended classes in the Department of Education while Ed went down the hill to economics and political science classes in the Fletcher School building. His dorm, with its dining hall, was only another block away. After several weeks of classes Ed started to invite me to his dorm to watch the Hunt-ley-Brinkley evening news and have dinner. Then, after dinner, I finished my homework at the Fletcher library. By the following spring Ed and I would both get Master's degrees.

Early in November, on my birthday, we visited Aunt Mary and Uncle Delos in New Hampshire. It happened to be an Indian summer day, balmy enough for us to play tennis in shirt sleeves and blue jeans. The clay court, next to a dairy cow barn, provided the rustic setting, as Mozart, with both pastoral themes and energetic tempos, rang out from the sound system at milking time. I was relieved that Ed didn't take tennis as seriously as my country club Kidder cousins who looked like pro shop mannequins, all crisp in their tennis whites. Ed never regretted playing singles with me. Even though I had trouble returning his net-bending serve, he insisted I was giving him a good game.

We ate lunch with Aunt Mary and Uncle Delos in their cozy wood-paneled kitchen. Over crisp lettuce from the cold frame, Ed answered my family's questions about his parents' ranch and talked about Pablo, the man who ran it. Pablo lived in a "mud hut," he explained, and managed the sharing of water rights with a neighboring Indian pueblo.

"Mud hut?" Aunt Mary asked in her Virginia drawl. "You don't really mean 'mud,' do you?"

"Oh, yes. Adobe is mud. It keeps a house cool in summer and warm in winter."

How did his family happen to settle out there?, Aunt Mary wanted to know. She had never traveled west of the Mississippi.

"My grandmother in New York sent my parents out to investigate some land the family had acquired long ago in the Ortiz Mountains, near Albuquerque. She wanted to find out if there was any silver, copper, or turquoise on it," Ed said. They didn't find any metals or precious stones but they decided to stay because they loved the landscape and the dry climate.

"Hmm, squatters," Uncle Delos quipped.

Ed laughed. I knew that after our departure Aunt Mary would telephone my father and Aunt Ethel and tell them about Ed. She would relate his adventures in the Southwest, where he and his twin brother ran turkeys through alfalfa fields. He was becoming familiar to my relatives and had already met my friends in Cambridge. I wondered what it would be like to marry him, live in Cambridge, and send our children to Shady Hill School. I was becoming comfortable with these ideas.

In the meantime, letters from Arthur arrived less frequently and seemed less ardent. Time and distance were eroding our connection, prompting Arthur's analytical comments. It took a week for my letters to reach him outside Beirut, and once he was posted to Cairo they would take even longer. Besides, he told me he had met a girl in Jerusalem who reminded him of me. He was "almost completely sure" he would never want to marry her "but long distances tend to blot out affection toward someone far away."

≈

Alfie and Diana married in mid-November at an Episcopal church in Concord, Massachusetts. Ed's parents flew east for the ceremony. Ed was to be best man for his brother and he invited me to the wedding as his date. At the reception Ed introduced me to his parents. They had been divorced for ten years and "Pa" had married his second wife, Keziah, known as Kay. "Ma" (Mary) lived with the partner she referred to as Miss Katherine, and together they ran a Mexican wedding-shirt business in Santa Fe. I had never met an openly lesbian couple before, yet Ed seemed to take his mother's life choice for granted; he said he was relieved that she was happier than she had ever been with his father.

Ed had already warned me that his father had a regal, no-nonsense manner, paired with the dazzling smile he used to get his way. He charmed me. His mother, a tall slender blue-eyed blonde, with the curls she had passed on to her sons, flashed her best jewelry, a solitaire diamond, as she reminisced about the twins' birth.

"It was a cold day in February and I could barely walk," she said, holding her cigarette in a holder like Marlene Dietrich. "And then there were *two* of them. In the delivery room I thought I was done, but twenty minutes after Alfie there was Eddy! When we returned from the hospital, the Irish baby nurse looked at them in their carriage and said"—here Mary imitated the nurse's heavy brogue—"'What have you got there, Mary? Edward and Alfred? The Kings of England?'"

I was intrigued by the fact that Ed was a twin. Being around twins, a pair instead of one, struck a resonant note. It reminded me of another pattern. There was my official, biological mother and there was Mady, who was much more important to me than my mother. A bad mother and a good mother. Doubles were familiar. I loved listening to Ed and Alfie's chummy, teasing banter as they lined up the wedding party for the photographer. I wondered if there was a good twin and a bad twin.

I introduced Ed to my father in New York at Thanksgiving. Dad had already met many of my men friends and made no secret of his preferences. "He's Britain's next Churchill. He knows his stuff," he had announced after meeting Arthur in London. He referred to David, who planned to return to the East Coast for Christmas, as "the engineer." Back in Cambridge after Thanksgiving weekend, I told my father on the telephone that Ed was probably going to propose. Intuitively, I could feel it coming as he wrapped his arms around me or held my face tenderly as we kissed. But I didn't know whether I would accept his proposal.

My father cleared his throat as he tried to digest this information. "What part of the Middle East is Ed from?" he asked.

I was stunned. Was this early dementia? Was he confusing Ed with Arthur, who really did live in the Middle East? Or did he think Ed looked Jewish? As a naturalized citizen who wanted to be one hundred and ten percent American, my Canadian-born father disliked other immigrants, and he must have thought Ed looked like a foreigner. I knew he disliked Jews even though I counted many Jewish women among my friends.

During my practice teaching that winter, I drove every morning to the Bedford High School in Bedford, Massachusetts, forty miles west of Boston. I was assigned to the American history classroom of a teacher who would earn credits toward his Master's degree in exchange for mentoring me. He was an experienced man with a strong Boston accent who had good control of the thirty students in his classroom. He told his personal Korean War stories and showed films like the popular World War II series *Victory at Sea.* When it was my turn to teach, it was daunting to take his place in the classroom. I had no control whatsoever. My heart sank as the students whispered to each other and passed notes. I wished there were an escape hatch behind the teacher's desk, so that I could drop out of sight whenever I wanted.

On a cold January night Ed and I had dinner at the Ritz Hotel on the Boston Common. We usually saved the Ritz for special occasions like birthdays or holidays, but Ed's birthday was another month away, and I had just turned twenty-three in November. I wondered why Ed was taking me there. At the Ritz he treated me to a delicious dinner with a first course of smoked salmon, capers, and onions, and then a tender roast chicken as the entrée.

After dinner we walked around the Common toward Ed's car, which was parked on Charles Street. I was feeling happy and warm walking on Ed's arm. Suddenly he stopped in the middle of the sidewalk and turned to me. It had snowed briefly while we were at dinner, but now the snow was coming down harder. I loved Boston in the snow, and I thought I'd never seen Ed looking as handsome as he did with snowflakes between his face and mine.

"I love you," he said, holding both my hands, his face close to mine. "Will you marry me?"

So, this was the reason for our fancy dinner! I wasn't entirely surprised. At this point I would have wondered about him if he had *not* proposed. Still, the question seemed simple for him, and the answer was complicated for me.

"I need time to think," I said. And Ed accepted my hesitation. By this time he knew about the "Arthur dilemma," as I called it, and he was willing to wait while I figured out what to do.

For several weeks I pondered my decision. Unlike my relationship with Arthur, which depended heavily on memories and mail, I saw Ed every day. If I saw Arthur again, would our earlier passion for each other be reignited? I was beginning to wonder. When Ed and I weren't studying or writing papers, we were going out to Chinese restaurants or having dinner with his friends, a married couple who lived with their young son in Brookline. I wasn't rushing into anything. I thought

I had found the work I wanted to do—I just needed time to acquire more skills. And I knew I wanted to be with Ed, who loved me. I could imagine myself living in the places where his work would take him if he had to leave Cambridge—in Washington, at a university, or abroad. I never pictured him in any dusty impoverished capital in the Middle East, where I had felt so uncomfortable.

But I wondered about life with a husband—any husband. There was no way to "practice marry" the way one could "practice teach." In the early 1960s most couples I knew didn't live together or have premarital sex to find out if they were compatible. I didn't know how couples worked out their differences. My parents never taught me how to negotiate. Marriage would involve sharing, and as an only child I didn't know a lot about that. In my single life I had shared rooms, apartments, refrigerators, sometimes even coats or sweaters. But now I'd also have to share a bed, a checkbook, a car, meals, friends, and much more. When I pondered all the unknowns in marriage, my hands got cold and clammy.

Finally, after several weeks of reflection, I said yes to Ed. I was twenty-three and Ed was twenty-six. Most of our friends were already married. I wanted to marry a man who made me feel safe and comfortable. He had shown himself to be flexible and easy to live with. I was happy that he didn't pressure me to sleep with him before our wedding date. If passion similar to what I once felt with Arthur wasn't there yet, I felt certain it would come once the initial excitement of the wedding wore off. He suggested getting married during the following summer, before his required two-week Army summer camp, and before Fletcher and the middle-school teaching job I hoped to find began in the fall. This would give us time to get settled in a new apartment.

About a month before the wedding I started to question my decision. Was I right in assuming that I would never have the chance to know Arthur well enough before making the big commitment? Was I right in thinking I could never give up my country? Had I fallen in love with Arthur, or with Ed?

I felt alone in my decision. I didn't want to talk about it with my father, who was still a bit suspicious of Ed. And it didn't occur to me to talk to Mady. She had been happy for me when I told her I was marrying Ed. "I can't wait to meet him," she said.

Who could I talk to? At the time I had no close women friends in Cambridge. I briefly considered seeing a psychiatrist, but decided instead to go to my gynecologist in New York. I hoped he could help me sort things out and, if he couldn't, perhaps he could refer me to someone who could. Was it normal premarital jitters?, I wondered. Or was there something more?

"Tell me about Arthur," the doctor said when I was seated in his office.

I told him how we met and that we'd had been corresponding for over a year and a half. I told him what I knew about his education and his work. I knew very little about his family except that they lived on a farm in Oxfordshire. Then I mentioned that he was very well read, and that he sometimes wrote poetry and had sent me a book of poems by W. H. Auden.

"Poetry?" The doctor leaned forward as if I had revealed an important clue to Arthur's character.

"Yes."

The doctor raised his eyebrows. And then he said, "You know that homosexuals have a weakness for poetry. He may very well be gay."

Gay? *Arthur?* What nonsense, I thought. I knew he was not homosexual.

"That's not possible," I said.

"Well, many times men are attracted to both men and women. It's something to think about."

I stormed out of his office.

That evening, while my father was out having dinner with Mary Case, Ed and I sat on the sofa and talked. He told me he had been worried from the beginning that I would leave and fly off to see Arthur in Egypt. He hoped I wouldn't do that. He loved me, and he wanted to marry me. He was sure we would be happy together.

Several days after this conversation on the sofa, I decided Ed was right—although I don't recall where we were when I finally said yes. Since then I have wondered about the important life choice I made when I was only twenty-three and when long-distance electronic communications didn't exist. Looking back, I never saw more than two alternatives: Marry Ed or wait for Arthur. But I could also have postponed all serious involvements and continued searching for a satisfying occupation. But at the time that idea was way off my list, never appearing as a legitimate third option. Although I was aware of my inexperience in making important decisions, I nevertheless took a giant leap into marriage.

Mindful of Arthur's hope that I would follow the dictates of my heart, I dismissed that idea as an oversimplification in the head–heart struggle. Couldn't my heart alone lead me astray? Or could the head *and* the heart become allies in making a good decision? If I relied on my head for guidance, I was choosing the man who had already proved himself available and reliable, one who enjoyed his family and who would join me in creating a new one of our own.

"Let's continue with our wedding plans," I said to Ed as we stood at the curb loading our bags before driving to Boston. "Let's decide where we're going to get married." Ed smiled and put his arms around me, lifting me into the air. We both laughed.

I was sure I'd made a good decision.

Chapter 8

Marriage and Mexico

When Ed and I started planning our summer wedding, I thought about Aunt Mary and her colorful garden in Contoocook, New Hampshire. Ever since my move to Boston I'd regarded their farmhouse as my second home. I wanted to wear fresh flowers in my hair and create an altar on a wicker table near the crabapple trees. Family and a few close friends could drive up from Boston, and the rector at Aunt Mary's church in nearby Hopkinton would perform the ceremony. Ed and I would prepare cold salads to go with the champagne, and we would order the wedding cake from a baker in Concord. In case of rain there would be a tent near the maple trees and we could set up tables in the barn.

I had first stayed at Aunt Mary and Uncle Delos's place with my parents and Mady when I was seventeen, just before my freshman year at Vassar. The visit did not go well. We drove to Contoocook on a hot day in August, and sitting next to Mady in the sweltering back seat of my father's Cadillac was unbearable.

"The air conditioning isn't working," I whined. "It's so hot back here I can't stand it." I yawned. I tried to sleep. I wanted to go back home to New York to resume my seventeen-year-old life, but I was stuck. And my father, the only driver then, scolded and growled.

Sam Brown, whom I thought of as my boyfriend, lived not far from my aunt and uncle, in Exeter, New Hampshire, on the campus of Phillips Exeter Academy, where he had prepared for Yale. I wondered if I should telephone him. In those days boys called girls, not the other way around, and I knew this. But, I reasoned, how could he call me if he didn't know where I was? He didn't have my telephone number in Contoocook.

But I had his—in Exeter—and when we arrived at the farmhouse I dialed it. His mother answered and told me he was hiking with friends in the White Mountains. She promised to try to contact him.

When Sam called back the next day I was elated. Maybe he really liked me after all! I had never been sure. He said he would drive down from the mountains and take me out to dinner the next day. I looked forward to my rescue from too many grownups.

Ever since a friend had introduced me to her cousin Sam during our spring vacation, I couldn't stop thinking about his deep sexy voice. At the Yale Spring Fling weekend we lay on the grass of his Davenport College courtyard, talking and drinking beer. He was an unusual young man, headed into pediatric medicine and not shy about repeating what he learned in his pre-med program—sayings like "Breast Fed Is Best Fed." I was embarrassed to use the word "breast" in front of a boy, but here was Sam, referring to breasts as if they were as ordinary as knees.

Late in the afternoon, as the sun dropped down toward the ridge west of the farmhouse, Sam pulled into the driveway and parked his Jeep in front of the Kidders' old barn. My heart was beating fast. He was still dressed in hiking gear—blue jeans, a plaid cotton shirt, and sturdy boots with laces. After making polite conversation with my parents and my aunt and uncle for a few minutes, we drove into Concord to see *The King and I*. Afterward we had pizza and beer at the local pizza parlor. I'd never tasted pizza before.

"You didn't finish your pizza," Sam remarked.

"I didn't really like it that much."

"Pizza? Why, everyone likes pizza! What's the matter with you?"

"Here," I said, pushing my plate over to him. "Eat the rest of it."

"Okay, okay."

I was hoping he would kiss me, but he was not in a kissing mood. From then on that evening we disagreed about everything. He talked about going to Rye Beach, along the coast, which I didn't want to do. He said he liked to be part of a crowd, and I said I didn't like crowds. That was strange to him. Maybe he was thinking I was strange, too. After the pizza he dropped me off at the house and drove home to Exeter. He promised to call me from Yale after I arrived at Vassar.

My parents were waiting for me when I walked into my aunt and uncle's living room. Mady had already gone upstairs to bed. My mother smiled at me and said nothing, but I could see right away my father was displeased.

"Why does he come to take you out wearing construction boots?" he asked me. "That's not the right way to treat a young lady."

"Because he came down directly from the mountains, Dad. Those were hiking boots. He was hiking."

"Those boots are not respectful. He ought to know better. He's how old?"

I got up in tears and headed for the stairs.

As I ran up to my room I yelled at my father over my shoulder. "Why are you so critical? Why can't you just leave me alone? Let me live my life!"

I couldn't stop sobbing. My date with Sam was a disaster, and now I wouldn't see him again for a couple of months or more. And my father made things worse. Clearly, having dates around my parents was not a good idea. My mother could be tactless, and conversations with my father were stiff and awkward—if not hostile. Vassar would be a better setting for my social life.

Five years later, on Memorial Day of 1961, I returned to Contoocook with my new friend David. By this time I was living in Cambridge, and I had my own car. Aunt Mary and Uncle Delos had just returned from their winter refuge in Delray Beach, Florida. They were eager to see me and meet David, who was about to get his Master's degree at MIT.

"How long can you stay?" Aunt Mary asked as we sat down by the fireplace for a chat.

"Forever!" I said, laughing. "I don't want to leave, ever."

And I didn't. I made myself at home. I had brought a load of laundry and I hung it out on the clothesline to dry. I helped Uncle Delos prepare Aunt Mary's breakfast tray. And the little bedroom at the top of the stairs, with the red and white patchwork quilt on the bed, became "my" room. I was happy to spend time with Uncle Delos and Aunt Mary. I felt a new sense of family and belonging in my relatives' welcoming home.

I also recognized what a gem of a place the Kidders had found and renovated. I could imagine it written up in a four-page color spread in *Architectural Digest*—"Updated Colonial Home Exudes Charm." I loved the brisk country air, the smell of wood smoke in the kitchen fireplace, the coffee brewing, and bacon frying. At dinner we always had fresh lettuce from the garden—even the slugs couldn't make a dent in this healthy crop.

For the first time I had an adult woman relative to talk to who was interested in cooking, gardening, antique furniture, interior decorating, and family genealogy. She was someone who would also comment on my clothes and volunteer an opinion about what was and what wasn't becoming. Soon we were discussing Aunt Mary's new living room curtains and trying new recipes together. I'd never done this either with my mother or with Mady. Aunt Mary was teaching me. And she never criticized or asked awkward questions. Here, too, I had found the right place to entertain prospective suitors. Always the gracious southern hostess, she could help me charm any young man I brought along for the weekend.

And so it was that six months later, on November 4, 1961, a warm Indian summer day, I brought a new man friend along to meet my relatives. This was my first important date with my future husband.

~

In March, 1962, during spring break, Ed and I drove to New York for a visit with my father. We wanted to talk about our wedding plans. After the ceremony in mid-July, we told my father, Ed would have to spend two weeks at Camp Drum, New York, in the Army Reserve. Early in August we'd go on our honeymoon to Mexico and New Mexico. There I could spend time with his parents and see the Southwest before returning to Cambridge for Ed's second year at the Fletcher School, where he was studying for his Ph.D. in economics. There I would continue my search for a teaching position.

"I don't want to be married in New York," I told my father. "Especially not in July when it's so hot."

I looked at his face, waiting for his positive reaction. Surely, I thought, the bride-to-be can make her own wedding plans.

"I want a small outdoor wedding at Aunt Mary and Uncle Delos's home," I went on. "July fourteenth, Bastille Day, will be perfect. It's a Saturday this year, a day of celebration in France. And it will be a beautiful sunny day, I hope, in New Hampshire."

I thought he'd go for this idea because he always liked Aunt Mary, and having the wedding there would make things easier for the Kidders. But I hadn't reckoned with my father's determination to have things his way.

"We'll have the wedding in the Chapel of the Fifth Avenue Presbyterian Church," he said, hardly taking a moment to consider what I'd proposed. "On West Fifty-fifth Street."

"But it's the wrong place for a summer wedding," I protested. "We want to be outdoors. And this has never been my church! I'm a confirmed Episcopalian, even though I don't go to church now. And neither does Ed."

The thought of collaborating with my father on an event as important as this gave me chills. He would plow right over my plans. And he was tone deaf—he gave no indication that he had even heard me. So there we were, our wedding plans vetoed.

My father cleared his throat and turned to me. "I'll talk to Mary," he said, referring to Mary Case. "Maybe she can help us get the use of the River Club for the reception."

The River Club is located in Manhattan on East Fifty-second Street, overlooking the East River. Its large public rooms are tastefully decorated with English linen prints and brocades. The food in the dining room, where my father, Ed, and I had often dined with Mary Case, was delicious.

Mary will know what to do, I thought. She has three married daughters, and my father will listen to her suggestions. At least my father agreed to help me get married. There were no other big obstacles. So without further argument I went along with the New York plan. After all, he would be footing the bill. I never thought about eloping. If the goal was to get married, then any means, any place, was acceptable. Looking back, I'm surprised at how malleable I was, how quickly I allowed my father to ignore my wishes.

In the end he hired wedding planners, and they did everything. It was like a corporate event, with few personal choices. All Ed and I had to do was provide lists of family and friends to be invited, select the bridesmaids and ushers, choose the bridesmaids' dresses, buy my own dress, and show up on the appointed day. The planners took care of printing and addressing invitations, ordering flowers, arranging for the photographer, hiring the musicians at the reception, renting the limousine, and arranging for the drinks and hors d'oeuvres at the River Club. At least I could choose the music for my walk down the aisle, and I picked a Purcell Trumpet Voluntary. And instead of flowers in my hair I wore a cathedral-length veil that had once belonged to my mother's paternal aunt, Lucy Kidder Bulkley.

On Boston's Newbury Street I bought a simple, short-sleeved wedding dress, and in New York I shopped at my mother's favorite linen store, Plummer McCutcheon, for monogrammed towels and sheets. It was sad to go trousseau shopping alone, without an older woman relative. But Aunt Mary never wanted to drive into Boston.

And Mady was unavailable to shop with me whenever I was in New York.

July 14, 1962, was hot and sticky in New York. The sky was white, not the royal blue New Mexico sky with cumulus clouds that Ed missed on the East Coast. The air was heavy, nothing like the fresh air we would have enjoyed in New Hampshire. In New York it was a day to stay indoors next to an air conditioner and watch the French celebrate Bastille Day, our wedding day, on television.

Even though it wouldn't take place at their farm, I was glad that Aunt Mary and Uncle Delos would attend the wedding—especially since I knew how much Uncle Delos loathed New York; he hadn't been there for years. Fortunately, they were able to spend the weekend at Aunt Ethel's in Englewood. And they could see their two daughters, my cousins, who came with their families from Baltimore and Chicago. Ed's father and mother came separately from Santa Fe without their respective partners.

I changed into my wedding dress upstairs at the River Club with Aunt Mary's and Mady's help. In the only photograph of Mady at the wedding I am sitting in a chair, and she and Aunt Mary are holding up the long lace veil behind me. Moments before, Aunt Mary had lamented the fact that the chapel decorations and the floral bouquets and arrangements at the reception had been delegated to a florist, not to a family member.

"What did you expect?" I asked her. "This is my father's doing. He's paying for everything. and he's showing off."

"Well, I suppose so," she sighed. "Tomorrow I'm going to take your beautiful bridal bouquet, with all those wonderful gardenias, and put it on your mother's grave."

I had never suggested such a gesture. Why hadn't she asked me what I wanted to do?

I would have given my bridal bouquet to Mady.

On the day of the wedding I was nervous. The night before, I had taken a sleeping pill. I had the jitters, and I still worried whether I was doing the right thing. I was so full of doubt that I had to numb myself with a tranquilizer in order to walk down the aisle. Ed, on the other hand, seemed to have no doubts at all.

Looking back now, I can see why I was so nervous about getting married. My biological mother and Mady had offered stark contrasts of adult womanhood. Mady had never, as far as I knew, been with a man. In our household her strength, authority, and competence were impressive. And she was self-supporting; she was free to come and go. My mother, despite her family inheritance, was utterly dependent on my father's caregiving. Even though I saw no social advantage in Mady's spinsterhood, I thought the quality of her life was much better than my mother's.

At this time I didn't know much about my parents' romance, except that my mother had hesitated before she finally said yes to my father. She wasn't sure whether to continue her state of "single blessedness," as she called it. I know this now, after reading their courtship letters: hers was a tentative yes, full of doubts. And the outcome, as I saw it, was catastrophic. My father's frequent comment to me—"Everything was fine until you were born"—raised a dark specter of marriage and childbirth that foreshadowed my mother's unraveling.

After the ceremony, everything went well at the reception and we were having fun dancing, cutting the cake, and sipping champagne.

"This is a wonderful party, Dad," I said, pausing as I whirled around the dance floor with one of my cousins.

"Maybe so. But I think everyone's had enough to drink and it's time to close the bar. And I can't do that until you and Ed leave. The limo is waiting for you outside."

"Time to go? Not yet!"

"Yes. Climb the staircase, throw the bouquet, then change into your going-away clothes."

What a killjoy he is, I thought. But I went along with his orders. I wouldn't have to obey him any more after this. So without an argument, I threw my bouquet and then changed into my brown linen suit and fastened a double strand of my mother's coral beads around my neck. My twelve-year-old cousin Leslie, an athletic tennis player, caught the bouquet. Then Ed and I climbed into the limousine that took us west on Fifty-fifth Street to the Gotham Hotel for our wedding night.

Our hotel room was small, but it had the essential item—a big bed. I told Ed I felt nervous, and excited. We held each other for a long time and he gave me a big kiss. Then he said he was starving. I realized I was too. We hadn't eaten all day, so we went downstairs to the dining room. There, across the room, we saw some of Ed's relatives, who told our waiter we had just been married.

Taking our order, the waiter hovered. "He the water, she the rose," he said in a heavy Italian accent. He mumbled about marriage and how lovely I looked. But I was furious. I wanted us to savor our first moments as husband and wife by ourselves, and here was this idiot. I fumed inside—I didn't have the nerve to tell the waiter to leave us alone.

When we returned to our room to take off our clothes and shoes, the bed suddenly collapsed. The mattress and several pillows slipped onto the floor.

"Oh no, look at the bed," I wailed.

"What the hell?" Ed knelt down on the carpet and peered under the mattress to see what the problem was.

"Shouldn't we call someone?" I asked. "This can't be our problem."

Already the wedding night magic was disappearing as we wrestled with the bedclothes, trying to find the broken part of the bed and waiting for someone to fix it.

"I bet this is an Alfie prank," I said. "Wouldn't he do something like this? He couldn't attach tin cans to the limo fender but he *could* disrupt our first night."

We called housekeeping and they sent the engineer. I imagined the men smirking in the hallway afterward. What kind of bad omen was this? I wondered. I couldn't help feeling superstitious. If the bed collapses, will the marriage collapse too?

On Monday morning after the wedding I telephoned my father.

I thanked him for taking charge of everything—I figured it was the right thing to do. Ed's and my wedding, the way my father wanted it.

"Well, he said, "I just paid for it in the market this morning. Five thousand dollars profit from the sale of another pipeline stock. How about that?"

I didn't know what to say.

"Good for you," I managed finally, resisting the impulse to slam the phone down.

I was disappointed in my father, bringing his commercial world into my joyous occasion, before we'd even left for our honeymoon.

After two nights at the Gotham Hotel, and lunch on Sunday with Ed's mother, we drove back to our new apartment on Chatham Street, in Cambridge, taking with us some of our more practical wedding presents. I stayed there while Ed left for Camp Drum for his two-week ROTC service.

When he returned to Cambridge early in August, we flew from Boston to Mexico City. I could have insisted on going to Bermuda, the traditional honeymoon destination, and Ed would have agreed, to please me. But I didn't want us to be so traditional. And Ed had talked so enthusiastically about his two summers in Mexico, where he had studied Spanish, and about Hoyt and Marty Frothingham, his cousins who lived there, that I went along with his idea. We would spend ten days in Mexico City, Taxco, and Acapulco. I was curious to meet Hoyt and Marty, who had raised both their sons in Mexico. From Mexico City we would fly to Santa Fe, spending half our time there with Ed's father and his second wife, Keziah, and the other half with Ma and "Miss Katherine."

I was leery about visiting Mexico—I had heard worrisome stories about people getting altitude sickness and diarrhea, or being held up by bandits. But as a new bride I wanted to please Ed. At the Frothing-hams' weekend place in Cuautla, outside Mexico City, we marveled at the dazzling view of the snow-capped volcano Popocatepetl and soaked in hot springs. A few days later, on the way to Acapulco, our rented car had a flat tire, but we stayed pumped up about the semitropical scenery and the miles of white beaches along the Pacific Coast. Only when scorching heat burned my feet on the beach in front of our hotel, when itchy hives reddened my arms and legs, and when broken air conditioning forced us to cool off in the hotel pool at midnight did my spirits begin to sag.

And this was only the beginning. By the time we arrived at my in-laws' home in Santa Fe, my period was late. I thought at first that the Mexican diet of tortillas and frijoles, or drinking straight tequila with a sprinkling of salt, might be the problem. Or Montezuma's Revenge, which had attacked us both more than once.

I tried to ignore the nausea I was feeling on our third night in Santa Fe, when Pa and Kay gave a party to introduce me to their friends—they already knew Ed. Declining all the passed hors d'oeuvres and taking only a few sips of wine, I greeted their guests as warmly as I could, letting Ed guide me around the *portal* of their adobe house. By the next morning I calculated that my period was more than two weeks late and I panicked as I replayed in my mind all our nights in Acapulco and Taxco, trying to identify the moment of conception. I didn't want to be pregnant. Having a baby so soon after our wedding would be bad timing. I was so caught up in the novelty of being married, with a brand-new wedding ring on my finger, and a man beside me every night who sometimes snored after we made love, that I couldn't take in the possibility that I might be pregnant.

Back in Boston, in our new apartment, my period still hadn't come. And I was beginning to feel sick in the mornings. I couldn't eat anything until lunchtime. I asked a friend, who was seven months pregnant with her second child, for the name of her doctor and got an appointment with her obstetrician, Dr. Yahia, the next day.

Chapter 9

Mother's Day

I drove to Dr. Yahia's office to provide a specimen for the pregnancy test. I had planned to start a new teaching job in a suburban middle school, but now teaching was up in the air. I'd heard about unwanted pregnancies—getting knocked up, we called it—and I'd always felt sorry for "those girls." This could happen to them but never to me. Now, though, I was in the same boat.

Before this, having a baby had never crossed my mind. But here I was in the waiting room of an obstetrician's office at the Boston Lying-In Hospital with my heart pounding. The nurse took the specimen and told me that the lab would have results shortly.

"Make yourself comfortable," she said with a big smile before she disappeared behind a door. I wanted to scream at her. There was no reason to smile.

I was leafing nervously through a magazine in the waiting room when Dr. Yahia came out and shook my hand. He was a tall middle-aged man with thinning reddish hair. He held an unlit cigarette in his left hand.

"Congratulations, Mrs. Hoyt, you're due early in May."

"I am—?" I stammered.

"Yes indeed. It's a perfect date. Fatten up the baby all summer to prepare for a Boston winter. And while you're here in the office today you should make another appointment. We want you to have a healthy pregnancy. The nurse will help you."

And then he was gone.

I didn't see what was so perfect about this due date—or any due date. I was too shocked. When I got back to the apartment I stared at my still-flat belly, wondering how such a tiny embryo could turn my newlywed happiness into gloom so quickly, making me nauseated and worried.

In the late afternoon when Ed returned from Harvard's Widener Library I was lying on the bed crying. Tears had dampened the pillow behind my head. Ed lay down beside me and cradled my face in his hands.

"So it was positive?" he asked gently.

"Yes," I said, sobbing.

"Oh, my God," Ed said. "How on earth did this happen?"

We lay on the bed for a while in silence before we started to speculate about when conception might have occurred. And where. I thought it might have been Taxco. Ed said it must have been one of the sultry nights in Acapulco when we swam in the hotel pool to cool off.

"What are we going to do?"

"Don't worry," Ed answered. "We'll figure it out."

Despite Ed's reassurance, I was dejected—and furious at the New York gynecologist, whose birth control method had failed. The next day, trembling with anger, I called his office and waited for the secretary to put him on the line.

"This is Sarnia Hoyt. I saw you in July before my wedding, and you recommended using contraceptive jelly."

"That's right," he said. "I recall your visit. The jelly is very effective."

"I'm calling to tell you that I'm pregnant even though I followed your instructions to the letter. I don't want to be pregnant yet! Next year, maybe. But not now!" I was screaming into the phone.

The doctor cleared his throat. "I'm sorry you feel that way. I know that becoming a mother, ready or not, is the most rewarding thing a woman can do in her life. Time and again I've seen it in my practice. After the birth the mother falls in love with her child."

"How can you be so sure?" I yelled. "You're an idiot!" And I slammed down the receiver.

Most evenings during the next month Ed and I sat on the sofa in our dark living room to talk about the baby. One night I was tearful as we sipped our gin and tonics, waiting for a chicken casserole to finish cooking. I had never thought about adoption or abortion before, but now these words had new importance. If we wanted to end the pregnancy we would have to do something. Soon.

I knew I couldn't opt for adoption. After nine months in my womb the baby would feel like a part of me. And I could never give it up. The fate of my child—not knowing what had happened to him or her—would always haunt me. That left us with only one option—abortion—which was still illegal in this country. It would require a trip to Japan, Sweden, or some other place. It would be expensive travel with money we didn't have, and Ed would lose valuable class time. In those years there were safe, but illegal, options for abortion in America, but I knew nothing about them.

At least I wasn't alone with my dilemma. In the words of one of our favorite songs, Ed stood by me. He said I should do whatever I felt I needed to do. We could fly to Japan or Sweden if we had to. And we would go together.

"But I do know that we can give the baby a good home," he said. "We can create a family."

I conjured up a vision of Ed cradling our baby in his arms. I didn't know enough then to picture him with spit-up on a clean shirt.

"I think we can do a better job of raising him or her than any adopting parents," he added. I didn't know how he knew this but I wanted to believe him. And after a few more days of living with this decision, getting used to the idea of becoming a parent, I knew down deep that it was the best choice. The only choice.

Early in the pregnancy Ed had started calling the fetus Eggbert.

Or Eggberta. It was already a person in his mind. He seemed ready
to shift gears and become a parent. I knew I would be the primary
caregiver, and that I would have to postpone any full-time career
plans. But I also knew that as an only child, with an aging father, I
would eventually want a family of my own. Ed and I were just getting
started sooner rather than later.

Despite my angst about the pregnancy, Ed and I were enjoying
our life together. Most Sundays that fall we drove to Medfield, a rural
suburb west of Boston, for lunch, followed by poker games with
Ed's Aunt Hattie and Uncle Fats Frothingham. Lunch was always a
simple meal because Aunt Hattie hated cooking—boiled potatoes, an
eye-round roast much too rare, and frozen peas. By the time lunch
was ready she would be tipsy and the peas would roll off the silver
serving dish onto the floor. After another round of drinks we were
calling them Uncle Hats and Aunt Fattie.

On one of those Sundays, Ed raised his wine glass at the dining
room table and announced, "We've got news for you."

"Well, I don't suppose you're pregnant yet," said Fats with one of his
broad smiles. "It's too soon. You've only been married a few months."

I could feel myself blushing.

"Oh, yes, we are," Ed said with a grin.

Fats's and Hattie's—and everyone else's—joy when we announced
the pregnancy pleased me, and yet when we went home later and I
confronted my expanding waistline in the mirror I felt depressed. We
had only just begun to explore our sex life together and now I was too
unhappy to participate with enthusiasm. I had always liked feeling tall
and thin but Ed admired my new shape—"a spinnaker on a broad
reach," he called it.

One beautiful fall weekend we drove to the North Shore for a buffet
dinner with one of Ed's ushers and his wife. Their suburban colonial
home was cluttered with the toys of their three little girls.

"Ed must have kissed you too hard," Bobby said, laughing, after
we shared our news. He was tall and boisterous and already I disliked
him. Shut up, Bobby, I thought. It's not funny. I smiled wanly.

In the years since then, I've learned how blessed I was to conceive so easily, but at that time I knew I wasn't ready to become a mother. I had been so busy with wedding plans, thank-you notes, and moving from one apartment to another that I didn't give a thought to having children. And I was too angry. I felt like a child having a child. Disabled by illness, my biological mother could not model the maternal behavior that might have guided me. She left almost all the parenting to Mady, whose loving kindness in our daily interactions endeared her to me always.

In October I wrote to Mady, enclosing pictures from our wedding. I didn't want to tell her about the pregnancy just yet—I needed to feel more comfortable with the new reality. I sent her a picture of Ed and me, along with the one of her and Aunt Mary holding my veil.

She wrote back:

> They all was good, and you look lovely on all, but the one I did like best, is the one of you and your husband. I found a frame for it and its now on the top of my desk, looking down on me. You both look so very happy — I am glad of that.

A couple of weeks later I telephoned Mady to give her the news. But I didn't want to tell her how I really felt about the pregnancy because I thought it would upset her, and I knew she wouldn't understand. In her world, women accepted their lot in life. They didn't expect to have choices, certainly not about pregnancy. But then, I thought, she had always been my number-one confidante. Why not tell her the truth?

"I'm not ready, Mady. It's too soon to become a mother." I almost choked on my words. "I'll have only a few months alone with Ed—I've never had a roommate like him before! And then there's going to be an even bigger adjustment with the baby."

"But it's a natural thing," she said. "Becoming a mother. You'll see. You'll be happy to have a little girl."

"But there's no choice about the baby's sex."

"That's true. So you just try again, and keep trying until you get a girl."

"Oh, Mady," I groaned. "You don't understand."

"This is God's will," Mady went on. "You have to accept it."

"But God doesn't have anything to do with it!" I cried. "It was bad advice from the doctor!"

A few months later, in February, I called Mady again to ask for her help. Again I hesitated because I thought I shouldn't ask so much of her. After all, she wasn't young any more. In 1963 she was almost seventy.

"Would you be able to come to Boston early in May? It would be wonderful to have an extra hand when the baby arrives." I couldn't imagine giving birth without Mady there.

Her answer, in a letter, disappointed me.

> I am planning on going a trip to Norway this year. I also had the same plans last year, but then I got sick and that was that. Hope things goes better now. Keep yourself happy and well, and that's my wish for you. I would not like anything better than to be some little help to you, but it cannot be that way. Much love, Mady

Reading this, I cried. *Cannot be that way.* I was surprised to learn that if she hadn't been ill she would have gone to Norway last summer. She would have missed my wedding! I couldn't tell from her letter if the timing of her travel plans was dictated by the cost of the passage, or whether the family in Norway had some influence. Either way, I could see that in her mind my needs and hopes had become secondary.

I couldn't count on Mady anymore. I had often asked for her help and advice, and she was always happy to give it. But now things were different. She had been off my father's payroll for four years. Maybe she didn't care about me as much as she used to. She had moved on, and so should I.

As my pregnancy proceeded I continued to study my body's betrayal. How did it dare do what I didn't want? Just because Ed's sperm had united with my egg didn't guarantee that I would become a good mother, or that Ed would become the father he wanted to be— nothing like his own father, who had frightened him when he was young. I could hardly take care of myself—how could I take care of a baby? The idea of an unexpected child haunted me, and I wondered about my mother and her experience. Hadn't I also been unplanned? The way my mother ignored me, it had always felt that way. How come history was repeating itself?

Four years after her death, I thought I had banished my mother from my thoughts. But furnishing our apartment with things she had put in storage when I was young was bringing her back to life. Here was a large oil painting of her as a four-year-old in a blue and white dress—I had never seen it before. Here too were her sewing table, rocking chair, tea cups and saucers, and her pale green and gold set of Jane Austen, the pages still uncut. She had resurrected herself and was walking around inside my head, saying whatever she pleased. I could see her with her messy hair, seated in an upholstered chair, her legs spread-eagled and her pink stocking garters showing on her thighs. Without a girdle to flatten the lines of her flabby belly, she had always embarrassed me.

I was surprised at the way pregnancy affected me. I developed a huge appetite and loved making tollhouse cookies. One evening a favorite cousin from Detroit arrived in Boston on a business trip and took us out for dinner at the Ritz Hotel. I'd never enjoyed fresh oysters before, but this time I devoured a whole dozen. As my belly grew I moved the desk out of the spare room into our bedroom and furnished that room with a crib, a changing table, and a small chest of drawers, as well as a daybed. At a store on Brattle Street I bought two maternity dresses, in pretty moss green and teal blue wool, and they gave me a new pyramid shape. I'd never been a fanatical cleaner, but

in the last few weeks before my due date I dropped down on my hands
and knees and scrubbed the nursery floor, instinctively preparing the
nest—and getting a backache.

During January, before I began to show, I worked as a substitute
French teacher at the Brookline High School. It was dark and frigid
in the mornings as I drove from Cambridge across the Charles for my
first class. By coincidence I was taking the place of another Mrs. Hoyt,
so students joked about the name that still felt new to me.

"*Je m'appelle Madame Hoyt. Comment vous appelez-vous?*"

I knew what to do with the students because I had notes from my
work teaching at Shady Hill. My classes went well, the administrator
was enthusiastic about me, and the pay was generous. I was enjoying
my job.

But one evening at a dinner party a friend of Ed's made a comment
that disturbed and puzzled me.

"So you can't support her?" he asked Ed. "She has to go out, pregnant, and become the breadwinner? What's the matter with you?"

Suddenly my status as a young married woman in the workplace
invited new scrutiny in the eyes of men. How could Ed look incom-
petent if I worked and he didn't, when he was a graduate student with
a promising career ahead of him? In another encounter, an employee
at the Massachusetts Department of Motor Vehicles insisted that my
new married name on my driver's license should be Sarnia Tillison
Hoyt, not Sarnia Hayes Hoyt. Hayes was my maiden name, and Tillison was my former middle name, ready to be discarded. We had a
loud and public argument before I convinced him it had to be Hayes.

As my May due date approached my father asked me to come to
New York to sign a will. His timing made me wonder. Did he think
I might not survive childbirth? My mother's estate had settled three
years earlier, and I was one of her beneficiaries. I had never drawn up
a will before, and my father explained that it was just "boilerplate." I
would leave everything to my husband and any "issue." I hated the
way lawyers referred to our baby as "issue."

When I arrived at the New York apartment I kissed my father hello and then went straight to the kitchen to meet his new housekeeper-cook, a tall, black-haired Hungarian immigrant Juliana. She said she was pleased to cook for me because my father had lost his sense of taste and smell and couldn't appreciate her *chicken paprikash*. She was sure I would enjoy it.

My father and I had our regular evening cocktail in the living room and as we sat down at the dining room table, he began to tell me my birth story.

"When we arrived at the Englewood Hospital," he said, "the doctors decided that because of her age Mommy had to have a Caesarean section."

Caesarean? Oh no, I thought.

He went on, "Then she got a staph infection and had to stay in the hospital almost a month."

"And where was I?"

"After a few days you came home with the baby nurse. Your mother almost died."

Was he trying to scare me? If this had happened to my mother, did he think this might happen to me? But I was only twenty-four, a good age for natural childbirth. She was forty when she gave birth. I wondered why my father was sharing this frightening story with me just weeks before my due date.

Then he changed the subject. "Your doctor has a strange name. What sort of a person is he, this Yahia man? Is he Japanese?"

I stiffened in my chair. Once again, he and his xenophobia questioned my judgment. He wanted to meet my latest alien, my obstetrician. I told him they could meet each other at the hospital, after the baby's birth.

Throughout my pregnancy I had regular appointments with the doctor. Alcohol was fine, he said, especially as a lubricant for sex. Cigarettes? Not a problem. One day I told him I was worried about getting help at home after the baby was born. Did he have any suggestions?

"That's easy," he said. "Get your mother to come."

"She died four years ago."

Dr. Yahia clucked sympathetically but said nothing. Month after month, it was the same. We were deaf to each other. Dr. Yahia made no notes to help him remember my mother's death. When he mentioned her again after that first time, I could feel the anger rising in my pelvis; I wanted to strangle him. I already knew there were plenty of reasons to dislike doctors, and here was one more. But there was no point in switching, I thought—one would be as bad as another.

During the last month Dr. Yahia relented and gave me the name of a doula-nurse. "But I want to caution you," he said. "She's not one hundred percent behind breastfeeding because she doesn't think the baby gets enough nourishment. With breast milk it's hard to measure intake." To this day I don't know why I couldn't find someone more suitable in all of Boston, but I was young and inexperienced.

Early in the morning on May 2nd I was surprised when my water broke. I had no idea such a thing could happen—when I read about it, I didn't know what it meant. We rushed to the hospital. There Ed was escorted to a waiting room while I was taken upstairs to spend the whole day alone in one of the labor rooms. Occasionally a nurse would come to check on me as my cervix slowly dilated.

Ed was not allowed to stay with me. He sat with other fathers-in-waiting in a smoke-filled room, studying for his oral exams. I had an anthropology book by Ruth Benedict, but anxiety killed my concentration. I was too nervous and excited—I could hardly wait to find out if we had a boy or a girl and to get my body back in shape.

The contractions were slow at first and as they came more frequently I asked for the epidural. I had never felt pain like this. But I recalled my twelfth-grade biology teacher saying that the brain is designed to help a woman forget the pain of childbirth. And that is what happened.

Neddy was born late at night after about fifteen hours of labor. The moment when the delivery room nurse laid my swaddled son on my chest and asked, "Breast or bottle?" will stay with me forever. My baby. My miracle. He came to life with endearing little bleats. There was no question in my mind: I wanted to nurse him. He weighed seven pounds, six ounces. He was beautiful and I was euphoric. A tsunami of love and tenderness swept over me as I lay on the gurney admiring him and his pink face. He smelled as good as a fruit pie coming out of the oven.

Suddenly I didn't care about having a girl. I was thrilled to be the mother of a boy.

The Sunday we came home from the hospital happened to be Mother's Day, the second Sunday in May. The doula-nurse who had doubts about breastfeeding welcomed us. I stared at her, wishing she would transform herself magically into Mady. But Mady was on a steamship crossing the ocean. This nurse's high-pitched voice, her posture, the way she touched my baby—everything about her was wrong. Banging pots and pans around in the kitchen, roasting the steak instead of broiling it—she was an alien invader. She refused to get me up in the middle of the night to feed the baby, and once I caught her giving Neddy a bottle of formula. After three days, I let her go.

Ed, Neddy, and I were on our own. Now we were a family of three.

I was unprepared for the profound physical attachment to my tiny child—the orgasmic feelings as Neddy nursed, reducing my uterus to its normal size; the way milk spontaneously spurted out of my breast whenever I heard his tiny cries. My whole body had been colonized by this small, vulnerable creature who was both me and not-me. All these things surprised and fascinated both Ed and me.

My college friend Barbara came promptly for a peek at Neddy. She had met both my mother and Mady when she stayed with me in New York while we were sophomores at Vassar. Barbara had been unfazed by my mother's messy hair and her rudimentary social skills. So when Ed telephoned her and asked her to stay with Neddy and me while he went away for his two-week ROTC training in June, Barbara moved in to help me. For two weeks she slept on the daybed, got up with Neddy in the night so that I could sleep, and continued with her day job at the hospital.

One evening I put a fussy Neddy in his infant seat and strapped the seat to a rocking chair. Seated next to him on the sofa, I used my foot to rock the rocker.

"Not like that!" Barbara said. "Go and sit in the rocking chair and hold him!"

As soon as I did this Neddy stopped crying.

"That's what the rocker is for." She laughed. "To soothe the baby."

I wondered sometimes what might soothe me, so that I could manage the shopping, cooking, and cleaning chores along with the new responsibility of caring for the baby. It seemed that mothering was so full-time I wouldn't be able to do anything else, except when he was sleeping. I would have to learn how to juggle everything.

Neddy transformed my life. Whenever I went out I pushed him in the stroller—to the market, the laundromat, to the park to look for other mothers and babies, and to the camera store to pick up color prints and more film. People admired him, making me feel proud of something I'd accomplished without even trying. Sometimes I fell asleep with Neddy at my breast; more often I used those quiet times to read. Eventually, as I began weaning him, I started to leave Neddy with a babysitter for a few hours during the week so that I could do errands in Boston and meet a friend for lunch.

Not surprisingly, I faced a new dilemma with babysitters. If I disappeared for a day and another caregiver took over, what would happen to the mother–child bond? How much time off could I take for myself without severing our connection? I never found any peace of mind when I was away from my children. I believed then that if I worked full-time my children would love their babysitter more than they would love me. I feared that my children would have the same complicated feelings about the hired help as I had had about Mady.

Like many young women of my generation, I had barely articulated my ideas about marriage and my role in it. But I knew that if I wanted an interesting life I had to have the right husband, one who would be the primary breadwinner and whose career choices would determine where we lived. I thought that in a male-dominated society only exceptional women could have a career, and I didn't see myself that way. I would focus on home and family, working outside the home part-time wherever possible.

In early November 1963, I invited Mady to visit us. By this time Neddy was six months old and he rode in the back of the car in a child seat when we drove to pick Mady up at the train. I couldn't wait to show him off. I thought of Mady as Neddy's grandmother.

Ed stayed with Neddy in the double-parked car outside South Station while I went to find Mady on the train platform. As soon as I saw her I waved and ran over to give her a big hug. She was dressed like an old lady with a hat and woolen gloves.

"Oh, it's so good to see you," Mady cried as I took her suitcase. "It looks like motherhood agrees with you."

I demurred with a scowl. There were so many things I wanted to do besides change diapers and cook dinner. I still felt unready for my new responsibilities and unsure of myself.

As we reached the car Mady hesitated slightly before she put out her hand to shake Ed's.

"Hello, Mr. Hoyt. I'm happy to see you," she said. "And where is that little fellow?"

I was standing next to Mady and I heard her. What? "Mr. Hoyt"? Oh no, not again! Stubborn Norwegian! From the time of our marriage Mady had been addressing my husband in this formal way, and I found it jarring. Yet she persisted in maintaining this distance even though I had begged her more than once to call him Ed or Eddy, the way my father did. Her greeting disappointed me so much that I didn't answer.

"Don't forget your seat belt," I said to Mady, like a scold.

For years she had been the person telling me what to do, but now our roles had shifted and I was bossing her around. It was the only way I could get even with her for being so unavailable the year before, when I had needed her so much, and now, too, when I could see she was too frail to be much help with a twelve-pound baby. I didn't want to notice this shift in our relationship—I wanted a storybook scene where the old nanny embraces the new mother and her baby as if he were her biological grandson.

Mady spent two nights in Neddy's room on the daybed next to his crib. I cooked chicken with mushrooms for our dinner one night and, without taking Mady's special request into account, I used heavy cream. By this time in her life, she had simpler dietary requirements and needed to avoid rich sauces. But I wanted to cook my delicious new recipe for her, and even with her aging digestive system I thought she would enjoy it. Looking back, I realize that once again I was letting out my frustration with our relationship.

Before dinner Ed offered her some sherry. As always, she refused.

"I'll say thank you very much, Mr. Hoyt, but I never touch a drop." And she never stopped calling him Mr. Hoyt.

～

On the morning of Friday, November 22nd, 1963, Ed got dressed in a suit and tie—instead of the sports jacket and corduroys he usually wore—and flew to New York for a job interview. Over lunch the director of the International Development Foundation (IDF) expressed interest in Ed's taking a newly created position running the organization's student programs in Bogotá, Colombia.

As Ed was flying back to Boston from New York, an old boarding school friend and I were finishing a soup and sandwich lunch in my kitchen. She lived in Cambridge with her graduate student husband, and they were expecting their first child in January. We were gossiping happily about mutual friends and discussing childcare when my neighbor knocked loudly on our door. As I opened it I saw the terror on her face.

"Kennedy has been shot in Dallas," she exclaimed, choking back tears. "Come and look at the TV. It's on every channel now. I just started watching."

My school friend and I looked at each other, speechless.

"Is he going to be all right?" I asked my neighbor finally.

"They've taken him to a Dallas hospital—we don't know yet."

My school friend gave me a hug and left immediately to meet her husband at their home.

Ordinarily, Ed and I would have sat down at the kitchen table when he returned from his New York interview and talked about the job offer and a future with IDF. But that evening, after we knew the President had died and national mourning had begun, we feared that the future would be bleak without his leadership. Like most Americans, we were despondent and distracted. For four days we took turns, bleary-eyed, with Neddy on our laps in front of the TV, watching the shocking events unfold.

In the following days we talked more about the job offer. Unlike many of his classmates at the Fletcher School, Ed had no plans to enter the Foreign Service. Ever since our engagement, when he was completing the first of his three years at Fletcher, I expected he would stay in academia. Armed with a Ph.D. he would teach economics at the college level. I wanted to live in Cambridge so that our children could go to the Shady Hill School. But we were intrigued by the offer from IDF. So when Ed decided to accept the job, we figured we could go off on this adventure for a couple of years. I would teach part-time and learn Spanish. Then we would return to Cambridge in time for Neddy to start preschool and for Ed to start teaching.

I'd never heard of IDF and neither had Ed. We learned that its head office in New York managed a successful student program based in Lima, Peru; soon, if Ed took the job, there would be another office in Bogotá, Colombia. They were all funded by several foundations. IDF's grandiose name, International Development Foundation, appealed to my youthful idealism and I wanted us to respond to JFK's policy initiatives for Latin America. It was a region with a rapidly multiplying population, where fifty percent of the people were illiterate, seventy percent lived in poverty, and two percent at the top of the social ladder owned half the wealth. Ed and I eagerly anticipated the opportunity to participate in IDF's mission to improve the lot of Latin Americans. I believed Ed would make good choices, and I never questioned his decision. But even if we had asked knowledgeable people about IDF at this time we probably would not have learned what it was really about. That would come later.

Chapter 10

Into Thin Air

In May 1964, a four-room furnished sublet apartment on East Sixty-eighth Street became our temporary summer home in Manhattan. As it was within walking distance of my father's building, he frequently joined us for dinner. On other days Neddy and I would stop by to see him on our way to or from Central Park. Even though he wasn't comfortable holding a squirming one-year-old in his arms, I know my father was happy to have a grandson.

I had mixed feelings about being back in New York. I was glad to be able to see my father regularly, and it was good that he could spend time with Neddy, but I missed Cambridge and our Cambridge neighbor, who had become a good friend. I dreaded a hot summer in the city.

Fortunately, though, the apartment had air conditioners in the two bedrooms, a dishwasher, and a pleasant doorman named Mike who played peek-a-boo with Neddy in the lobby. I had forgotten how easy it was to live in New York. There was a good butcher, a pharmacy, and a greengrocer around the corner on Second Avenue; and at a Third Avenue fishmonger's I found soft-shelled crabs and shad roe just coming into season. Everyone made home deliveries—all I had to do was set up an account, call in the order, and soon groceries appeared. New York would be even easier once we sold our car and stopped looking for parking places on the street. This was going to be a good summer, after all.

My father's housekeeper, Juliana Keleman, was happy to see us again. She found it unsatisfying to cook for a man like my father who couldn't taste—who relied on textures and temperatures for his meal-time pleasures—and she was pleased when Ed, Neddy, and I came for dinner. Now in his seventy-fifth year, Dad was still working part-time at Smith, Barney and dreading retirement.

Although our move to New York put us farther away from my aunt and uncle in New Hampshire, it brought us closer to Mady. She came into the city from Weehawken once a week to babysit with Neddy so I could do my errands.

I couldn't "hire" Mady. It would be awkward to pay her for babysitting, and I knew she wouldn't take money from me. So I decided to show my appreciation by driving her home to Weehawken in my father's car. She was happy to avoid the crowded Port Authority building. She never refused my requests for help that summer—she kept saying what a good boy Neddy was.

Two evenings a week Ed came home early so that I could study Spanish with a teacher at Hewitt. Her upswept hair-do and the soft European inflections in her voice captivated me immediately. She agreed to help me with grammar and conversation until we left for Colombia. Her studio apartment, with high ceilings and casement windows, was only ten blocks away, and my two evenings each week with her provided a welcome respite from child care and the preparations for our move.

It happened that Ed's and my second wedding anniversary, July 14th, fell on the day before a Spanish lesson, so I greeted my teacher that evening with the news that I'd been married for two years. But instead of saying *casada* (married) I said *cansada* (tired). She laughed. On reflection, I thought both words described how I felt as I ran around the city, shopping for a refrigerator, a washing machine, electrical transformers, clothes for Neddy to grow into, and toys. All three of us needed immunizations, and Neddy needed his first passport.

While we were in New York I wrote a letter to the director of the American School in Bogotá, Colegio Nueva Granada, about a teaching position. He mentioned that there would probably be an opening in the high school faculty to teach modern European history to two sections of tenth graders. To prepare for this possibility I spent several afternoons working on lesson plans at my father's apartment, and during those few hours Mady came to take Neddy to the park.

"Why are you going to work when you have a small child to take care of?" she asked. She was frowning as she sat in an armchair holding Neddy in her lap while he drank from his sippy cup.

"I'll have plenty of time with Neddy," I reassured Mady. "I'll work mornings and then I'll have the afternoons and evenings with him until bedtime. Plus vacations."

Mady wasn't buying it. "You'll have plenty of time for teaching—this little fellow needs you now," she said. "Why do you want to work when you don't have to?" she went on. "Your husband is a good provider."

Mady couldn't understand my dream of becoming a first-rate teacher, a useful professional. She often muttered about men who couldn't provide adequately for their families. I didn't know then how much she had helped both her sisters financially—Tomine and her four children in America and Anne Kristine in Norway, a young widow with six children. Neither of their husbands had been "good providers."

As the summer months passed and the day of our departure for Bogotá drew closer, I felt anxious. We were moving to a new country—a place I'd had to find on a map—and to a capital city I'd seen only in pictures. I imagined Bogotá crawling with parasites, amoebas, and virulent bacteria. We needed immunizations for dengue fever, malaria, hepatitis, and yellow fever. We had a small child to care for and I didn't know a soul. My worries were adding up.

And then there was the altitude. Bogotá lies at nearly nine thousand feet above sea level, two thousand feet higher than Santa Fe, where I had headaches, no appetite, and breathlessness for a few days after our arrival. What would it be like higher up? In an old biology textbook I learned that people who live in the higher Andean elevations acquire twenty or thirty percent more red blood cells than people at sea level, and this helps them absorb more oxygen. Ed was already acclimated to high altitudes because he had grown up in Santa Fe. But what about Neddy and me?

Before we left for Colombia we decided to visit my aunt and uncle in New Hampshire. Sharing my fears with Aunt Mary would help me feel less apprehensive, so I looked forward to her Virginia hospitality, her tender deer-tongue lettuce, and her fat, juicy asparagus. We drove up to the farm in late July. Sitting with Uncle Delos in their cozy kitchen, I basked in the smell of the sweet smoke from logs burning in the fireplace. Every time we visited I wished he would share his memories of my mother, his younger sister, but he was a shy man who didn't talk about her. Instead he described his farming experience and the dairy cows he and Aunt Mary had when they lived in rural Maryland. Uncle Delos was not much of a talker on most other topics. He left that to Aunt Mary. He was happy canoeing on the Blackwater River, which flowed through their property, chopping wood, and hitting golf balls into freshly mown hay fields.

On our first day at the farm, Aunt Mary and I stood side by side watching Neddy and Ed ride around in the wagon behind Uncle Delos's tractor. Gently wrinkled and white-haired in her late sixties, she was still handsome, yet nothing like her youthful self, with the reddish blonde hair she had passed on to her grandchildren. Clearly, Aunt Mary had adjusted to the move from her leisurely existence in Virginia to farm life in New Hampshire. How did she do it? Was there something she could tell me that would help me in Colombia?

"I feel like we're jumping off a cliff," I told her. "Trying to fly without wings. I have no idea where we're going to land."

"Well, it's some distance, and your father must be unhappy."

"I guess he is."

"Look," she said. "It was a huge change for me when we came up here. This is Yankee country! I depended on Uncle Delos to help me create the life we would both enjoy. I'm sure you'll find a way to do the same in Colombia."

"So how did you manage it?" It seemed important to understand how she won so many friends in New England.

"Well, we needed to meet people in Contoocook because we didn't know anyone when we moved here," Aunt Mary said. "I had heard that one of our neighbors, Martha Hastings, had a tennis court as well as some nice waterfront on a lake, with a beach. I decided to make a phone call to someone I'd never met. That's how I found out she was organizing a tennis round robin. I hadn't played tennis in years but Delos missed the club in Charlottesville where he was often club champion. Very graciously she asked us to put our names on the list, and I agreed, thinking we'd play a couple of rounds. Then people would see how good he was and ask him back. Delos could cover most of the court, and hardly needed me. But it turned out that we played and played because we kept on winning. I was exhausted and in the end I couldn't move. I ached all over. But it did the trick. From then on we met everybody within twenty miles, and Martha Hastings has become my good friend. And when the grandchildren come to visit they get invited over to her place to swim and play with her grandchildren."

I was impressed. "Does Uncle Delos still play?"

"No, his back bothers him too much now. I know that when you get settled in Bogotá you'll find your own niche. But maybe not with tennis."

I wondered what Ed's and my life would be like. How would we meet people—would we find another kind of round robin?

"I don't know a thing about Colombia," Aunt Mary went on. "Except that it has good coffee and beautiful emeralds. But you have a good husband—we like him very much. He's handy in the kitchen and he makes a delicious *crème brûlée*. Now is the time for you to lean on him. So lean."

Lean? I wondered how to lean on a man who leaned right back on me and who worked late, so that I was often left on my own. At home he ruminated about his new job. Just a week earlier he had come home with the news that his "security clearance" had come through.

"What does that mean?" I asked him.

"I don't know. Probably some routine thing—they have people on staff from Eastern Europe," he said. "They need to check everybody."

I was so busy packing two steamer trunks with extra diapers, overalls, and jackets and shirts for Neddy to grow into that I put "security clearance" out of my mind.

~

Aunt Mary was right about my father. He was not happy about our leaving—he'd gotten used to seeing us regularly that summer. He also lamented that Mary Case, his lady friend, had declined his marriage proposal. She was too busy with her grandchildren and didn't have enough time for him. Juliana, his housekeeper, was too loud and emotional. The stock market was misbehaving. His golf game was terrible. And now his only grandson and I were moving to a foreign country. And it wasn't even a place like London that he would want to visit.

"Why can't you stay home in your native land?" he moaned.

I usually ignored his complaints, filling the conversation with small talk about Neddy. My marriage had given me an escape hatch from my father: Ed and Neddy now competed with him for my attention. I tried to be patient with him, but I couldn't do anything except listen.

Sometimes my father came for dinner when Mady was spending the night with us. Like divorced parents with a common interest in the same child, they had reunited over our dinner table, and I felt sad watching them. They would shake hands and address each other formally. "Mr. Hayes." "Miss Mortensen" or "Nana." After a close association as employer and employee for nineteen years, they now had little to talk about. My father and Mady, heirs to an old class system, couldn't change. If they spoke to each other at all, they talked about Neddy, the weather, and their health—her rheumatism and his regular exercise, her part-time job and his looming retirement.

Later, after my father went home, when we were washing the dishes, Mady remarked how much my father had aged. I turned a deaf ear. His aging was his problem, wasn't it? I had never witnessed an elderly relative become disabled. Aunt Ethel was a vigorous eighty-two. Mady, too, was doing well at seventy-one. Was my father going to need my help? I hoped not, because with a toddler on my hands, I couldn't do much for him. Besides, we had often sparred and my old resentments lingered.

At the end of August Ed and I had dinner with a couple who had just returned from a two-year assignment in Bogotá. The husband, an intense, articulate man, had just started working with IDF in New York, and his pretty, reserved wife spoke wistfully about the comfortable life they had left behind in Colombia. It was a life they were sure we would enjoy, with household help and a vibrant social scene with other young families. Their fluent Spanish, their easy familiarity with another culture, and their delicious Colombian coffee impressed me. The world they lived in seemed larger than mine. I wanted to become worldly and sophisticated, too. As I jotted down information they gave me, I began to feel better about our adventure. I couldn't know it then but their most valuable gifts to me were the names and phone numbers of their pediatrician and their good friends, Richard Eder, *The New York Times* correspondent and his Argentine wife, Esther.

~

We landed in Bogotá so late we couldn't see the rugged Andean landscape around the city. A Hungarian refugee, Csanad Toth, one of Ed's IDF colleagues, and his wife, Judy, met us at the airport. In the chilly night they accompanied us to our temporary housing, a furnished modern apartment complex in a residential part of the city. They were both fluent in Spanish, and I knew I had to catch up.

When we woke the next morning Csanad reappeared with groceries, including bottled water and milk for Neddy. I made coffee for all of us and then they left for the day to look for office space for IDF.

As they closed the door behind them, a sinking feeling ran through me. Here I was alone with Neddy, only sixteen months old, in a strange city. Through the windows I saw a high plateau, with puffy white clouds hanging almost within reach on the edge of the mountains. A bright sun felt closer to the earth's surface than usual. On a patio outside the window I could see other foreign tenants smoking and sunbathing. Like us, they were in transit, looking for permanent housing in Bogotá, or awaiting a new assignment elsewhere.

Both Ed and I were used to leaving home. Ed and Alfie had left the highlands north of Santa Fe for their high school and college education in other states. And every summer for five years, beginning at age seven, I had left New York to go to camp in Vermont. That first summer I left with all the enthusiasm of a piglet on her way to the slaughterhouse. But after a while leaving home seemed normal.

Now, in Bogotá my wanderlust had reached its limit. I was farther away from home, in a stranger place, with more responsibility than I had ever had. Determined not to let the unknowns daunt me, I got busy preparing Neddy's bottles and running after him outdoors on the warm grass. On that first day, though, I started to feel a pain in my head. We were only a hundred miles north of the Equator on a fertile savanna at an altitude of 8,612 feet. Except for our family visits to Santa Fe I had never spent time at high altitudes, so I hadn't known how my body would respond. But now I knew.

Two weeks later my headaches disappeared. My body had adjusted. We were learning to find our way around the sprawling city and enjoying the fact that even Ed's modest salary in American dollars made a comfortable apartment affordable. Everywhere I looked in the residential areas of the city *muchachas* in pastel-colored uniforms pushed *niños* in their strollers. Other women swept, dusted, washed, and polished furniture and floors in apartments like the one we moved into shortly after arriving in Bogotá. It was located downtown on the second floor of a building in Teusaquillo, an old residential neighborhood of traditional Spanish colonial houses. Two blocks away was a little park where we occasionally found other mothers and children. An American family with three children, the Luscheis, lived in the third floor apartment upstairs and they became our friends. Through our new landlord's daughter-in-law I hired Emilia, a young woman with long black hair and a missing front tooth, to help me take care of Neddy.

Shortly after we moved into our apartment, Ed flew to Caracas on a business trip. He was meeting with an IDF employee who lived on the Venezuelan coast northeast of Caracas. I was tempted to accompany him; it would have been a chance for Neddy and me to escape the cold damp of Bogotá and warm up on a Caribbean beach.

But what happened the next day made me feel glad that I had decided to stay in Bogotá. I woke up a little uneasy without Ed in bed next to me. I listened for the familiar noises from Neddy's room. He had a favorite stuffed animal, a furry orange crab, and at night with his head on Crabby's flat body and his buttocks in the air Neddy would sing and rock himself to sleep in his crib. By morning Crabby would be pushed aside with the other toys, the crib would have skated halfway across the room, and Neddy would be standing at the head of the crib calling me.

But today was different. No sound came from Neddy's room. When I opened the door I saw he was still asleep. His face was bright pink, hot and sweaty to the touch. I flew out of the room and grabbed the thermometer from the bathroom cabinet. Neddy was crying now, loud wails that turned his face a deep pink. I managed to wrestle him out of his sleeping suit, remove his soaking diaper, and insert the rectal thermometer. The mercury immediately shot up to 104.

I knew I had to move quickly, as terror gripped me. I was all alone in a strange city in the clouds, barely speaking the language, without a car, with the name of a pediatrician I had never seen given to me by someone I'd just met in New York.

I looked at Neddy. He was fine the night before when I put him to bed. Now he was miserable. How could he get so sick so fast? I put a cold compress on his sweaty forehead, cradling him in my arms as I dried his damp hair with a towel. I was trying to recall the name of the pediatrician I'd heard about in New York. Where had I written down his phone number? Did his name begin with an "R"? I wasn't sure. In my new Colombia address book I scanned the R's until I found "Restrepo, Dr. Juan Luis."

Please, dear God, help me, I muttered as I dialed the doctor's number.

"El doctor Restrepo," said a female voice after the first ring. Thank God, I thought. I prayed that the doctor was available. I told the secretary about Neddy's temperature and his other symptoms.

"*Bueno.* This is what I want you to do," she said in accented English. "You will need your overnight bag. Take your son to the hospital. Immediately. The doctor will meet you inside the main entrance." And she gave me the address of the Clinica del Country.

Clinica? Hospital? I'd never taken my son to a hospital. How would I recognize the doctor? And without a car I'd have to carry Neddy out to the street and hail a taxi. I hated Bogotá cabs. They had a metal cross dangling from the rear-view mirror, colorful pompoms framing the rear window, and *mariachi* music blaring. Not the right mood for a worried mother.

Why was Ed far away when I needed him most? The phones were so undependable I couldn't call him. I longed for Mady, too. She was at home in New Jersey, four thousand miles away.

The taxi stopped in front of the white modern-looking Clinica del Country, and I got out holding Neddy wrapped in his blanket. A doorman helped with my bag. Just inside the doors I saw a tall, dark-haired man with a high forehead. His name tag said "Restrepo." A nurse produced a stroller, and we followed the doctor into the examining room.

"Pneumonia," he said after he had palpated Neddy's chest. "We're going to put him in a clear plastic oxygen box and give him antibiotics.

He's going to be fine. But I want you to stay with him on the couch in his room."

"How long will it take for him to get well?" I asked, my voice shaking.

"I don't know how long. That depends how fast the fluid in his lungs gets reabsorbed into his system. But he will get better, I can assure you of that."

Thank God. I felt relieved. Dr. Restrepo was saving Neddy's life. I was so glad Neddy and I hadn't accompanied Ed on his trip to Venezuela. And if I had left Neddy alone with Emilia, she would not have known what to do, and I wouldn't have been able to instruct her over the phone in Spanish.

Neddy came home from the hospital after three days, and I soon began to feel I could trust Emilia for a few hours with him each weekday. I called the director of the American School, who invited me to the campus for an interview. A taxi dropped me down the hill in the parking lot and I made my way up the path to the administration building. Fragrant eucalyptus trees with shaggy barks shaded a series of ranch-style modern brick buildings on a steep hillside overlooking the savanna. A student escorted me to an office where I met Norman Roseman, the principal of the high school and my future supervisor. He was a dark-haired intellectual from New York, with a big smile and an ironic sense of humor about Colombian politics and arrogant Bogotános. He told me I would be taking over two sections of modern European history from an experienced teacher who already had a heavy teaching load. About half my students would be Colombians, the rest Americans.

Several days later I stepped out of the yellow bus in a wool dress with a sweater and heels for my first day at school. Norman seemed interested in my subject matter and he had suggestions about ways to engage the students. He encouraged me to experiment. I invited *New York Times* journalist Richard Eder to speak to them about his recent interview with Fidel Castro in Havana, which led to discussions of Communism and socialism. Ed's colleague Csanad Toth entertained the class with stories of his participation in the 1956 Hungarian Revolution and making Molotov cocktails. I tried other ways to dramatize historical events and important figures. Instead of writing a midterm paper my students wrote their own play about Napoleon and Josephine and performed it for the upper grades.

After a few months, I felt more comfortable in the classroom and happy with our new life. I had the part-time work I wanted, and Emilia helped with Neddy and household chores. As a bonus Neddy was learning Spanish. He asked for *jugo* in his sippy cup and *mermelada* on his toast. We had bought a used car and joined a tennis club. We also moved closer to the school, into an apartment with a sweeping view over the city from six bay windows. And we were making new friends easily—a Colombian couple, as well as other Americans and Europeans in the expatriate community.

Among our new friends were the Randalls, a couple with three daughters in the lower school. Evie taught there and Drake worked at the U.S. Embassy. We began to spend most Sundays with them at the country club. Emilia and their *muchacha* came along to watch the children in the shallow pool, while we played tennis.

One day during the school summer vacation, Emilia was pushing Neddy in the stroller when she noticed a man in a rumpled black suit watching her from across the street. She had heard rumors from other *muchachas* about a kidnapping in the neighborhood, she said, and her story alarmed me.

Ed and I, together with the three other tenants in our building, already had a *vigilancia* service: An armed man patrolled outside our building's front door for twelve hours, from six in the evening until six in the morning. Here in this impoverished country I knew that anyone—anytime, anywhere—might try to kidnap my beautiful child for a ransom. Colombia had a history of violence dating back to the warring political parties in the 1940s. After hearing Emilia's story I told her never to take Neddy in the stroller by herself. I would always drive her up the hill to the playground on school grounds, three blocks away. On weekends we decided not to travel into the insecure countryside but to confine ourselves to the country club, in the outskirts of the city. If we wanted to see other parts of the country we would fly.

Until then I'd felt proud of us for getting along well in a different world from the ones we had grown up in—shopping in Spanish, even being sick in Spanish. But now I was beginning to wonder if we weren't paying too high a price—Colombia was dangerous.

At the same time that I was worrying about our family's safety, I was becoming obsessed with the idea of having another baby. I didn't want Neddy to be an only child like me. I had always longed for a younger brother or sister. Our son had been conceived so easily, and I wondered if I would be so lucky the second time. I wanted to get pregnant soon so that Neddy could have a sibling close enough to his age to play with—I didn't want to wait. Mady always said I should have a girl.

After school closed for the summer I signed up for an intensive Spanish course at the University of the Andes. As the deadline for renewing my teaching contract at Colegio Nueva Granada approached, I decided not to teach the following year. Teaching had tied me down. I could let it go for a while and then return to the classroom when Neddy was older. I wanted the freedom to travel with Ed and Neddy. I wanted to play with my son on the white sand of a Caribbean beach. I was tired of spending hours on weekends creating multiple choice tests and correcting papers. I wanted to continue improving my Spanish and see more of Colombia.

When we invited friends over for dinner we talked about Colombian politics and our jobs. They understood that Ed had connections with the Embassy and the sociology department at the liberal Universidad Nacional. He told them that IDF was working closely with students in community development—many of them had close ties to the charismatic leftist priest and sociology professor Camilo Torres.

IDF was training and organizing teams of students from various disciplines—law, medicine, civil engineering, agriculture—to go out into the countryside and to see for themselves how the *campesinos* lived and try to work with them to create better, healthier living conditions. Some students would help dig latrines and others would talk to mothers about infant health. This was a long-term program, the directors of IDF said; as students eventually moved on into political leadership positions they would have more experience with their country's problems.

A prototype for this program was successful in Peru because that country's progressive president, Fernando Belaúnde, stood behind it and befriended IDF's representative in Lima. Ed hoped that with the right support the same program could also be run successfully in Colombia. Csanad and Ed wanted to work with Camilo Torres, rather than any community organization in the conservative government, because the students admired and listened to him. Camilo was going to help give IDF legitimacy in Colombia.

What we hadn't known when Ed accepted the IDF position was that the organization had actually recruited him to fight on another battlefield of the Cold War. After the Bay of Pigs fiasco, when the U.S. misjudged Cubans' support for Fidel Castro, the CIA was searching for better ways to gather information and influence policy-making, as it attempted to stop the spread of Communism in the Western Hemisphere. The CIA wanted to use IDF in its covert information-gathering about left-wing students in Colombia, Peru, and Chile.

When he flew to South America for orientation, in the summer of 1964, Ed learned about the CIA connection. At first he was excited about its cloak-and-dagger aspect, for he knew that the foundations funding IDF were conduits masking the fact that the Agency was providing the money. Nonetheless, he was intrigued with the work and happy to live and work in Spanish. But as time went on he found it necessary to lie to the students. Some of them probably suspected that IDF wasn't as altruistic as it seemed—that it had a hidden agenda—and after a while Camilo might have felt he was being used to legitimize IDF. Ed said he too was becoming increasingly uncomfortable.

In July 1965, just before we left to go to New York for a vacation, Ed and Csanad gave a reception at our apartment and invited the students they had been working with at the university. They were all hoping the priest Camilo Torres, their professor, would come too and speak about land reform and the fight against poverty.

It occurred to me that the students must have been wondering what we gringos were all about. The situation, as Ed described it to me, was delicate. We had both noticed photos in the newspapers of students welcoming Camilo home from trips abroad and carrying him on their shoulders. Now it seemed he was becoming so radical that he risked attracting the wrong kind of attention from the conservative government, as well as resistance from his bishop. If that happened, the liaison IDF had been carefully cultivating with the students and Camilo would backfire.

Everyone at our reception was anticipating Camilo's arrival—he was often late. Listening to Ed's conversations with his colleagues and students, I had noticed how often they mentioned Camilo. So I was looking forward to meeting him and hoping I could understand him with my limited Spanish. When he finally arrived at our apartment, a tight circle formed around him, so that all I could see was his high forehead and his curly dark hair. I had to excuse myself to put Neddy to bed. From his room down the hall I was sure he could hear the students' voices getting louder; I wanted them to quiet down so that I could get him to sleep. Then I could go out and meet Camilo. But within ten minutes, as I was telling Neddy a Crabby story, the living room grew silent. Camilo had already left. I told Ed how disappointed I was, but he assured me there would be other opportunities to meet Camilo.

~

Early in January I began to suspect I was pregnant, and a few weeks later my Colombian doctor confirmed my hunch. I was due in September, and so was Alfie's wife, Diana.

In February I received a telegram from Juliana in New York:

YOUR FATHER GOES TO HOSPITAL SURGERY.
COME HOME.

I put in a call to my father, but the long distance telephone service wasn't working. I couldn't get a line. After three days of trying frantically to get through, I gave up. I sent a telegram asking for more information but got no answer. Finally, I decided I'd have to travel with Neddy to New York to see my father and help him deal with his health emergency.

I didn't want to leave Ed or Bogotá. It was the dry, sunny season in the mountains, and in New York it would be a windy, cold March, where we would be stuck indoors with colds and fevers. Standing at the bay windows of our apartment overlooking the city and its beautiful sunsets, Neddy liked to watch planes land and take off at the airport in the distance. "Avianca," he would say, with a perfect Spanish accent, pointing to a plane.

On the morning of February 22nd I was packing our bags when I took a break to have a cup of coffee and read *El Espectador*, the daily newspaper. There on the front page was a shocking photograph of the bloodied body of Camilo Torres, killed by government troops. He was only thirty-seven, killed during his first military engagement. The lead article explained that following in the footsteps of Che Guevara, he had grown a heavy beard and become a revolutionary guerrilla in the mountains. As a professor of sociology and dean of the department at the national university, he had taught many of the same students who were signing up to participate in IDF's community development programs.

Three days after Camilo's death, Ed drove Neddy and me to the airport for our flight to New York. He and I sat in silence, thinking our own thoughts about Camilo and the future of IDF in Colombia. It was difficult to leave Ed at this moment of sadness and uncertainty. I knew from his uneasy talk and the way he gazed off at the little villages we passed on the airport road that he was worried.

Neddy, of course, was full of excitement about our flight, alternately standing up on the front seat of the car when he wasn't sitting on my lap. Where was the plane, he wanted to know. He was wearing his little square red blanket, a traditional Colombian *ruana*, which had a slit down the middle as the opening for his head. "Avianca?" he asked. "Yes, Avianca." I pulled a toy plane out of my purse, gave it to him, and told him we were going to see his *abuelo* in New York.

"*Abuelo?*"

"*Si, abuelo*. Your grandpa."

Chapter 11

Back to New York

*N*eddy and I arrived at my father's apartment on a cold, gray afternoon early in March. I was anxious. Juliana's telegram had said that my father needed surgery and that I must come home. What kind of surgery? I wondered. She didn't say.

When we walked into the apartment, my father was sitting in his favorite chair in front of the window, reading the paper. We hugged and Dad gave Neddy a playful handshake. I noticed his hand trembled a little. Then I studied him as he stood up. He didn't look sick. Despite his stooped posture he looked like my durable father, with his closely clipped gray moustache, the few stray white hairs on top of his head, and the crisscrossed wrinkle lines at the back of his furry neck. He was wearing a good bow tie and custom-made jacket. Except for the muffled noises of traffic from Madison Avenue, the apartment was quiet—there was no sign of dinner preparation coming from the kitchen.

"Where is Juliana?" I asked.

"I don't know," he said. "This morning after breakfast she left with a suitcase."

"Left? What do you mean? When is she coming back?"

"I don't know."

"But she telegrammed me about your surgery."

He raised his eyebrows. "What surgery?"

I went out to Juliana's room, off the pantry. It was bare except for a set of sheets and towels folded neatly on the mattress. It looked like she was gone for good.

And what about the surgery? Was that a ruse to get me to come home?

"What's going on here?" I asked my father, trying to control my temper. "Are you having an operation? Have you been to the doctor? Why did Juliana write me you were having surgery?" I tried to keep my voice down so I wouldn't upset Neddy.

"When I first saw the doctors, they said I'd have to have surgery for my constipation," my father said. "They wanted me to stay in the hospital for observation—to figure out why the space between my large intestine and my rectum occasionally closes up on me."

I was embarrassed talking about body parts with my father, but I knew there was no one else to listen. I had to try to understand.

"And then what did the doctors say?"

"Oh, you know, they just kid me along, to keep my spirits up. After a few days they said I didn't need the surgery after all. I just have a spastic colon, caused by nervous tension. I feel better now and want to stay this way."

I calmed down as I unpacked our suitcases, found toys for Neddy, and set up the portable crib and stroller I had stored in a closet. While it was still light outside Neddy and I walked to a nearby toy store on Lexington Avenue and I bought him a tricycle for the park. When we got back to the apartment I called Mady in Weehawken.

"How could Juliana just walk out without leaving a new phone number?" I was almost screaming into the receiver.

Mady said she would gladly help as long as I needed her. Just hearing her voice and knowing she would come to the apartment the next morning reassured me. I wondered if she would be strong enough to manage Neddy. He was almost three years old and full of energy.

That evening my father, Neddy, and I went out to a local restaurant.

After dinner, we walked home. As we stood at the front door of the apartment, my father fumbled with his keys, trying to figure out which was the right one to open the door. I resisted the urge to grab his keychain and open the door myself. I was beginning to understand why Juliana had left.

Later that evening I sat with my father in the living room while he smoked his pipe. "Do you have the name of the man at the bank?" he wanted to know. "And the lawyer? And the doctor? Do you know whom to call in an emergency?"

My heart sank. No matter how often I told him I had all the necessary information he would repeat these same questions, over and over. He seemed to know that he couldn't remember things any more, and that he needed help. I reminded him that he'd written me several letters to Bogotá with all the phone numbers and that I kept them in a safe place. I didn't tell him that his handwriting had gotten much harder to read. He was always proud of his penmanship.

"What about the safe deposit box? Do you know the number?"

"I have that too. But you sound worried. What's the matter?"

Silence. Finally, I asked his permission to speak with his doctor.

The next morning I took Neddy with me in the stroller to an address four blocks away. Dr. Hochman welcomed us into his office, its walls lined with framed diplomas. I was surprised to find a young man with a full head of dark hair. He didn't look much older than me.

I told him why I had flown to New York. I still didn't understand what was wrong with my father's digestive system, I said. He explained that my father's earlier symptoms suggested that there was a blockage in the large intestine and they wanted to rule out colon cancer. And after a few days of observation and some X-rays, they decided he didn't need surgery, He had irritable bowel syndrome, and with some pills to promote relaxation the doctor felt things would improve. This made sense to me.

I told Dr. Hochman that I thought my father had become more forgetful since our last visit to New York. I asked if there was some medication that would improve his memory.

"No, there isn't. Your father is getting old," he said. "And senile. And with that goes memory loss, which will worsen over time. I think we're seeing early symptoms of Parkinson's and arteriosclerosis."

"Parkinson's?" This was news to me. Had my father seen a specialist who had made that diagnosis? Just because he was seventy-six didn't mean he had to be sick. He had always been in robust health. His weight never varied and he got plenty of exercise. My mother had been the sick one. My father didn't go to doctors or dentists—his teeth were perfect. I was convinced he had the wrong doctor. He needed someone to make him well again.

I sat with my thoughts in silence, trying to absorb what Dr. Hochman was saying, but my mind kept wandering. My stomach growled. I was no longer suffering from morning sickness and I was famished. I was also in deep denial about my father's health.

The doctor kept talking. Parkinson's was a progressive condition of the central nervous system, he said, and it could only get worse. He was treating my father with L-Dopa, which controlled only the worst symptoms. Inevitably he would begin to walk with more stiffness in the muscles—he would shuffle.

I could follow only part of what Dr. Hochman was saying. Neddy was getting bored with his picture book so I knew we had to leave. I thanked the doctor and said goodbye. Back at home, I was happy to find Mady in her old room. We put Neddy down for his morning nap and then I told her about our visit with the doctor.

"We're all getting old," she said. "Your father has been healthy for a long time, but you can't reverse the clock. We all have to go sometime."

It began to dawn on me that since my last visit my father had been slowly declining. I'd been far away in Colombia occupied with my young family, my pregnancy, my own life. I hadn't noticed. Now my father was pulling me back into his orbit. How could I continue the pregnancy for another five months, take care of Neddy, live with my husband in Bogotá, and also be an attentive daughter? What did I owe my father, anyway?

I knew the first thing I had to do was find a good caregiver. She would be the linchpin, holding his household together. I would stay in New York for as long as it took to find her. Then I could go back to my home and my husband in Bogotá.

I knew it wouldn't be easy. Being around my father had always meant being on my guard—in recent years it seemed to me he could erupt any time. My ideas were "bunk." My choices of what to do and where to live were "cock-eyed." Now, when my father really needed me, and there was no one else to call on, I had become acceptable despite my wrong-headedness. He had to trust me.

He looked worried, and I figured he was also depressed and lonely. He had retired from Smith, Barney at Christmas, 1965, which left him untethered from the stock market and the colleagues and clients he had always enjoyed. I had to try and build him up: protein, iron, well-balanced meals. More exercise. When he felt stronger he'd feel better. His new housekeeper, whoever she might be, would have to pay attention to nutrition. More fruits, more vegetables. Maybe a protein supplement. And less alcohol. Maybe she could also encourage him to see some of his old friends. I wrote myself a reminder to call Mary Case and another woman he had been seeing from time to time after my mother died.

Mady stayed for a couple of days at a time and then went home to Weehawken, leaving me alone with my father and Neddy. After about a week with this arrangement in my father's apartment, I knew we couldn't stay there any longer. I was losing my patience. I disliked the cramped kitchen. I hated going down to the dark, dingy basement to do laundry. Neddy needed other children to play with and adults younger than Mady to run after him.

In desperation, I booked a two-bedroom suite for Mady, Neddy, and me at the Hotel Westbury, one block away. I didn't care what it cost. Then I wouldn't have to cook—there would be the hotel restaurant, where my father could join us for meals, and room service twenty-four hours a day. My father could also go to a favorite local restaurant where they served a hot breakfast he liked.

For several days Mady, Neddy, and I lived comfortably in our suite at the Westbury. Room service came and went. There were TV cartoons for Neddy. But then Mady caught a cold. She was constantly blowing her nose and coughing. She was exhausted, she said. She couldn't sleep. She wasn't used to being around a young child for hours at a time; she would have to go home to Weehawken to rest.

As the days dragged on, all I could think about was escaping from New York and going back to my husband in Bogotá, where I had reliable help. I missed Ed and our life together. I missed watching him rough house and play hide-and-seek with Neddy. I missed hearing and speaking Spanish and spending Sundays at the tennis club. With no telephone connections between New York and Bogotá, I couldn't find out what was happening at IDF. Above all, I missed feeling Ed's arms around me when we snuggled in bed.

One evening I hired a babysitter, and my father and I went out for dinner in Greenwich Village with a couple of his old friends. Jack was also a friend of my mother's but I had never met him or his wife, Janice. My father had already explained to them that I was visiting from Colombia with my son and we were staying at the Westbury.

"I'll have to leave a little early so I can get back to the hotel—the babysitter has to leave by nine o'clock," I told our hosts.

"Oh," said Janice. "I have an idea. I have a lovely young friend at church who is looking for a good au pair situation. Could you use someone like her? She would be able to live in."

Janice went on to describe Johanne Schroeder, who was German, fluent in English, intelligent, fun, and imaginative. She was also desperate to leave her current job.

"I would love to meet her," I told Janice.

I interviewed Johanne the next day, and I could tell right away she would be perfect. She was pretty, tall and slim, with long blonde hair and pale blue eyes. She was full of fun and games and she never seemed to tire. One minute she would have a serious expression on her face, and the next she would break out into a broad smile and giggles. She had only a slight hint of a German accent, and she enunciated her words carefully. I could sense her intelligence. She sat down on the sofa with Neddy and talked to him as if he were a six-year-old schoolboy instead of a toddler who spoke more Spanish than English. All along I'd been wishing for my very own Mary Poppins to drop out of the sky with her umbrella, and now here she was in the form of Johanne. I couldn't believe my good luck. She started work the following Monday.

Until now most of Neddy's words were Spanish because that's what he heard in Bogotá. *Jugo, mermelada, avion, papi, mami.* I never worried that he wasn't very verbal because I knew he was hearing both languages and needed time to sort them out. And now I could see how, with Johanne working on his English, he could soon become bilingual.

"How would you like to go to Bogotá with us?" I asked Johanne.

"That would be wonderful. I've always wanted to learn Spanish."

I told her that a teacher from the American school, just up the hill from our apartment, could probably tutor her twice a week. Johanne promised to be our au pair for a little more than a year, until the new baby was nine months old. And she would stay with us whether we lived in Colombia or if we returned to New York.

The day before Johanne came to see me at the Westbury, my father and I had interviewed a potential caregiver for him—a grandmotherly widow. She was gentle, kind, and patient, and she liked my father. She could cook simple meals, check on his medications, and accompany him to his appointments. And she was able to start immediately. We decided to hire her.

After four weeks in New York, I was finally free to return to Colombia, with both Neddy and Johanne. We arrived in Bogotá on the afternoon flight and Ed met us at El Dorado Airport. We had been unable to communicate over a long distance line so he had lots of news. In our absence, the U.S. Embassy had advised Ed to stop socializing with his contact at the CIA, and Ed had begun to dislike his job, especially its covert side.

Ed was concerned about IDF's future in Colombia. He could see that its relationship with the Colombian government had begun to erode. He was convinced that our home and the office phones were being tapped and that the government had learned that his Hungarian colleague was planning a visit with a former Colombian president who had a large populist following opposed to the current regime. This could be perceived as the United States meddling in the internal affairs of a foreign country. Ed had always had trouble reining in his Hungarian colleague, whose political activism had begun on the streets of Budapest in 1956 under fierce Communist repression. Instead of allowing him to visit the former president by himself, Ed accompanied him to try to minimize collateral damage. He feared that a meeting would add fuel to the government's belief that IDF was a dangerous leftist organization. Within a few weeks, though, IDF summoned Ed's colleague to New York, fired him, and then helped him find another job at the Agency for International Development (AID) in Washington.

By this time Ed was disgusted. Declining an offer from IDF to manage another program in South America, he decided to quit IDF altogether and go back to New York to find a "normal job." Our time in Colombia was running out, and if we were going to return to New York I would have to fly before the beginning of the seventh month of my pregnancy—in mid-June.

Although I knew that Ed's decision was right for him and for our family, I was disappointed. I would miss our expatriate life. I preferred living abroad to traveling as a tourist. I liked being immersed in a new language, especially one as beautiful and useful as Spanish, and I enjoyed our varied social life with journalists, bankers, and the cultural attaché at the U.S. Embassy. But I knew my father needed me in New York.

∼

We arrived at Kennedy Airport in the middle of June 1966 and went directly to another summer sublet on East Seventy-fourth Street, seven blocks from my father's apartment. The owners had moved to their summer house in upstate New York. I knew they would need to return in time for school in the fall, and we would have to vacate the apartment before then, around the same time as my due date.

Suddenly we had become gypsies. Where would we go? We had outgrown the available space in my father's apartment—we couldn't stay there for more than a few days. I knew I had to plan ahead so that we could be settled somewhere when the baby arrived. Where would we live after our summer lease ran out?

As my due date approached a quiet miracle occurred. Our landlord was offered—and accepted immediately—a senior position at the U.S. Treasury. He and his family were going to move to Washington, D.C.; we could extend our lease for another two years. With this happy turn of events, I had plenty of time to relax, take long naps, and daydream about the new baby. As Labor Day arrived, I was so placid in my pregnancy that I ignored the fact that Ed no longer had a job.

But my father noticed. One evening when we were having dinner with him he turned to Ed and said, not entirely kindly, "You're going to be the father of two children very soon. Don't you think it's time you went to work?"

My father's words made me cringe, even though I knew he was right. I wasn't worried, for I knew something would turn up. Besides, we had enough savings, and we'd been able to keep Ed's health insurance. I was confident that he'd find a good position. It was simply a matter of time.

Ed worked through the summer at IDF's head office and made one more trip to Colombia. Upon his return he began job hunting. With his master's degree in chemical (petroleum) engineering, it made sense to apply to the international oil companies, but he had his heart set on working at the Brookings Institution, a liberal think tank in Washington.

Brookings, it turned out, was not an option. As soon as the people there found out he had been working at IDF, they wouldn't consider him for a policy position: His résumé was tainted by his CIA experience. They couldn't be sure he wasn't still on the CIA payroll and they didn't want to take a chance. And the oil companies were slow in responding to him.

As the weeks passed, Ed became deeply discouraged. One day he came home looking especially gloomy. He had just had his third interview with Exxon. He went into the kitchen, poured himself a strong drink, then collapsed on the bed with a crippling headache.

"What's the matter?" I asked. "Tell me what happened."

"They aren't going to hire me." He groaned.

I suggested that we go away for a few days to get some fresh air. So in July we drove to New Hampshire for a reunion with my aunt and uncle on their farm. Johanne came too. Color slides show her wearing a red bandanna and sitting with Neddy in a hay wagon behind Uncle Delos at the wheel of his tractor. All three are smiling.

Back in New York I continued to ready the apartment for the new baby while Ed went on more job interviews and followed up leads. Unlike his work with IDF, they were all positions in the business world. I was less concerned about his unemployment than about the possibility that he might end up working on Wall Street.

Ed and I are opposites—he likes numbers and I prefer letters. He likes apple peels, I like the fruit. I thought a job in business or finance could cause friction in our marriage. If his dinner-table talk centered on stocks and bonds, I would go crazy: I would feel I was living with my father. Yet in my more rational moments I knew Ed and my father were very different. Ed was much more relaxed and irreverent than my father. Most important, he made me laugh.

During my pregnancy we enjoyed going to movies and cooking dinner. I also liked seeing members of his family—the Hoyt aunts, a cousin, and an elderly Hoyt relative who lived near us. We had dinner with old friends at a Brazilian restaurant, and with my old college friend Mary and her husband, Bill. Ed teased me about my bovine condition in the third trimester, when my waking life focused on eating—and trying not to gain weight.

Contractions began during the late afternoon of September 6th, and Jonathan was born in the early hours of September 7th at Columbia Presbyterian Hospital. In the delivery room, with the obstetrician urging me to "keep pushing; the baby is almost here," I was sure he would soon cry out "It's a girl!" But instead I heard, "Congratulations, Mrs. Hoyt. You have a healthy baby boy!" I lay back on the table, disappointed at first to learn we had another son. Two boys. I remember Mady saying "You just keep trying until you get your girl." Maybe. But for now I was relieved that Jonathan was healthy and normal. And Neddy finally had a sibling. I thought he'd be happier with a brother than with a sister and I hoped they could become good friends. I wondered how I would handle their inevitable rivalry.

I spent a few days on the maternity floor at Columbia Presbyterian, the hospital where my mother had died eight years earlier. Was I risking bad luck by using a doctor affiliated with her hospital? I wasn't superstitious. Yet as I lay back on my hospital bed with a sweet new baby in my arms, I wondered whether her ghost, like Hamlet's father, roamed the hallways, ready to undermine my mothering or shake my confidence. Shouldn't I have protected myself by choosing an obstetrician affiliated with another hospital, unencumbered by all those memories of relief and guilt after her death?

After two months of job-hunting Ed was offered a position in the training program of the International Division at Morgan Guaranty Trust Company. Expecting this to be a temporary job until he could find the one he really wanted, Ed started work there in late October 1966.

During the winter of 1966–1967 I had plenty of help at home so that I could enjoy the new baby. Johanne loved holding and feeding him a bottle, so much so that I often had to shoo her away and claim my prerogative as his nursing mother. Mady visited regularly from Weehawken and admired my smoothly running household. "The floors are so nice and shiny," she said one day.

I arranged to have old family furniture moved to our apartment from the storage warehouse in Englewood, and with Johanne's help I painted Neddy's room in bright colors. With new wooden blocks to play with, he had many more toys than he'd ever had in Colombia.

In the warehouse I also found a wicker hamper packed with silver and a hatbox filled with old family photographs that my mother had put away twenty-four years earlier, when we moved from the Englewood house into Manhattan. There were formal studio portraits, photo albums, and pictures going back to nineteenth-century daguerreotypes, most without names or dates. Eager to know the identity of these fashionably dressed people, I made a date to visit Aunt Ethel at her home in Englewood.

She welcomed me warmly and we sat down together on her sofa. This time I hoped I'd learn more from her about my mother. Eight years after my mother's death it seemed that her family had closed the subject of her illness. My cousin Bud and his family, my aunt and uncle in New Hampshire, and great aunts Ethel and Alma never mentioned her name. And my father said nothing.

But I had lingering questions. She may have been dead to her world but now that I was also a mother she was alive in my mind.

"What happened to my mother?" I asked Aunt Ethel. "Why was she sick for so long?"

Aunt Ethel sank back against the sofa pillow and looked straight at me. Even now, at eighty-six, she had a lovely face framed by short fluffy gray hair.

"I don't really know," she answered. "Her illness was baffling."

Baffling.

"No one knows what went wrong," Aunt Ethel went on. "We knew about the diabetes, of course. But your father took good care of that, with the nurses and the insulin injections."

So what was the baffling illness? I asked myself, as Aunt Ethel continued.

"What we couldn't figure out," she said, "was her strange behavior. What caused her to become so hyperactive and talkative, needing only three hours of sleep each night, and then suddenly retreating into the isolation of her bedroom, too depressed to come out and talk to anybody? Your father and I didn't know. It was so unlike the Margaret we had always known. No one could understand it."

I stared at the burning logs in the living room fireplace, trying to absorb what Aunt Ethel was saying as the February afternoon light faded.

As we chatted, Aunt Ethel and I went through the contents of the hatbox I'd found in the storage warehouse. It was full of scrapbooks, loose candid pictures, and studio portraits of my mother, her parents, her brothers, and grandparents—collected images of a privileged life. There was my mother building a snowman, her brother Delos standing beside her in a woolen hat. A studio photograph taken in her early twenties showed her dressed in a silk print dress, her hand resting on the head of her black Scottie. She looked composed; there was no sign of any strange behavior.

Aunt Ethel and I worked together quietly, sorting the pictures into piles. I wrote down names and dates wherever I could. At one point, Aunt Ethel peered at me over her reading glasses and said gently, "I think you shouldn't dwell too much on your mother."

Why not? I wondered. Isn't it natural for a daughter to want to know more about her mother? I had put her out of my mind too long.

"I'm not dwelling on my mother," I assured Aunt Ethel. "But I would really like to understand her. Is there anything more you can tell me?"

Aunt Ethel looked away, as if deciding whether or not to give up a precious nugget of information. Then she said quietly, "Even the doctors didn't have any good answers."

"But what did they try?" I asked, remembering my mother's many physicians and her extended hospital stays.

"There were some treatments," Aunt Ethel said. "But I think the doctors were as stumped as we were." She hesitated again. I looked at her expectantly.

Finally she said in a low voice tinged with sadness, "Lobotomy was the only treatment left. It was the last resort."

What was she talking about? *Lobotomy?* How could that be—and how come I'd never heard about it?

At that time, I knew practically nothing about the surgery, although I knew it had something to do with the brain. When did it happen? During one of those mysterious stays in the hospital? Who performed it? And how did it affect her?

Aunt Ethel had few answers. She had opened the door to thinking and talking about all this, but the thought of opening up my mother's brain made me too uncomfortable. I wondered how the decision to go ahead with the surgery was made. Aunt Ethel was my best—most honest—source of information and yet she had little to tell me.

But she did know a lot about my mother's mother, my grand-mother, Emily Bliss Kidder, her eldest sister. And she admitted that my grandmother's behavior was sometimes strange, too. She recalled once seeing Emily on the porch of her house. Pregnant then, she was showing off her large belly to her five younger sisters. She swirled her long skirt around her and laughed hysterically. "Volatile" was the word Aunt Ethel used to describe her.

I was the direct female line—descended from at least one disturbed person, maybe even two. It all depended on what Aunt Ethel meant by "volatile." Maybe I was doomed to go crazy. I wondered about this, but not for long. I wanted to deny all of it. I had my husband and sons and many good years ahead.

Baffling. Volatile. These were the only clues Aunt Ethel could give me about the family mystery.

"Be good to your father," she said as we wound up our afternoon visit. "He had a big burden to carry."

"I know," I said, without really knowing at all.

Chapter 12

Fire Island

*I*n the summer of 1967, when Neddy was four and Jonathan ten months, Ed and I rented a cottage in Point O'Woods. This is one of several communities on Fire Island, a long, narrow barrier beach that protects the south shore of Long Island from the often turbulent Atlantic. Between Fire Island and Long Island is Great South Bay— calmer waters ideal for sailing, swimming, and fishing.

I knew about Point O'Woods because my mother had rented a cottage there in the early 1930s. My father courted her there, Aunt Mary told me. Aunt Mary also recalled that one summer in the 1930s she and her daughters, my cousins Nancy and Emily, had visited my mother in Point O'Woods. They had explored the island's sunken forest, undulating sand dunes, salt marshes, and mud flats, good for clamming. But I had never been there. Manhattan friends said it was still a popular summer resort for young families. With no cars allowed on Fire Island, cottage owners and renters use bicycles and wagons to transport luggage and groceries.

One Saturday in May, Ed and I had gone to see Point O'Woods for ourselves. Disembarking from the ferry, we followed the path from the dock to the cottage we planned to rent. It cut through a

With Ed, Ned, and Jonathan at Point O' Woods, Fire Island, New York, 1967

seven-foot-high dense green hedge with a sweet fragrance and fresh sea breezes. As we walked past the post office, the grocery store, and the ice cream shop we saw parents carting their small children in ubiquitous wagons. There was a yacht club, a full-time family doctor, tennis courts, and a casino where teenagers hung out.

The Club at Point O'Woods, on a grassy dune overlooking the ocean, was important in my planning. Staffed in the summer by college students, it had simple but comfortable rooms and served three meals a day. When my father's housekeeper took her vacation in July he would be able to stay there and dine with us most evenings. I could keep an eye on him. He could walk safely on the foot path between the Club and our cottage. We decided to go ahead and rent the cottage.

Johanne said good-bye to us in the middle of June. She promised to visit us from time to time but now I was pleased to be on my own with our two boys. Just family. I didn't hire a summer mother's helper because Mady was going to visit for a week, and Ed would come week-ends and take his two-week vacation in July.

I was eager to see Mady. I knew she would help with the children—chatting with Neddy about his toys and drawings while she gave Jonathan his bottle. And I would enjoy her company. I didn't want to make physical demands on her, and because her hair never turned gray, I always assumed she was younger than her chronological age.

Now I know that in 1967 she was seventy-four.

Right after Jonathan was born Neddy noticed that he didn't talk. And he couldn't help build sand castles. We assured Neddy that Jonathan would soon become a playmate, but in the meantime Neddy was making friends with another four-year-old, Howdy, next door. On weekday mornings two college girls came around with a wagon, collected Neddy, Howdy, and other four-year-olds, and took them to a sandy playground for sports and games.

Jonathan was a placid, blond blue-eyed child who had regular bottles and naps. While he slept, Mady and I sat in wicker rocking chairs on the screen porch and reminisced over our coffee mugs.

"Remember one afternoon I went to pick you up at Debbie's house?" she said. "I rang the bell but nobody came to the door. I rang and rang, and still nobody came. So I tried the door and it was unlocked. I walked in and all of a sudden her father walked out into the living room. He was so surprised!"

"I bet!"

"I always thought Debbie was kind of wild."

"And she thought you were awfully strict."

"That could be." Mady grinned.

"I think the other mothers admired my shiny braids—you always kept my hair out of my eyes, with pretty bows on my pigtails." Now I had one thick long braid down my back.

"You had lovely hair. You still do."

"Thank you," I said, tearing up a little as I poured us another cup of coffee. Norwegians are big coffee drinkers, and Mady liked hers black and strong from the percolator so that the coarse coffee grains escaping from the basket left a residue at the bottom of her cup. She and her friends would tell their fortunes from the patterns in the grains.

Ed and I met several Norwegian trolls on a North Cape cruise.

"I wonder what it will be?" she mused out loud one morning as we were slowly sipping our coffee.

"What do you mean?" I asked.

"Don't you think these grounds are shaped like an eye?"

I looked at the bottom of her cup. The grounds had a vaguely oval form and above it there was a fuzzy line shaped like a crescent moon. Was this an eyebrow?

I asked Mady if she remembered telling me the story of the one-eyed trolls. They had only one eye among the three of them. They took turns using it—each had a hole in his forehead to put it in. When the leader had the eye the other two followed, holding on to him.

That evening I served the children Spaghetti-O's, a new canned dinner made out of little pasta O's in tomato sauce. All I had to do was open the can, and their dinner was practically done. I usually added a bit of cooked onion and hamburger and served it with a vegetable.

"That's not much of a supper for these boys," Mady scolded while they devoured their Spaghetti-O's, leaving bright rings of tomato sauce around their mouths.

"I know," I said, wary of her watchful eye as I experimented with shortcuts. "I'm sure you're right. Sometimes I just take the easy way out. But I don't give them sweetened cereals in the morning. Every day I make oatmeal for their breakfast, with Old Fashioned Quaker Oats."

Mady nodded her approval and then asked, "Why don't you get another girl like Johanne? Wasn't she a big help?"

"Yes, she was. I really needed her when we moved and when Jonathan was born. But I want to raise my boys myself, with part-time help."

"Too bad," Mady said. "That eliminates a good job for somebody."

Her remark surprised me. She had been opposed to my part-time work when Neddy was younger. I thought our close bond would help her see the childcare question from my perspective. But we were on opposite sides of the divide. Every time I hired a babysitter, which wasn't often, I saw myself becoming more and more distant from my sons, the way my mother distanced herself from me. Mady, on the other hand, saw things pragmatically: To her, I was a busy mother who needed help.

I was torn. On the one hand I longed for another Mady to take care of my children and me. And on the other, I wanted a close attachment with my own children. I couldn't have it both ways. At that time I didn't realize that a relationship with a part-time caregiver could be a plus for my boys. I was too afraid of becoming the kind of mother I didn't want to be, a mother like mine, a mother I couldn't love.

Having Mady around that week erased these thoughts from my mind. I relaxed and enjoyed being a mother because I had Mady's company—whether she was sitting at the table while the children ate or standing next to the tub with a huge towel to dry them off after their bath. She comforted me. In small matters she might criticize— she never did accept the Spaghetti-O's—but she would always stand up for me, telling me what a wonderful mother I was. How proud she was of me. I was her girl.

I knew there could never be another Mady.

Thursday morning Mady came down the stairs more slowly than

usual. She sat down in her bathrobe at the kitchen table, where Neddy was drawing a shark with sharp triangular teeth.

"This shark is going to eat you!" he said, handing the drawing to Mady.

She stared at it. Then she turned to me.

"I can't see it," she said in a soft voice.

"I'll turn on the light," I said. "It's dark in here."

"*Nei*, it's not that. I can't see anything," she said, her voice rising.

I took a closer look at her face. Her small brown eyes were so good that she never needed glasses, except to read. They looked the same as always. Then like underground springs they started to well with tears that trickled down her cheeks. She dabbed both eyes with a handkerchief and blew her nose.

I put my hand in front of her face. "What do you see, Mady? Can you see my hand?"

"No, I see nothing."

"Not even the shape of it?" I knew Mady had lost some vision in her left eye years ago, from complications after a cataract operation. The big problem now, it seemed, was in the right eye—her good eye.

"No," said Mady. "No. You don't understand—I can't see anything." Her voice was squeaking high and low as she took deep breaths, trying to stop sobbing. She croaked like a Canada goose.

"I always wondered what it would be," she said. "I never thought it would be *this*."

What it would be. Those were the words she had used when she looked at the coffee grounds in the bottom of her cup just days before. I didn't believe in fortune-telling, but I shivered, remembering her question: "Don't you think these grounds are shaped like an eye?"

Now I put my arm around her shoulders. "What do you mean, 'it'?"

"I mean, what is the particular illness God has chosen for me in my old age? I never guessed it would be blindness. But that is how God has decided to punish me. I just have to be grateful for the good health I've had for so long."

Mady had always embraced a punitive fatalism. "All good things come to an end" was one of her mantras. But her view of blindness as a punishment distressed me. I wanted to help her look at it differently, without this harsh judgment, and get treatment.

"Wait a minute. Calm down," I said, feeling anything but calm myself. "Let's find out what's going on before we jump to conclusions."

After Neddy went to his play group, I put Jonathan in the stroller and Mady and I walked to the doctor's office. With one hand she held on to the railing of the ramp and with the other she stabbed at empty space, grasping for obstacles.

"It's okay, Mady," I assured her. "I'm right here beside you."

But she didn't hear me—she moved stiffly up the ramp to the office.

Dr. Barrett was tall and rangy in his tennis whites and sneakers. I introduced Mady and she told him what had just happened.

"Well, at your age, sudden loss of vision in one eye can happen," he said as he reached for the head mirror. "But it's not that common. Let's have a look."

Dr. Barrett shined the light in her eyes and asked her to count the number of fingers he held in front of her. But Mady couldn't see anything. Then he asked her to read the top line on the eye chart, on the far wall. Still nothing.

"I can't do any more here," the doctor said. "I can only offer a speculative opinion because I'm not an ophthalmologist. Miss Mortensen must see a specialist immediately."

My chest suddenly felt hollow and my mind raced ahead with questions. What if she couldn't ever see again? Was there enough money for extra help? I knew I'd be needed to help deal with everything, or at least to assist Mady's relatives. Was I up to the task—what with my own family responsibilities and my father, who was becoming more dependent on me?

I thanked Dr. Barrett and led Mady down the ramp outside his office. On our walk home I tried to say something funny about being one of the one-eyed trolls leading her to safety, but after a while we both worried in silence.

Back at the cottage, I called Ed at the office and told him what had happened.

"Oh, my God," he said. "She actually can't see at all?" I told him what Dr. Barrett had said, that Mady needed to see a specialist as soon as possible. It was an emergency.

"Let me check with the medical staff here at the bank, and I'll get right back to you."

I knew Mady would be uncomfortable if we made arrangements for her; they would be too expensive. But I thought we should do whatever we could. Time might be important.

"Let me see if we can get a helicopter to evacuate her from the island," Ed said. "If we can get her to Bay Shore quickly we can get an ambulance to take her to one of the specialists uptown at Columbia Presbyterian."

"Good idea," I said. "Why don't I call you after I've discussed this with Mady? You know how she is—she doesn't want to spend money on herself."

"Okay; well, let me know." I knew I could count on him.

Mady and I talked about what to do next. She had often accused me of acting helpless—now I wanted to show her how resourceful I could be. She thanked me but said she didn't want to see the specialist. Not yet anyway. First she wanted to see her own doctor in Weehawken. And the idea of a helicopter—well, that was out of the question. She would take the ferry.

The next day I accompanied her on the boat to Bay Shore where one of her Long Island nieces—someone I didn't even know about—met us and drove her to Weehawken.

Two days later Mady telephoned me. It was bad news, she said. Then she handed the phone to her nephew Arthur, who summarized the doctor's findings. "Her loss of vision, a common development in older far-sighted people with small eyes, is incurable," he said. It resulted from a painless swelling of the optic nerve that connects the eye and the brain. The diagnosis had a long name—non-arthritic ischemic optic neuropathy.

Mady's news made me sad and angry—sad about my powerless-ness, angry at whatever had conspired to cause this terrible loss. After six years of marriage, starting a family, and following my husband to South America and back, I was beginning to enjoy living in New York. But now the sudden news about Mady's blindness hung like a black cloud over us.

In the fall, after Neddy had started nursery school, I got a babysitter for Jonathan and drove my father's car to Weehawken to see Mady. Seated together on the sofa in her cozy living room, we talked about her future. I tried to persuade her to look at her blindness differently, not as a harsh punishment for her alleged sins.

I knew it would be hard at her age to make this adjustment. I tried walking around her living room with my eyes closed and I couldn't stand it for more than a few steps.

"How can we help?" I asked. I had spoken with Ed's favorite cousin, Helen, who lived near us. She was familiar with government programs and would know how to find the right support.

"You know how much Ed cares for you"—I always referred to him as Ed, though Mady still called him Mr. Hoyt. "He has good connec-tions, and knows about health insurance. I'm sure you're eligible for lots of support services. You can get mobility training and learn safe ways to cook light meals. You can get a seeing-eye dog. You could learn Braille. There are Talking Books, Meals on Wheels, companions to take you out for walks. The Lighthouse for the Blind has a list of volunteers...."

I prattled on while Mady sat on the sofa, sighing audibly—deep sighs filled with anguish. I was pouring all my energy and hope into her so that she wouldn't feel discouraged, but it wasn't working. Every time I looked at her bleak expression and her sagging shoulders I saw despair.

Mady shook her head. "It's no use," she said. "You can't teach an old dog new tricks." Another mantra. Her eyes, so useless for seeing, could only leak tears. When her sister Tomine came downstairs to help with their dinner, I said my good-byes and headed home, sobbing the whole way.

The next time I spoke with Mady on the telephone she had made up her mind. She had decided to return to Norway, where she would be eligible for benefits as a Norwegian citizen. Her American social security checks and health insurance, together with her savings, meant she could afford all the care she ever needed. She had been talking with a nephew in Norway who was positive he could get a good room for her in the Old People's Home in Kristiansand, on Norway's southern coast. Her grandniece and her young family lived only a few blocks from the Home. As soon as the space was confirmed, Mady said, her sister, Tomine, would help her pack and she would fly to Norway accompanied by her niece.

As I listened to her reasonable plan, my heart sank.

"I don't want you to leave," I murmured. But I knew Ed and I had little to offer. We were no match for the persuasive arguments of nieces and nephews who assured her she would receive excellent care in Norway—care they had already seen when their own parents lived at the Old People's Home.

As we talked on the phone, Mady kept reminding me that I had plenty to do with my own family. She was right. Monitoring care for my father, who was beginning to need round-the-clock nurses, was taking more and more time. Although I didn't do his bookkeeping, I cooked for him on his housekeeper's day off. He came to our apartment for dinner every Thursday evening and occasionally he spent the night in the extra bedroom. I went to his apartment for lunch on Fridays to check in with his housekeeper. She served me a hamburger while I sat at the table with my father and talked with his male nurse.

One day when my attempts at conversation with my father failed, I remembered the photo album he had made of my first ten years. I set it down on the table in front of him, and opened it to the years 1942–1943. There were pictures of him in Englewood with his dog, Denbigh Dan, on a leash and another of him holding me on his lap with Denbigh sitting by his side.

My father studied the photographs. "You got carsick when I took you and Denbigh for a ride," he recalled. "You oofed your cookies!"

I had heard about this accident before and I was sorry this was the one memory that popped into his clouded mind when he thought about me and his dog. I had soiled the upholstery in his beautiful Cadillac.

"You miss Denbigh Dan, don't you?" I said.

There was a glimmer of understanding on his face as he nodded.

∼

I didn't go to the airport to say good-bye to Mady when she flew to Oslo in early July. Members of her family were going to see her off, and I knew they would all speak Norwegian together and I would feel out of place—and probably the most distraught.

That afternoon, at the time when most flights to Europe took off from JFK, I sat on the beach in Point O'Woods with Neddy and Jonathan. For more than a half hour we watched all the jumbo jets on their flight path over our heads. I told the boys to look for the one with the blue initials SAS on the fuselage. I told them we were looking for the plane taking Mady away, to her home in Norway, where the trolls and the reindeer live.

At the end of the summer Ed and I decided not to return to Fire Island and its poignant reminders of Mady's last visit.

"I'm tired of being here on the ridge," he said. "Too close to our neighbors and their noisy Sunday brunches. And I don't care about the beach. Let's do something different next year. Tell you what," he went on. "Let's rent Roger Griswold's family's place in Maine. Seal Cove, on Mt. Desert Island. He's been talking about renting it out for his father, who's getting senile. I'm pretty sure we'll get a break on the rent."

"But it's better here for the kids. And closer to New York," I protested.

"I know. But let's give it a try and see. Roger says it's beautiful, and they have a swimming pool for the kids. If it doesn't work we can always come back here."

"Okay," I conceded. "I suppose it would be fun to see where my mother spent her summers." Maine had always intrigued me because my mother and grandmother had summered in Kennebunkport. It was as if I were tracing her steps, hoping to get closer to her, to connect to her and the grandmother I'd never known.

And so we decided to spend the following summer in Maine. Neddy, Jonathan, and I stayed there for five weeks and Ed took vacation time, commuting by air from New York to Bangor on weekends. Located on twenty acres of apple trees and meadows, with views of the water and the Camden Hills, the property at Seal Cove had a tennis court as well as a sun-warmed salt water tank at the water's edge. The coastline dazzled me—the mustard yellows of seaweed clinging to the rocks at low tide, cormorants flapping and drying their wings after fishing expeditions, and lobster fishermen in the cove hauling heavy traps. Neddy and Jonathan became happy hikers, picking blueberries along the trails as we climbed the gentle hills. I didn't know it then but the landscape was exactly like that of the southern Norwegian coast, where Mady had grown up.

At the end of our stay we found it hard to leave. But we knew we couldn't do it again. Ed's weekend commute between Bangor and New York was too long and uncertain, with the marine weather and fog. We would have to find an affordable summer place closer to Manhattan.

When we returned to New York in August, we moved into our own seven-room co-op apartment on the corner of Ninetieth Street and Madison Avenue. I was pleased that our frugal habits during the first four years of our marriage had allowed us to save enough for this purchase. My father had never invested in real estate, but I could see there were benefits to owning property in New York. And there was always the hope that the apartment would appreciate in value while we lived in it.

Nevertheless, many of our friends and neighbors on the Upper East Side questioned our choice. "Ninetieth Street is so close to Harlem," they said. Indeed, Harlem, the area north of Ninety-sixth Street, had become a center of unrest among African-Americans, which reflected the national upheavals of the 1960s. The day we signed the contract to buy the apartment, June 4, 1968, was the day Bobby Kennedy was assassinated. He died only two months after Martin Luther King was shot to death. The Civil Rights Movement and the Women's Movement were in full swing. And then there was the Vietnam War, which I opposed so fervently that I canvassed registered Democrats in our neighborhood to help get out the vote for the Democratic presidential candidate, Eugene McCarthy. At the same time I tried to be a supportive wife, nurturing mother, and attentive daughter to an ailing father.

Ed's banking job isolated him from much that was going on in this political environment. It confined him to banking circles that offered limited participation in the momentous social changes that were occurring all around us. He averaged one week of travel to Latin America every month.

Our lives had begun to seem static in a rapidly changing world. Old friends were divorcing their husbands and remarrying. Some were taking on bigger professional responsibilities. Ed and I had lived abroad; it was hard to see where we fit in at home. Ed was so focused on his work and I on our family that we often didn't feel connected to the turbulence around us or to each other.

With both Neddy and Jonathan in school for part of each day, and Ed busy at the bank, I began to think about what I could do. I wanted to try something other than teaching and I wanted my work to be portable. I'd enjoyed teaching in Bogotá and at the Shady Hill School in Cambridge, and I was proud of how my skills and confidence had grown, but I wanted a new challenge, something that might satisfy me on a deeper emotional level. I was searching for a creative outlet.

Ever since I read James Agee's *A Death in the Family* in 1964 I had dreamed of being a writer. In all the novels I'd ever read, I'd never experienced the sorrow I felt when Agee's character Jay Follet dies. What techniques did Agee use to evoke such sadness? What did it take to engage a reader so deeply?

I was not an English major in college, and I had a lot of reading to do if I was going to become a writer. I had read many classic works in French, but because it wasn't my language of emotion I read them to expand my vocabulary. I'd never read a Russian novel or short story. And Virginia Woolf was a new experience. I began to enjoy the time I had to read and experiment with writing before I started to think more seriously about writing stories myself.

I wasn't sure what kind of writing I wanted to do. My first impulse was to write for children, using my family experience. After our visit to the lobster pound in Maine, where I saw the boys' fascination, I imagined the story of Larry the Lobster who, with the help of a small boy, escaped from a trap and went on to have adventures with a harbor seal in a Maine cove. I wanted to combine my inclinations as a teacher, helping children learn new words like "crusher claw," with a good story. I would have fun, and soon my books would be best-sellers. How hard could that be? I asked myself.

Certain that I had a good idea, I signed up to learn more in a course called "Writing for Children" at The New School. There I quickly discovered I was not alone—that many other aspiring writers think they will begin by writing books for children.

After writing Larry the Lobster and doing the layout, I researched the market. How many other children's books could there be about lobsters? Soon I discovered Larry's competition as I browsed the children's book section at my local library. *Titus Tidewater* was a nice little story with an alliterative title and charming illustrations by the author. The books in the section seemed so simple but as I soon learned, very few children's books are simple at all. Simplicity is not the driving force behind *Blueberries for Sal; Goodnight, Moon;* or *Harold and the Purple Crayon.*

I was disappointed, but I wasn't discouraged. I kept thinking about story ideas and exploring other kinds of writing. I accepted the idea that writing was a lonely business and that I would have to work hard at it. I would write, then I would revise. And I began honing my skills and getting useful feedback in writing workshops—at The New

School, at Columbia School for the Arts, Sarah Lawrence College, the West Side "Y," the Writer's Studio, and the 92nd Street Y.

In the years that followed I started to zero in on certain markets and sell my work to newspapers like *The New York Times, The Boston Globe,* and *The Miami Herald* and publications like *Miami Magazine* and *Singapore Business.* I wrote pieces for the style, travel, and education sections of these magazines and one investigative piece on day care for *Miami Magazine.* I was especially pleased when *The New York Times* published my essay "An I for an E," about my name, on the Op-Ed page of July 1, 1985.

By 1970, my father was not doing well. He now needed round-the-clock care, in three shifts. He still recognized me but he spoke little. I talked frequently to his nurses and with the legal secretary who opened his mail, monitored his insurance, and paid his bills.

On Saturday afternoon, the fourteenth of March 1970, I was in bed recovering from a sinus infection while Ed took the boys to the park. I was starting to read a new novel but I fell asleep in the middle of the first chapter. Late that afternoon one of my father's nurses telephoned. His breathing was getting shallow, she said. He had no appetite, his pulse was slow, and he had a fever of 104.

Four months earlier we had helped my father celebrate his eightieth birthday with candles and cake. Now, after four years of senile dementia, Parkinson's, and arteriosclerosis, he had developed pneumonia. I knew he was slipping away.

That night Ed and I went to bed early. I was asleep but Ed was awake when the phone rang at two in the morning.

"Papa Hayes died," he said gently. He put his arms around me.

I had been dreading this moment. I'd have to get up, get dressed and make decisions. But I was so tired and sad I didn't think I could.

"Are you okay?" Ed asked, still holding me.

I rubbed my eyes and straightened out the pillow.

"I wish I could go with you," he said.

"I wish you could, too." I kissed him.

Out on the wet, deserted street I hailed a taxi to my father's apartment. Ed stayed home with Neddy and Jonathan, who were asleep in their bunk beds.

The doctor on call at the City Health Department met me at the apartment to sign the death certificate. I walked over to my father's bed and put my hand on his cheek and kissed him. He was still warm. When I arrived home just before dawn on Sunday morning, I couldn't sleep, so I stayed up, wrote a short obituary for *The New York Times*, and phoned it in to the paper.

Later that day I called Mady at the Old People's Home in Kristiansand and gave her the news.

She expressed her sorrow and asked me how I was getting along.

"What are the funeral plans?" she asked. She had always been fond of my father.

"They've taken the body to Frank Campbell's Funeral Home," I told her.

"I hope you can get some rest," she said. "How are the boys? I wish I could be there to help you."

"Ed's here," I told her. "He's not traveling, thank God. He's going to take a day off from work for the funeral on Wednesday."

When I woke up on Monday morning, I saw it had snowed two inches during the night. I planned to take a brisk walk on the path around Central Park's reservoir, hoping to clear my mind. After delivering Neddy to the school bus, I pushed Jonathan in his stroller along the snowy sidewalk in front of the church on the corner of Ninetieth Street and Fifth Avenue. Even as my father's condition worsened, I hadn't contacted any church, nor had I given any thought to what kind of service to have. Yet I knew he would want something, at least as much as he had done for my mother.

As if on cue, there in front of us was Fritz Creamer, the young assistant to the rector at the Church of Heavenly Rest, who was wearing his collar under his open jacket as he shoveled the sidewalk. I didn't know him personally but I had heard about him from a Fire Island friend, who sent her boys to the Sunday School.

"Hello, Father Creamer," I said, noticing his boyish good looks.

"You don't know me but I'm a friend of one of your parishioners and I have a problem."

"Certainly," he said. "How can I help?" He leaned on his long-handled shovel and smiled.

Already I felt better. I explained that my father had just died and that I needed to plan a service for him. Would he be willing to officiate?

And so we worked it out that it would be a traditional Episcopalian service in a nondenominational chapel and that we would hear the comforting words "ashes to ashes, dust to dust" and "I am the resurrection and the life." Fritz suggested that I think about what hymns and readings I wanted to include and then call him at his office.

On Tuesday, March 17th, St. Patrick's Day, I delivered a suit, shirt, and tie to Campbell's Funeral Home for my father's service. I remember walking down Madison Avenue carrying a clothes box and navigating a green tide of Irishmen drinking beer and singing. On my way down in the elevator I had met Judy, one of our new neighbors. She asked where I was going.

I gave her the news. "My father died on Saturday night," I told her, "and I'm bringing one of his suits to the funeral home for his burial."

It was not the answer Judy was expecting; she hardly knew my family or me. I could read the surprise in her eyes as she and her husband mumbled their condolences.

The next day she sent us a chicken casserole with rice, a salad, dressing, and dessert.

"In Iowa, where my mother comes from, the first thing you do after a death is go to the kitchen and cook," Judy explained. I appreciated her kindness and we soon became good friends.

After the service at Campbell's, Ed, my cousins Nancy and Emily, and I were driven out to Englewood, where my father was buried next to my mother in the Bliss family plot. This time there was no reception at Aunt Ethel's because she was already living in a nursing home in Tenafly.

A week later, with more rest and a clearer mind, I realized I'd need to spend at least a couple of months vacating my father's eight-room apartment. He had lived there for twenty-seven years. Closets were filled with old estate papers, letters, checkbooks, clothes, shoes, hats, golf clubs, and fishing and hunting gear. There were documents in the safe deposit box at the bank and in the safe inside the bedside table in my father's room. Except for some antique dining room furniture and Persian carpets, I didn't want anything I found. So I decided to spend weekday mornings at the apartment, sorting and cleaning things out when a babysitter could stay with Jonathan before dropping him off at preschool.

Going through my father's papers was a daunting task. By the time I reached the bottom drawer of the mahogany desk in the dining room, I had been working at my father's apartment every weekday morning for more than two months. I had already cleared out the bank statements and my mother's correspondence, so I wasn't expecting to find anything in the desk except boxes of extra stationery and some postage stamps.

But as I rummaged through the bottom drawer I was surprised to notice a six-inch stack of letters tied up with a blue satin ribbon. A quick glance at the handwriting revealed they were written by both my parents. Were these love letters? Or letters they'd exchanged when one of them was traveling? My body churned with excitement as I contemplated what to do with this personal correspondence. I carried the stack of letters into the living room, poured myself a glass of Cabernet, and settled into my father's easy chair. Then I untied the blue ribbon around the letters and began to read.

Chapter 13

Sail and Anchor

The first letter from my mother, Margaret, to my father, Alex, was written in July 1931 while she was vacationing with friends in Prout's Neck, Maine. She was thirty-three, and he was forty-two, a broker on Wall Street. Neither had ever married. My father was infatuated. Early in August he took a weekend off and drove from New York to Maine and back—a trip of seven or eight hours each way—to spend one evening sitting with her on the rocks and watching the sunset over Casco Bay.

It took me about ten minutes to read Margaret's first four letters, all postmarked Prout's Neck and mailed in July and August. I was intrigued by a statement she made in one letter—"You don't know Maine till you've seen its coast"—but she offered no clue to what Alex had said to prompt it. In early October, she wrote two short notes on New York's Fairfax Hotel stationery and then, two weeks later, a long letter postmarked Cadiz, Spain. For the next eight months most of my mother's letters came from Palma, in Mallorca. A few more came from Cannes, Geneva, and Paris. I learned that she was traveling with Anna Ross Weeks, an old friend of her mother's.

As I sipped my wine, I asked myself, why Spain? I wasn't expecting her to make such a big move. Suddenly she shifted from news about her bridge and tennis games, and Maine's coastal fog, to reports about Spanish food, culture, and the language on a ship called the *Marques de Comillas*. Then I read a startling sentence: "I told you about the man in my cabin."

At that point, completely mystified, I tied up the letters and headed home. I wanted to share my treasure trove with Ed. Together we'd find out about that man in her cabin—and much more. I put the packet of letters in my tote, carried my empty wineglass into the kitchen, and headed out to Madison Avenue.

Ed wasn't home when I opened the door to our apartment. This was no surprise—he often worked late. I thanked the sitter and sent her home, then gave Neddy and Jonathan their dinner. After I put the boys to bed I unpacked the letters, organized them chronologically on the coffee table, and began to read. The first letter from my father, written on Christmas Eve, 1931, followed nine letters from my mother. They had probably met in Englewood sometime during the late 1920s, and it was clear from the letters that he was already smitten. "You certainly are giving me cause to worry in telling me about all these romantic men you are meeting. You got to be careful.... Maybe you want to keep me on my toes."

His tone sounded familiar—he often spoke to me in the imperative voice to hurry me up when I was late. It was my mother's voice, on paper, that astonished me. Here she was the healthy, independent woman I had never known, and I felt proud of her. I was happy to learn that there were many years when her life was easier, when her worst miseries were head colds and seasickness. "She wrote beautiful letters," my father always told me. As I read her words, I wept, thinking about the connection we never made, the good times we never had. She and I had spent most of the last twenty years of her life more apart than together. And even when we were together she seemed aloof, as if she were moving around behind a scrim that was never backlit to reveal the details. She was almost invisible to me.

Now in these courtship letters I was witnessing her in action. I had never seen my mother drive a car. Here she was telling my father about her journey from New York to Maine and how much she disliked the Boston Post Road. I observed her taking the initiative, solving problems, and making decisions. Most important, she was having fun—she seemed happy. I loved her. And the effect she was having on my father took my breath away:

> *Don't think for a minute, my dear, that I want to change you in any way. I want you, and love you just as you are.... Your shyness and reserve which I adore so much attract the right kind of friends to you and repel the others. This is the way it ought to be.*

It took me a little while to feel comfortable reading what they had written to each other—my father, the ardent suitor, and my mother, the flirtatious, adventurous woman I had barely known. I soon found their courtship engrossing. He was already very much in love with her as he waited for her to reciprocate his feelings: "I'm absolutely sure I can bring happiness and contentment to you," he assured her in one letter.

An hour later, absorbed in my eavesdropping, I almost didn't hear Ed's key turn in the lock. "Guess what I found!" I called out to him.

"What—a diamond ring?"

"No. Even better. My parents' love letters."

"Really?"

"Yes. Starting in 1931, ending just before their marriage in 1934. One hundred and sixty-four altogether. It will take a while to go through them." Then I led him into the living room and pointed to the letters organized into piles on the coffee table. First I showed him my mother's long October 19th letter about the man in her cabin.

"Amazing. How did she get rid of him?"

"She doesn't say. Let me read it to you: 'It was not long after he was evicted that we were introduced and we are now good friends, he serving as a useful dancing partner on many occasions.'"

"Hmm," Ed said. "There must have been a mixup as they were boarding the ship. I'm sure she made your father jealous, writing stuff like that. From intruder to dancing partner."

"She was a real tease."

After Ed and I had dinner, we sat down on the sofa and started going through the letters. Some, we noticed, were written on creamy vellum monogrammed paper. Many were smooth and sturdy to the touch; they had 2-cent stamps on the envelopes and were franked with the names of places like New York, Paris, Englewood, Point O' Woods, Long Island, Prout's Neck, Palma de Mallorca, Charlottesville, Virginia. Some were only one or two paragraphs long; most ran to more than six or seven paragraphs. Several from my father were engraved with the word "Pinelawn," the name of the house he shared with three other bachelors in Englewood. Other letters—my mother's—were written on hotel stationery. On the envelopes my mother specified the ship the letter would sail on, then "via Cherbourg." Each letter had been opened with a knife and on the envelope my mother often noted the date she had received it and when she had answered it. Many of them were marked "Keep."

"Look at this," I said to Ed.

Full of excitement, I showed him a few samples of my father's ardor.

> I did hate to see you go away, and I wanted you here so I could see you, play around with you, and maybe occasionally hold you all snuggled up in my arms in the hopes that you would be won over, and return my love and affection.

"And how about this one?" I said.

> Write again soon and often and this time I am
> sending you a big armful of love and affection.

"Wow!" said Ed. "He wrote that? I didn't think he had that in him."

"What do you mean?"

"Well, you know, he was so buttoned up. I didn't think there was so much emotion there."

"Yes, there was," I said. "I think we'll learn more as we continue reading. I'm going to sit here and go through the letters from start to finish."

"I want to know what happens," Ed said with a grin. "Let's read them together."

And that's what we did. I read a letter, then passed it on to Ed. It didn't take long for me to get caught up in my parents' communications, letting their words fuel my imagination about their romance. The letters conjured up the world of their youth—the Great Depression—which was already familiar to me because of conversations I had overheard as a child. I also recalled nostalgic trips to Englewood in the car—with my mother seated next to my father, the driver, while I squirmed in the back seat.

Mutual Englewood friends must have introduced my parents in the late twenties or early thirties—married couples always try to hook up their single friends, especially someone Margaret's age. And as an attractive bachelor, my father was in demand. In one letter he mentioned having ten invitations for a Saturday evening.

I imagined one of my parents' dates on a bright Sunday in the spring of 1931. After a round of golf, they might have come back to Pinelawn for a glass of sherry and some Welsh rarebit or codfish cakes, my father's favorite. Pinelawn was an old Dutch colonial, with a fish-scale slate roof, surrounded by a large shaded lawn. After both her parents' deaths, my mother had moved out of the rambling thirty-six-room mansion where she had grown up and rented a two-bedroom apartment not far from Pinelawn.

I could see Margaret leaning against Pinelawn's mantelpiece and twirling strands of her dark, shoulder-length hair with her long fingers. After their golf game she would have changed out of her golf outfit into a calf-length tweed skirt with a V-neck woolen cardigan over a silk blouse.

"How did you get the name Alexander?" she might have asked him. "Was that your father's name?"

He would have explained to her that Alexander was the name of his father's brother, a physician and surgeon who practiced in Sarnia, Ontario. When he was a boy growing up in the village of Springfield, Ontario, he said, he thought Sarnia was the biggest city in the world. He would have laughed then, thinking about the long journey he had taken from his hardscrabble Canadian youth. He didn't want to tell her about his boyhood—the memory of its poverty embarrassed him. He brushed the topic off with the comment that it was "uninterest-ing." I learned later that it was so tough that only he and two sisters out of the brood of eight Hayes children survived long enough to reach adulthood, marry, and have children of their own.

There was something appealing about Margaret's silhouette, Alex noticed. She was tall, slim, and athletic—a good tennis player, with long arms that could reach almost any backhand or overhead. She was also a good partner at the baseline, chasing the lobs while he looked for his chances at net. As they sipped sherry by the fireplace that Sunday, she cocked her hip, letting one of her elbows rest on the mantelpiece. He stared at the almost perfect V-shape of the widow's peak of her dark hair, which framed her heart-shaped face. She was lovelier than all the women he had ever known, and he adored every-thing about her—her deep-set dark eyes, the softness of her sweater, her silver and moonstone necklace. He enjoyed her sense of humor. And he loved when she leaned against him so that he could smell her perfume. It made him feel strong and manly.

As their friendship developed, letters helped them communicate even when they were both in New York as well as when she was away in Maine and Spain. At this time, just before the late October inauguration of the George Washington Bridge, which shortened the commute from Englewood to Manhattan, my mother preferred to stay at the Fairfax Hotel, on East Fifty-sixth Street. From there, on October 5th, Margaret sent Alex two short notes to his downtown office at 65 Broadway. Alex must have thought he had finally succeeded in launching a serious romance with her until he opened the first letter:

What a fog I am in at the moment! This afternoon I decided to set sail on Saturday of this week. It will be an awful scramble to make it but we found that the two later boats we thought of taking have been taken off and nothing goes to Barcelona for another month. I shall be glad to get away from New York but I was looking forward to our dates on Sunday and Monday. You don't know how guilty I feel breaking them like this.... Will you forgive me?

She was breaking dates he had planned with her for the long Columbus Day weekend. He must have been shocked at this sudden turn of events. Now all he could do was wait patiently for her return.

Margaret stayed in Palma de Mallorca, in Spain's Balearic Islands, for several months. She studied Spanish, saw friends in the expatriate community, and went to parties. Although she doesn't mention him in any of her letters, she may have been curious to visit the place where her favorite piano composer, Chopin, lived with his lover, George Sand, in 1838. But Mallorca also made practical sense because a married couple she had met through my father had a vacation house in Raxa, outside Palma. The husband lived with my father at Pinelawn, when he was working in the States. But most of the time the couple lived in Palma and in Lisbon, where the husband worked in the cork business. Staying in Palma gave my mother a chance to see his wife, her good friend Helen.

In Palma, where she and Mrs. Weeks rented an apartment and did their own cooking, my mother enjoyed visits with Helen:

> Yesterday I spent the day with Helen at Raxa. Took the train out in the morning and walked to the house. The country is a perfect dream of beauty now. Really the almond blossoms are too lovely for words. Helen and I sat out on their sun porch and I feel all thawed out and I am sure my cold is better as a result. We had lunch on the porch, too. She gave me some chewing gum you had presented to her on the day of her departure. I chewed and thought of you.

Margaret left Palma in March 1932. She traveled via Marseilles and Cannes to Geneva, where she talked with some journalist friends ("a nice crowd, with their work cut out for them") and bought herself a ticket to a session at the Disarmament Conference of the League of Nations. Then she went on to Paris. She did not return to New York until May.

During this eight-month separation she seemed to become more appreciative of Alex's steady attention. Their letters got longer and more detailed; it was clear that they looked forward to writing and receiving them. Alex would decline invitations to dinner with friends just so that he could stay home alone in his room at Pinelawn. There, in the old house, which creaked and groaned on windy nights, he would sit at his desk and think about Margaret as he wrote:

> Here I am answering your letter within two hours of receiving it, not because I felt the necessity of doing it, but the urge was there right in the spot and I feel very happy in writing to you, even though I haven't

*much to say. My thoughts are of you anyway. Wish
you were going to be here tomorrow and over the
holidays.*

Back and forth the letters sailed, by steamship. She described her adventures, the early warnings of political and economic troubles in Spain, her late-night parties, and her unconventional travel arrangements. The more she flirted, the more he pursued.

*My trip from Cannes was one of the funniest I have
ever taken. By the greatest good fortune I discovered
that a friend was taking the same train — a night trip.
So, at least I had someone to talk to and he being
a Cuban I even tried my Spanish on him. I had a
reservation in a first class compartment, absolutely
the only thing I could get, what is here known as
a "couchette." Well, if you can believe it, I slept
with three men and a dog! My Cuban friend was
in the next car, unfortunately (or fortunately) — I
don't know which. In any case, sleep was quite
impossible under such odd circumstances and as the
thermometer in our compartment registered 80 that
was another obstacle to a good night's sleep. French
people cannot endure fresh air and of course I was
out of luck. But can you imagine such a night?*

Alex flooded her with news from home. There were people Margaret and Alex knew well who were so depressed by the Depression that they found it difficult to get out of bed in the morning. Other men Alex knew at the office also couldn't handle the economic pressures. In October 1932, when Margaret was staying with her brother Delos in Virginia, Alex sent her shocking news:

The man whose desk was on my right committed suicide a few days ago.... Also, a man came to my desk and intimated to me he was about ready to bump himself off—trying to arrange his affairs so no one would be hurt. I told him what I thought about it all and how weak he was. All this was not pleasant but I guess I am hard-boiled because I can throw these things off in no time at all.... But it does seem that some people do not know what to do or how to handle themselves when hard times strike them. They are most unfortunate. Myself, I think hard times have developed and brought out understanding among people.

"Look at the way my father thrived in hard times," I said to Ed. "He wrote my mother that he was happy about 'the leveling of the playing field.' He thought the Depression would 'separate the people who had some backbone from those who did not.'"

I put the letter down and looked at my watch. It was getting late—well past ten o'clock—but I wanted to keep reading. At this point Jonathan woke up and asked for a glass of water. I brought him the water and then tucked him in again while Ed and I took a break.

"What do you think about his remarks about the Depression?" I asked Ed. "Not surprising, given his Republican politics."

"Not much compassion there," Ed said.

"I'll say."

What was the attraction between Margaret and Alex? From my mother's perspective, my future father had what some men she knew in Englewood did not have—a steady job and experience in the financial industry. He had been hired in January 1929 by C. D. Barney and he held on to that job during the lean years that followed the

Crash nine months later. Then in 1932 he was hired by the Guaranty Company, which eventually became known as Smith, Barney.

Margaret believed Alex was a broker who knew how to find customers and take good care of them. But she didn't like his cigars and the holes in his sweaters. Some of his clothes needed attention—he could use some fresh bow ties. She could overlook many things, though, in a man who seemed willing to do almost anything she asked. He would deliver her sedan, her trusted LaSalle, to wherever she was staying in the country, then return to the city by train; he would also run errands, lay a fire in her fireplace, cut firewood, and take her to her favorite roadside tavern for a quick supper on a moment's notice. He even switched from cigars to a pipe for her sake.

No doubt she found all of this devotion refreshing. I imagine she liked his Canadian background, so different from the old-money American families she had grown up with. Englewood was full of Ivy Leaguers who got lifetime memberships in exclusive clubs after they graduated from college. Unlike them, Alex wasn't stuffy, and he had a twinkle in his blue eyes. She liked his optimism and his seemingly unlimited capacity for work. And she shared his love of the outdoors—taking long walks on top of the Palisades, chopping wood for the fireplace in his lumberjack shirt, and eating a stack of pancakes floating in Canadian maple syrup. He brought her a new can whenever she ran out.

What did my father see in Margaret? Did he pursue her because she was rich? His finely tuned antennae must have picked up the sound of inherited money in her voice—but it was hard for him to separate her wealth from her charming reserve, which he could puncture with a good joke. She laughed easily. And she didn't watch every penny the way other women did, so it was fun to be with her. But her wealth was only part of the package.

Perhaps he pursued her because she played the upright Emerson piano at his house—plunging into familiar music without even looking at the keyboard, hitting only an occasional wrong note. Or perhaps it was the way she sprinkled her conversation with French and Spanish phrases. He couldn't tell the difference because he didn't speak any foreign languages but he liked the way the words sounded. So worldly.

"Voilà," she'd say with exaggerated precision after opening a can of peaches on one of her rare trips to the kitchen. Or *"Qu'est-ce que c'est que ça?"*—"What's the matter?"—as if she were scolding her car when it wouldn't start right up. And always, after a kiss goodnight, *"Hasta mañana."*

Maybe he liked her family connections: Her older brother, Mansfield Kidder, served as Mayor of Englewood, and so did her uncle Dan Platt, the husband of her mother's sister, my Aunt Ethel. But he also liked the fact that she was not popular—he didn't want a wife who ran around to parties and nightclubs.

In my father's mind my mother belonged to the gentry—those socially secure, correct people, like the Dwight Morrows and the Thomas Lamonts, who dominated the social and political scenes in Englewood through their money, ambition, and civic leadership. Most of them were successful Republican lawyers and businessmen, or partners in the investment banking house of J. P. Morgan. They commuted to the city on the train that ran between Bergen County and Hoboken, where they caught the ferry to Manhattan. They contributed generously to local churches and hospitals. They ran everything. They were Anglophiles, most of them, and their homes showcased English furnishings, with well-worn Persian carpets scattered on wooden floors, polished brasses around the fireplaces, overstuffed chairs, leather-bound books, and etchings and watercolors on the walls.

The women belonged to the Junior League and the garden club. They played tournament tennis and golf. When they weren't occupied with the children and their large, rambling houses, they stayed busy with good works and played bridge or an old-fashioned card game called Bezique.

This was the world Alex wanted. As a naturalized American, with Irish-Canadian ancestry and U.S. World War I military service behind him, a handsome face, and deep admiration for the Crown of England, he was easily accepted. He was sure he and Margaret could fit in there as a married couple.

Alex kept hoping she would accept him as a suitor even though he knew he was no match for her worldliness. He had never traveled to Europe, nor had he ever known a woman with so much freedom. He wanted to be her anchor—he thought she needed one, the way she had sailed off so suddenly to Mallorca. He wanted to be her husband.

My mother's sudden departure for Spain surprised me, too. Was she running away from him—and his marriage proposal? I had no idea she was capable of such independent action. Her letters made her sound like a free spirit, a woman ahead of her time, a feminist who didn't need a man. The letters raised other questions. Why was she still single? At one point Alex reminded her that they had known each other for five years. Why did he persist for so long? Why didn't he give up?

During the summer of 1932 Margaret rented a beach cottage a block from the ocean in Point O'Woods, on Fire Island. She and Alex exchanged letters all summer. Alex also visited on weekends. On one of those visits Margaret's nieces Nancy and Emily were staying at the house too. Nancy, age eight, asked why Alex didn't sleep in the same room with Margaret. Their mother, my Aunt Mary, explained to Nancy that ladies don't have men in their bedrooms if they're not married.

Margaret enjoyed repeating this conversation to Alex.

After a weekend in early August, Margaret wrote Alex a letter that foreshadowed her dark moods. He had left Point O'Woods late Sunday afternoon to catch the train back to the city.

> You should have stayed down here till Monday morning and you would have seen one of my depressed moods, but in a mild form. I soon got over it. But even the weather contributed to the blackness. Such peculiar looking clouds I have never seen.... we went to the Inn and heard Negro Spirituals, and

*I seemed to cheer up after hearing that well known
one, "Nobody knows the trouble I've seen. ..." I
began to think my troubles were not so bad after all.*

I turned to Ed. "Listen to this," I said, my hand shaking, as I read the letter to him. "I think this is the first hint that my mother had mental problems before I was born."

"See," Ed said, putting his arm around me. "It wasn't your fault."

I laughed. Ed made me feel better. Her words—"one of my depressed moods, but in a mild form"—made it clear she had already suffered worse bouts of depression than the one she had just experienced.

After reading the next letter, from my father, I said, "Look at the way he responds to her letter about her depression."

*Forgetting about yourself for a time, it would be a
relief to you to tell me what makes you depressed. I
don't think there is any reason for it at all. I might
be mistaken, but why not use me. You will find me
a pillar of strength in straightening out some mental
kinks. I am used to standing on my own feet. ...*

"He's not much of a psychologist," Ed said. "How about 'mental kinks'!"

"And look at the way he changed the subject from her problems to his strengths!"

My father had ignored the warning signs. The more he heard about her vulnerabilities, the more he wanted to rescue her.

"He didn't get it," I said to Ed. "He thought their marriage would solve everything. He didn't see she had real problems. Her vulnerability inspired him, and that must be why he persisted longer than most men would."

After we read another month's worth of letters, I began to yawn. It was past eleven o'clock, and I was exhausted. But I wanted to finish— or at least get to the point where my parents considered themselves engaged. I picked up a long letter from my mother, dated September 2, 1932.

"Look at this one," I said to Ed. "I think it's important." I handed the letter to him. He read it aloud.

> *I don't see much ahead for me if I propose to continue this state of single blessedness. I am not the type of girl who attracts attention at all. In fact, a great many men probably think I am a desperate bore! And that is one of the many reasons why it is so agreeable to be noticed and flattered and have such a fuss made of me by you, because it hasn't happened often. . . . I don't seem to have handled life's problems as I should. I don't know how to tell you what bothers me, because it is hard to put my finger on. I wouldn't for the world cause you any suffering intentionally. A good many girls are far too casual no doubt, and perhaps you think I am, but I am not.*

And from Wall Street, my father responded immediately:

> *Right now you are just merely satisfied with single blessedness. You do not even begin to know what happiness is waiting for you right around the corner. You don't know what joy you can have until you are married. My love for you has changed me a great deal. It makes me more human, more happy,*

and more interested in life in general, not only with
you but also with other people.... If you like the
attentions I have been extending to you I want you to
know my dear that it has all been most natural with
me, and I have been getting more happiness out of it
than you have. I love it all.

Ed and I looked at each other, puzzled. "This doesn't make any sense," I said. "He was never married before but he wrote as if he knew all about it."

"He was a smart broker—marriage was a good investment."

I began feeling sad for them, knowing what the future held in store and what a burden my mother would become. Part of me wished my father had given up.

I turned to Ed, who was yawning as much as I was. It was close to midnight by then, but we couldn't stop reading.

We soon learned that the fall of 1932 was the beginning of my father's most vigorous effort, with the help of the Post Office, to win my mother. It coincided with FDR's campaign against Herbert Hoover to win the presidential election. In September my father drove to Springfield, Ontario, to visit his seventy-nine-year-old widowed mother. While he was there Margaret wrote him that she loved him "a little bit." He was overjoyed—he wanted "to turn handsprings on all fours." Early in October she drove south to visit her friend Marjorie in Pittsburgh and her cousin "K" in Baltimore, and finally spent five weeks in Charlottesville, Virginia, with her brother Delos, his wife, Mary, and their two girls. There she accumulated twenty-five letters from my father in which he told her why he loved her.

Alex acknowledged their class differences. He had already learned about her social class from his business and college friends, but there was much more she could teach him, he said, and she would find him a willing pupil. He wanted to "pull himself up to her level." He was "not good enough for her."

"These letters remind me of *The Great Gatsby*," I said to Ed. "My father could be writing about Daisy Buchanan. She was the golden girl. It was all about social class."

There was naval imagery in his letters, some of it contradictory. She was a rudderless ship—all sail and no anchor. She admitted that she needed an anchor badly—something to work for and somebody to help her on her journey. In some letters he would be her anchor, but in others she would anchor him. The anchorage he visualized was the banal one of home and hearth—he reading to her and she knitting him a sweater near a roaring fire. But if she refused him he would "take it like a man."

In another letter he switched metaphors and spoke of her as a "sturdy oak" that, paradoxically, needed his protection. He recognized her mental fragility as he referred to "ensuring her peace of mind," bringing her tranquility. He wanted to absorb all the "shocks and bumps" for both of them.

His odd use of military language—referring to her as his "worthy opponent" in battle who had "barricaded" every approach so that he needed to bring out the "shock troops"—culminated in early November 1932, when she telegrammed him from her brother's farm outside Charlottesville. "I surrender STOP the victory is yours," she wired.

"I accept the honorable captive," he replied.

Much later my father would reminisce with me about this sequence of telegrams and my mother's use of the word "victory." He seemed amused that he had discovered the winning tactic and used it. Like General Grant at Appomattox, who allowed Robert E. Lee to keep his sword because he was such a worthy opponent and a great fighter, he was allowing her the privilege of a noble defeat.

"But really, my dear," he concluded on November 7, 1932, "there is no victory—no vanquished. It's an acknowledgment, an appreciation of the fine love we have for each other. Nothing could be sweeter."

For her part, she relished the parallel between his successful campaign and FDR's landslide victory at the polls on November 9, 1932. On November 7th she wrote, "I don't know whether you are a Democrat or a Republican but I elect you as my president."

He wrote back:

> Will vote for Hoover at Highwood but according to all the dope Roosevelt will win by a tremendous majority. Understand that Europe is on the edge of a volcano — mostly financial.... All these things mean nothing to me now, however. It's your love and affection for me that's bigger than all these things.

And so they became engaged. My father shared his victory—his hard-fought battle for my mother's hand—with President Roosevelt, a man he despised.

But more than a year passed before they married.

I asked Ed about this. "They considered themselves engaged at the end of 1932 but they didn't marry until March 1934. How come?"

Ed thought for a moment. "Financial problems could have been part of it. Look, here she writes that she spent five weeks in Charlottesville for financial reasons."

"But this must be a smokescreen," I said. "How could a woman who buys herself a round-trip transatlantic passage, who maintains and garages a car, and who books good hotel rooms be short of money?"

"And then rents a beach house the following summer," Ed added. "It doesn't make sense."

"More than likely it was my father. His prudence. And maybe my mother's caution as well. I remember his telling me that he didn't have enough money to buy her an engagement ring. Eventually he found her a beautiful Art Deco emerald and diamond ring."

"Yes," Ed said. "Times were tough then. And he may have had some old debts to pay off so that he could start married life free and clear.

He needed to look prosperous enough to marry into this family. He couldn't be perceived as a gold digger."

"But I still think my mother had her reasons for fearing marriage. Remember her expression 'single blessedness'? Where did *that* come from?"

"We'll never know." Ed sighed.

"Maybe so," I said. "But I can't help wondering."

I stood up and stretched my arms up in the air, taking a deep breath.

"At last they're engaged," Ed said as he yawned. "He had to work so hard to woo her. Several years. It must have been exhausting."

"Yes, you were lucky. It took only one year," I said, hugging him.

I gathered up the letters and retied them with the blue ribbon, leaving the stacks on my desk. It had been a long night.

Chapter 14

Kristiansand

Over the next few weeks, I reread all my parents' letters, and they transformed my mother in my mind. It was thrilling to meet her again as a healthy, sophisticated woman, ahead of her time. She had postponed marriage until her thirties, she had traveled independently, and as a pacifist she had focused on important issues in international relations. She read Walter Lippmann's columns in the *Herald Tribune*. I could imagine her standing up and speaking out publicly, expressing strong opinions. "War is not a solution to anything," she wrote my father in 1932 during a visit to the League of Nations in Geneva. "It's insanity on a massive scale."

The mother I met in these letters was fearless and resourceful—easy for me to mythologize and idealize. I was proud of her achievements as a pianist, a linguist, and a tennis player. Above all, I admired her writing. Even my father told me she could have been a successful contributor to women's magazines—a mother I would be proud of. But as I read her eloquent letters, I couldn't forget how disabled she'd become later. And I worried that I might become mentally disabled too. I didn't want to think of myself as someone with severe limitations. Yet the truth was that by this time, several months after my father's death, I was falling apart. I was depressed. I depended on sleeping pills at night and tranquilizers during the day. I yelled at my sons for no reason—and then tortured myself with guilt.

During the winter that followed my father's death I called Susan, a college friend whose father had died at the same time as mine. His sudden fatal heart attack shocked her and her sisters. Yet within a couple of weeks following his death, Susan was back at her part-time job. We had lost our fathers at the same time. But while Susan seemed energized, I felt paralyzed. Why were our experiences of loss so different? Why was I unable to pierce the gray gloom around me?

I went through the motions of being a wife and mother, but I wanted to stay in bed all day. Life, it seemed, was about death. First my mother and then my father had died. Any day now Aunt Ethel would pass away. And Mady lived so far away, in Norway, she might as well be dead. I gazed out my eleventh-floor bedroom window at the brick apartment building across Ninetieth Street, wondering how it would feel to fly out the window, cross the side street, and land on its penthouse terrace. That terrace wasn't so far away. This fantasy worked its way into my brain and stayed there.

One day, getting a tenuous grip on myself, I dialed Susan's number. A Philadelphia native, she had recently moved to the Upper West Side, with her husband and small daughter, after living abroad for several years. We made a date to go skating at the Wollman Rink in Central Park later that week. As we circled around the other skaters on the rink we were surrounded by a bright ring of skyscrapers. Afterward we had dinner at a Chinese restaurant.

"Do you feel settled now in New York?" I asked as we sat down in a booth and waited for our menus. Our cheeks were pink from the cold night air.

"We love living here," Susan said. "It's fantastic. So much to do. So many fascinating people to meet and fall in love with. And I like my new job."

I'd never thought of New York in such positive terms. Maybe I could also feel at home here, despite my sad memories and my inner struggle about hiring babysitters.

As our green teas warmed us I began to relax. After ordering cashew chicken we talked about some of our mutual friends and interests, and soon I felt comfortable. I decided to risk our friendship and tell her about my childhood in New York as an only child, my mother's illnesses, and my attachment to Mady.

I had never told anyone outside the family about Mady or about my mother's lobotomy.

As we talked, my whole body began to shake. I tried to keep my trembling hands out of sight but I still had to use my chopsticks to eat. Pretty soon I couldn't speak. I was sure Susan was aware of my distress and embarrassment.

"Why didn't you know what happened to your mother?" she asked, taking a cigarette out of her purse and lighting it.

I could see she didn't understand my shame.

"Why didn't they tell you? She was your mother, after all." Susan took a long drag on her cigarette, then looked up and blew smoke at the ceiling.

"I don't know," I mumbled.

"I recall a woman in Philadelphia. She had the same operation. People said it changed her."

"How?"

"Hard to say. I didn't see her—I was too young. It's what people talked about, though."

I wanted to hear what had happened to this woman, how she was "different" after the lobotomy, but Susan didn't find the subject so compelling. She wanted to talk about signing up her daughter for skating lessons, and she thought I could help.

After our dinner I took a taxi home to the Upper East Side. I worried about the way my body had trembled when I revealed my secret. I felt ashamed. How could I face Susan again, now that she knew the truth about my mother? I expected her to abandon me as a friend. But later it seemed to me that she never noticed anything amiss. She took everything in stride, as if I had revealed nothing more than the name of an old boyfriend. It was so confusing.

Later that night, I told Ed about my dinner. He didn't know what to think about my panic attack, although he tried to reassure me. But I knew that reassurance wasn't enough. My dark moods and angry flare-ups convinced me I needed help. I told Ed I wanted to see a psychiatrist. Neddy and Jonathan needed a mother who wouldn't explode with anger over minor problems. I needed to feel better. I'd been trying to use my father's recipe for living—showing the world what I was made of, with a stiff upper lip—but it wasn't working. Who was I, then? Shy, rigid, moody, insecure, and, despite outward appearances, miserable and angry.

I still felt anxious the next day when I called my gynecologist to get a referral to a psychiatrist. As I left my name and number I knew it was too late to change my mind—I had started the ball rolling. Part of me was about to embarrass my family by consulting a shrink, and the other part wanted to open the bedroom window and fly across the street.

Several days later, I took a deep breath and dialed the psychiatrist's number. I figured his secretary would give me temporary cover, so my heart sank when I heard the doctor himself offering me an appointment.

Was I doing the right thing? I had no idea about different psychiatric treatments, and I was anxious I might be following in my mother's footsteps. I had her bad teeth and her bad feet, so I probably had her bad brain, too. I might be sent to a psychiatric hospital far from my family and friends. This thought upset me all over again. But even with these ideas filling my mind I didn't feel I had any choice. I had to face my demons and talk about my flying fantasy.

Sitting in the doctor's stuffy waiting room, I felt my heart skip a beat when he finally came out of his private office and shook my hand. He was a tall man with kinky brown hair, a big forehead, and glasses. When we sat down I noticed his huge feet, even bigger than Ed's, and his long legs, which he crossed and recrossed on the brown leather ottoman of his Eames chair.

"What brings you here?" he asked in a soft voice.

I hesitated. "I'm depressed," I said finally.

"How long have you been feeling this way?"

I was thinking how cheerful Susan sounded. How did she do it? Was this a skill I could acquire?

"It feels like I've always been depressed. It's just gotten worse lately."

I felt shy talking to a stranger, but he paid attention to everything I said. Nothing surprised him.

And so my treatment started in February 1971. I began to tell the doctor my story—my mother's mysterious illnesses, my marriage, my work experience, our two sons, Mady's return to Norway, my father's recent death, and the sleeping pills and tranquilizers I'd been taking. I told him I felt split in half, bouncing back and forth between two extremes. Did I belong with Mady, the loyal and loving Norwegian nanny who had raised me? Or with my distant, disabled mother—and her concerns about my moral life? Mady, the capable mother figure, or my biological mother, who claimed her place in a socially correct family? Mady, who hugged me? My mother, who pushed me away?

During the first few sessions the doctor asked about my sons and my husband. Then there was a question that seemed to come out of nowhere—did I have orgasms? Uh-oh, I thought, here we go into my sex life. I clammed up; I didn't want him to know what my husband and I did together, and I was afraid he'd discover that despite my education there was a great deal I didn't know, that I was a novice at living. I often had the feeling I was missing out on fun and laughter. But once I had assured the doctor that my marriage was intact, that Ed was not having an affair, he suggested psychotherapy twice a week. I had no way of knowing whether he was the right doctor for me. He wanted to work with me, but he couldn't provide any guarantees. He simply held out some interesting possibilities.

"You might want to be less inhibited," he suggested. "More spontaneous."

Was I inhibited? This was news to me.

"Yes, I suppose so," I said.

"And more comfortable with intimacy?"

"Yes." I said. Recalling my dinner with Susan, I thought he must be right. I had never disclosed my story, not even to my closest friends, and talking to Susan that evening had left me trembling and upset.

The doctor and I began by talking about my childhood. My father had always told me that I'd had all the advantages—good schools, friends, nice clothes, extra activities like skating and piano, trips to Europe and summer camp. He felt confident that he had provided everything a daughter could want or need. And I believed he was right. I'd had a happy childhood. I'd gone to good schools and to a selective women's college.

But the doctor reinterpreted what he'd heard.

"You may have been privileged," he said. "But in many ways, you've been deprived. Emotionally deprived."

Deprived? What was he talking about? I could feel my defenses coming to my rescue, pulling a shade down over a window. Little by little the doctor continued to suggest that despite my family's comfortable position I had never had a real mother, that I'd seen my father as my mother's caregiver rather than her partner, and that the whole family had trouble expressing feelings. Our family was loosely knit and there had never been any real intimacy among us. He said my story reminded him of the Emperor's New Clothes. I had grown up in a culture of denial. It was wonderful that I'd had Mady to love and to love me, but she was only a good substitute for a real mother.

After several weeks, with defenses crumbling, I started to cry and I didn't stop. I'd never felt so miserable or alone. What the doctor had said was probably true. I began to see how much he could help, and that I needed this help, especially with language. The language of feelings. When the doctor called me "vulnerable" he surprised me with his ability to tune into my feelings. For the first time, I felt understood in a way I could never have imagined. With his help I could get answers to a lot of questions. I could learn why I blew up about minor problems and how I could manage those feelings.

As the work progressed I wasn't just irritable. I was enraged. I worried that my therapy was coming too late because much of my anger was directed at my father, who was gone. How could I vent my anger when its object could no longer feel the brunt of my attacks?

"There are plenty of opportunities to deal with anger," the doctor assured me. "That's not a problem." He didn't want to let on that he himself would become a target, and that one of the benefits of our work together was that I could "practice" expressing my feelings to people in appropriate ways. Eventually, all he had to do was respond to one of my comments with "What's that all about?" and my anger would flare up because he was making me work so hard to talk and explain. I felt like a child learning to walk.

By June I felt less depressed. At times I felt moments of pure joy. As we played with the boys or visited my in-laws in New Mexico, I had the strong sense that things were working out the way they were supposed to. Slowly, therapy was opening doors that had been sealed shut.

"Let's talk about my mother," I said to the doctor one day.

"What about her?"

"What was her illness? Does it have a name?"

"From what you tell me it may have been bipolar disorder or schizophrenia. But it's impossible to know for sure."

Did he think my symptoms fit into one of those two categories? I worried. But it turned out he didn't want to talk about these illnesses or about my mother. He wanted to keep the focus on me and my feelings about her.

~

By 1972, our family had outgrown the apartment at Ninetieth Street that had been our home since 1968. Beginning in February, when I contacted a Realtor friend, I started apartment hunting in the East Nineties. One day our broker told me about an eleven-room apartment only three blocks away, at the corner of Fifth Avenue. "It has an interesting layout," she said, "and it's just come on the market. We should look at it soon."

We went the next day. The moment Ed stepped out of the elevator and into the sunny entrance hall of the apartment, he was dazzled: He had found a bright corner that reminded him of his beloved New Mexico in dark, dreary New York. The morning sun streamed into the eastern side of the building, into three of the four bedrooms and the library. From the fourth bedroom there was a narrow view of the park.

Ed turned to me. "Let's buy it," he said.

I was flabbergasted. Had he lost his mind? "You're not serious!"

"Yes, I am. I can borrow against my profit-sharing at the bank to make up the difference between the proceeds from selling our apartment and what we can offer the seller."

"But we don't really need all this," I said. "It'll be too big—too much to take care of. And besides, this financial commitment makes me nervous."

"With Neddy and Jonathan cooped up all winter in an apartment, there's no such thing as 'too big,'" Ed said. "Look at this long hall. They'll have a great time here playing hide and seek and throwing a ball back and forth."

Many people we spoke with about our plans cautioned us. "It's the DMZ," they said. "You'll be only three blocks from Ninety-sixth Street, too close to Harlem." But I liked the idea of giving the boys more space, and we were willing to take a chance.

And so we bought Apartment 11C at 1115 Fifth Avenue, in 1972, and moved in July. Having grown up in a small eight-room apartment, I was secretly pleased that Ed had pushed hard for more space.

∼

One afternoon early in 1973, my therapist asked about Mady. By this time it had been more than four years since I'd seen her, and a lot had happened—my father's death in 1970, Aunt Ethel's death in 1971, our move, my psychotherapy. We had even found a simple weekend house to rent every other weekend in the Hudson River Valley.

Ever since Mady's return to Norway, she and I had been corresponding, with the help of either her nephew or her niece. At the bottom of the letter she always wrote a few words that looked like hieroglyphics, followed by a misshaped signature, "Old Mady." My eyes always welled up when I saw it.

On special occasions—Christmas, Easter, Mady's and my birthdays—I called her on the telephone in her private room. I sent her knitted shawls, balsam-filled pillows from the Adirondacks, and maple sugar candy—gifts for all the senses except her vision, which had never returned. And for Christmas she always asked Anne Kari to send knitted snowflake mittens to me and the boys.

"Have you ever thought about going to see her in Norway?" the doctor asked.

"Yes," I said slowly. "But the distance and the cost would make it difficult. And if I took my sons along it might be hard to spend quiet time with her."

"I think you should go. Figure out a way. She's a very important person in your life. If the name you gave her, Ma-dy—a combination of *Ma*ma-Dad*dy*—means anything," he said, "she was both mother and father to you."

What he said was so true that I'd burst into tears. He understood. Why had I denied her importance for so long? Was it because it was so difficult for my family and friends to see how she fit into my adult life? Was it because she didn't come when I gave birth to Neddy? I barely understood that I had this deep attachment to a woman who neither talked nor looked like me. But she loved me and I loved her.

For days after the doctor suggested I go to Norway, I pondered what to do. Ed encouraged me, and finally we decided that I should take Neddy at the end of our family vacation in August, leaving Jonathan at home with Ed and the housekeeper. Neddy was ten years old and he had already studied the Vikings and read about the Kon-Tiki raft. He wanted to go with me. And if the visit went well, the four of us could fly to Norway the following year.

∽

As our plane taxied up to the gate at the Oslo airport, Neddy and I saw the Norwegian flag fluttering in a stiff breeze. The sight of it, the bright red field with the blue and white cross, filled me with happiness. I knew I'd feel like a stranger in Oslo but I also felt I was coming home. Home to Mady.

As soon as we arrived at our hotel Neddy and I called her.

Mady answered the phone on the first ring. "Welcome to Norway!" she said. "Where are you?"

Her warm voice. Her dear, lilting voice. It sounded just the same.

"I can look out the window and see the Parliament building at one end of the street and the royal palace at the other," I told her.

"Then you're staying at the Grand Hotel, aren't you? On Karl Johansgate?"

"Yes, very central location."

"And very expensive," Mady said. "Kings and queens stay at the Grand Hotel. They're not looking for bargains, I'm sure of that. Couldn't you have found something a little cheaper?"

"Probably." Dear, frugal Mady. She would be disgusted with me if I reminded her that money existed so it could be spent.

The next day Neddy and I boarded the train for Kristiansand, on the southern coast, where Mady lived in the Old People's Home. The town, I had heard, was a vacation destination, with swimming and sailing; during the long summer days Norwegians anchored their yachts in the harbor. It also had many old streets and houses, open plazas, and historic churches.

I felt anxious about seeing Mady again. So much had happened during the five years since she left America. What would she be like? We would have both changed. Would she have forgotten English? Would she look a lot older? And would I be able to manage my moods?

On its way south the train rolled through tunnels gouged out of the mountains. As it pulled into the open Kristiansand station I scanned the narrow platform. When I spotted her—an old woman in a light coat clutching her white cane—I felt fearful and excited. She was eighty now and almost unrecognizable as she groped her way through the crowd.

"Mady!" Neddy and I shouted.

A strong gust of wind could have knocked her over. The other Mady, the one I remembered, the one who carried me and ran after me, was gone. Her face, once etched with delicate wrinkles, had become a landscape of mini-crevasses. Again I had to choke back tears of happiness mixed with sadness as I kissed her cheeks, hoping she wouldn't detect my tears.

A stocky middle-aged man standing behind Mady stepped forward and introduced himself.

"Hallo, Mrs. Hoyt," he said. "I'm Peder Mortensen, Tante Petra's nephew. Welcome to Kristiansand." He had driven her to the station and now he would drive us to the hotel.

I recognized his name from Mady's letters. We shook hands. He was one of her few relatives in Norway who spoke English. I thanked him for his help with our correspondence, and he assured me that Mady was being well taken care of.

"She has everything. She even takes taxis everywhere—and this is a luxury in Norway," he added.

"That's good," I said. "She always gets cold in the wintertime. She needs many layers of clothing!"

"She has a fur coat!"

"That's wonderful."

As we talked I looked at the woman in front of me: Mady was much diminished. The years had taken their toll. My mind flew back to my adolescence. My teenage rebellion had begun in eighth grade, and Mady got the brunt of it. In 1951 my New Year's resolutions—carefully noted in my diary—included "to do mostly what Mady asks me to do and not be rude to her." Many times I heard her sobbing in her room, next to mine. Her distress would make me feel so guilty I would knock on her door and ask if I could come in and apologize. If I didn't, I was afraid she might leave forever. Yet she always opened the door to me and then we hugged each other in forgiveness.

In Kristiansand we were lucky to have two sunny days, so that Neddy and Tore, the white-blond ten-year-old son of Mady's niece, Anne Kari, could play outdoors in the garden of the family's home. She lived two streets down the hill from the Old People's Home in a neighborhood of white clapboard houses. Neddy was happy to stay with Tore and play with bows and arrows before Mady and I joined the family for dinner.

We sat on the terrace and talked. We both squinted in the late afternoon sun. Other residents came over to meet Mady's English-speaking visitor. She introduced me as "my baby." Now that I was trying to feel mature and wise, the "baby" joke was not amusing.

"Ed is doing well in his job," I told her, as I tried to summarize the past five years. "After five years in the Latin America group, he has moved into a new group doing business with large U.S. corporations."

"Ooh," Mady said. She sounded impressed.

Mady and I in front of the Old People's Home in Kristiansand, Norway, 1973.

"So when are you going to have a third child?" Mady asked. "Three is a nice-size family."

I was surprised that she brought up this idea again. I thought we had settled it.

"We decided not to have another child," I said. "Two boys is also a nice-size family, and a third child would be too many. Now they are old enough so that we can do more things together. Next year—"

"Oh, that's too bad," Mady interrupted me. "I think you should have a daughter. A little girl would be wonderful."

How could she say that? It was none of her business! But I didn't want to raise my voice. I knew what she meant to say—that I was like a daughter to her and she wanted me to have the same experience. Yet I was still annoyed. It didn't take much for me to feel that Mady was giving me orders.

"But you don't know what it's like—two boys, two different schools and vacation schedules, and a busy husband. Life is too full already."

"I do know. But a girl would be so nice for you."

"Well, I can't just order up a girl, special delivery! Mother Nature might not cooperate."

I couldn't believe we were arguing like this. I knew I needed to stay calm, so I wouldn't feel guilty later. What I really needed was a gin and tonic.

"Next year we can bring the whole family. Jonathan will be eight, Neddy eleven."

"That will be wonderful," she said.

As the warm afternoon sun moved and cool shadows covered our chairs on the terrace, we went inside and took the elevator up to her bedroom on the second floor. It was small but it had three windows overlooking the city and the river. On the far side, a dining table with two chairs and a crocheted tablecloth stood in front of the windows. A side chair had a needlepoint cushion she had made—I noticed its similarity to a seat cushion she had once made for me. The gifts I'd sent her—the fragrant balsam pillow, the soft woolen Colombian shawl—were all there.

We sat down together on her bed, which was covered with a gold bedspread. There at her side I tried to imagine being blind.

"This is a nice room, Mady," I said. "It has a good view. And it's a nice size."

"That's what they tell me," she said. The lines around her small brown eyes shifted into a frown. "One day Peder and his son came up to my room. I was downstairs having lunch. They thought I should have more light near the bed, so they moved all the furniture around. When I got back to the room, I realized what they had done. I was so angry. I couldn't find anything! I made them put everything back exactly the way it was. And put my purse back under my pillow. That way I always know where to find it."

I couldn't help laughing. I could just hear her cranky, irritated voice, bawling out Peder and his son, who were only trying to help. I'd heard her petulant moods often enough. She held nothing back.

Trying to distract myself, I plugged in Mady's electric kettle, then filled her teapot with tea leaves and boiling water. We sat in silence, sipping the hot drink from her teacups and munching on shortbread.

"What time is it?" she wanted to know. We were expected for dinner with the family at Anne Kari's at six. "It must be almost time to walk down to her house," she said.

I stood up to help Mady put on her coat. Time was passing fast and I needed to make sure she knew how much she mattered to me. How grateful I was. How much fun we had, especially at Watch Hill, where she got me included in the children's afternoon games.

"Mady, I hope you know..." I began. Then I hesitated. How would she take what I wanted to say? Would she hear a thank-you? Or a good-bye? I didn't want to say good-bye. Yet maybe this visit would be our last—and I couldn't bear that.

Mady smiled. Maybe she was thinking about her own memories. "Hold my hand," she said. "It's a nice walk down the hill."

Mady knew this path so well that she was able to follow it without much help. As we knocked at the front door of Tore's house, his parents and his younger sister, Elisabeth, greeted us.

I was happy for the distraction of this gathering with Mady's relatives. It softened the impact of our departure and the inevitable let-down.

After dinner, Neddy and I prepared to leave. Anne Kari, a thin woman about my age with long dark hair, had promised to take Neddy, Tore, and me wherever we wanted to go in her car. As we still had daylight, I knew Neddy would like to go down to the wharves.

"We're going to watch the unloading of the car ferries from Denmark," I said to Mady. "And maybe we can also see the sailors climb in the rigging on the frigate *Sorlandet*, tied up at the dock."

"*Nei.* Don't go down there," she said, with alarm in her voice. "You can't tell what will happen. They steal from you. Things have changed."

I'd heard *nei* much too often. How many times did she call me back from wading in the warm shallows of Long Island Sound or the Rhode Island beaches? She didn't know how to swim.

"Don't be silly," I said. "There's still daylight after supper and people walking along the quais. Nothing will happen." I knew there was no way to keep Neddy from exploring all the activity along the busy waterfront.

"*Nei, nei, nei.* You mustn't do that. I'll be so worried if you go."

"But you've been telling me that people are so kind and helpful."

"No, I'm sorry. I insist that you not go down there where the boats are. If you do, you must call me when you get back. Otherwise, I won't sleep a wink."

"Don't impose your fears on everybody else!" I growled as I threw on my jacket and stalked out of the house. Once in Anne Kari's car, seated next to Neddy in the back seat, I started to feel terrible about getting upset.

On the waterfront, Neddy and I walked along the quai and I took a picture of him in front of the frigate *Sorlandet*. After a short time he said he wanted to return to the hotel. He had discovered the mini-bar and he wanted a soda.

Before I turned off the lights, I put in a call to Mady to tell her we were safe. But I knew the reason I was angry at her was that I wanted to make it easier to leave.

"Dear Mady," I said on the phone from our room. "I'm so sorry I got angry. Neddy and I have had a lovely time visiting you. And next summer I'll bring the whole family."

"That will be wonderful to look forward to," she said. As always, Mady had forgiven me.

~

The following June, Ed and I and the boys flew to Bergen, then took a hydrofoil and train through Stavanger to Kristiansand. Once again Peder brought Mady to the rail station and once again we treated Mady to halibut and boiled potatoes at a local restaurant. Mady continued to call Ed "Mr. Hoyt." This time, though, Peder also drove us to the coastal village of Grimstad, where Ibsen was born, and then to Mady's birthplace, Sögne, so that we could all swim off the dock at her niece's house. As our hostess served us coffee and apple cake, we admired the red and ochre farmhouses that dotted the rocky coastline across the bay.

On the day in 1976 when we left Mady to continue our European tour in Copenhagen I was in turmoil. Silent questions about how long she would live and when I could see her again tied my stomach up in knots. I wanted to visit Norway again as long as Mady was alive. After we returned to New York I booked a flight to Norway for early July 1976. I planned to visit her alone, without the rest of my family, but this was the year of the American Bicentennial, and Ed thought it would be fun for all of us to watch the tall ships sail into New York harbor. It was a historic celebration, he said, and I agreed it would be an event to share with our sons.

"Let your trip wait another year," he said. "She's still able to communicate and get around."

So I cancelled my reservation for July 1st and wrote Mady a letter outlining my new plan to come again the following summer, in 1977.

It never occurred to me then that Ed's position at J. P. Morgan would interfere with my trip. One evening at dinner Ed told me he was going to be transferred to run a new bank branch in Miami, and he was excited. So just at the time I expected to be sitting next to Mady on the terrace of the Old People's Home I would instead be organizing a move from New York to Florida.

"Miami? Why would anyone want to live there?" asked a friend when we told him about our future transfer. Indeed, our summertime move out of our Manhattan apartment into a suburban house in a semitropical climate required a big adjustment. I commuted to the hardware store on new errands, like buying equipment to remove the mildew and its pungent odor from our closet floors and shoes. Even though we had room air conditioners, I bought ceiling fans to stir the warm humid air overhead.

One day early in September the pest-control man took me outside and pointed to a small plot of ground outside Neddy's room. Little green plants were poking up through the damp soil.

"That's marijuana," he said.

"Oh?" I exclaimed. I had never seen marijuana before, not as a plant nor as a reefer.

Ned looked sheepish as he kicked the soil with his flip-flops. "You could be arrested," I said. "It's illegal to grow this stuff."

He stared down at his feet as I pulled up the plants and put them in a plastic bag. As he had found no other boys his age in the neighborhood, I kept him busy painting outdoor furniture. So I was relieved when the hot Florida summer was over and we could all fly north as we accompanied our son to his new school, Phillips Exeter, in New Hampshire. To mark the occasion he requested that we call him "Ned," not "Neddy," and we agreed. When we returned to the Miami house without him, I was unprepared for the sight of our son's forlorn room and its empty, unmade bed. During our recent summer of his rebelliousness I'd looked forward to the day when I could depend on other adults to help keep him out of trouble. Now the sight of Ned's oil paints, skateboard, and swimming trunks tore at my heart. As I sat weeping on the bed I wondered if he felt the wound of separation as much as I did.

~

On a chilly day in December 1979, I sat on the screened patio of our Florida house. The mail had just been delivered, and among the usual bills and brochures I spotted a familiar-looking onionskin envelope, postmarked Kristiansand. Inside was a typed letter signed by hand: "Best wishes, Peder." My heart sank.

Five years before, in 1974, I had asked Peder to buy flowers when the time came for his Tante Petra's funeral. It wasn't just the news of her death that made me start to sob when I realized that the time had come. What devastated me was finding a photograph neatly tucked inside the folded letter. It showed a white coffin covered with a spray of pink carnations and the inscription "With love, Sarnia and family." The coffin stood in the aisle of a church, in front of the altar.

I sat on the patio, almost breathless, trying to absorb the image.

The tall stand of bamboo next to the house sighed and swayed in the breeze as I studied the color photograph. Mady gone. Mady already inside a coffin, buried in the frozen Norwegian earth. I stuffed the photograph back in its envelope—I couldn't bear to look at it any more. Just then I heard a rustle in the dead leaves around the goldfish pond. Our cat, Lioness, was stealthily approaching, looking for geckos. Then she suddenly reared up on her hind legs to swipe at some ants marching in formation up a pink wall. I pulled her away and settled her on my lap. The softness of her fur, the playful gestures of her paws, and her prickly nails comforted me. I was reminded of how much Mady liked my cats, always feeding them their favorite delicacies. Maybe I could get along without Mady, but still keep her close, as long as I recalled her favorite things: her wisteria brooch and pearl bracelet, and the Lord's Prayer, which we recited together at bedtime.

The news of Mady's death came at a time when I was no longer in touch with her family in Kristiansand by phone. I knew she had been transferred to an intensive care facility for the elderly along the river. There, according to Peder and Anne Kari, she no longer recognized members of her family. And at the time when I saw the photograph of Mady's white coffin, I was distracted by events in my own family.

Three years after our transfer to Florida. and one week before I learned of Mady's death, Ed had been offered the much-coveted job of running the Petroleum Group at the bank's office in New York. It was a great opportunity. He would return to New York right after New Year's and commute home every weekend until the boys and I could join him the following June.

Sitting on my Florida patio, on that chilly December day in 1979, I pushed Mady's death into a remote corner of my heart. Without time to feel my loss, I buried it. As it turned out, years would pass before I would be able to confront the depth of my attachment to her and make my peace with her passing.

Chapter 15

The Global Employee

$\mathcal{B}$y the time Ed, the boys, and I arrived in New York on June 15, 1980, our tenants had moved out of our apartment. We had planned a major renovation of our kitchen and dining area, so we moved directly into temporary quarters in a neighborhood hotel. Seven months later, with our living space nicely transformed, we moved back into the apartment. That fall Jonathan began eighth grade at Dalton, a more progressive coed school than his other schools, and Ned started his school year abroad in Barcelona, where he became fluent in Spanish.

During the months we spent waiting for our renovation to be completed, I missed Florida and hated the ugly buildings around our hotel. I wasn't used to New York's noisy, crowded streets, and I had trouble sleeping. But I knew that eventually our life in limbo would end. And slowly, as we reconnected with our old friends, it did.

The following spring I learned that the *Farmington Bulletin,* the quarterly magazine of my boarding school, was going to devote its next issue to "Families in the 1980s." The editor was looking for an essay about a nanny. I phoned her and offered to write about Mady, and she encouraged me to go ahead. The essay, I hoped, would help me organize my thoughts about Mady: I had to stop playing hide-and-seek with the truth.

Since her death in 1979, her niece Anne Kari and I continued to exchange Christmas cards, maintaining the slender link between New York and Kristiansand. Despite this connection, I could feel Mady and her family slowly slipping away. I wanted to keep her memory vivid and to frame many pictures of her as she was when I was young. Yet I could find only one photo of my mother, Mady, and me.

I began the essay with a physical description—her spinsterish looks and her matronly shape in the long-sleeved uniform: no lipstick, no makeup, and no bra. "She wore her brown hair bobbed so that the waves made a series of hairpin turns from the crown of her head to the neck, ending in a sausage roll."

Like Mademoiselle, the overweight Swiss nanny who dominated the young Vladimir Nabokov's life, Mady made her presence felt after I had climbed into bed. From the dark silence of my room, with the door of our shared bathroom slightly ajar, I was acutely aware of her, especially when she turned on the light, casting a bright pink stripe across my blanket. I would hear the water running in the sink when she brushed what was left of her own teeth and put the false ones to soak in a grim smile on a glass shelf. Then the light would dim, as she followed her bedtime routines in her own room—sometimes applying a slice of raw onion to a bunion, and leaving a kitchen odor in her room.

When I had an upset stomach she prepared a mixture of bicarbonate of soda and water. Despite my protests, she also favored soapy enemas, milk of magnesia, and folk remedies like camphor oil rubbed on my chest for a stubborn cough or on my back for a sore muscle. But swollen glands were her main enemy, and she used an ice-packed rubber collar repeatedly to reduce the inflammation, until finally, in the spring of 1944, my tonsils were removed.

I included many other memories in the essay: "I snuggled with her in her four-poster bed on cold winter mornings, listening with her to Arthur Godfrey or the news. She worried and telephoned the doctor when my temperature shot up to 103. She braided my pigtails, mended my dolls' clothes, knitted my prettiest sweaters, and sewed on nametapes. And she helped adjust my lace veil on my wedding day."

I went on to explain the embarrassing fact that my nanny had stayed with our family far longer than most nannies. In doing so I had to breach the carefully constructed secrets around my mother's mental illness and her psychosurgery: "My mother returned to live with us again just as I was leaving for Farmington, at fourteen. But by this time, in 1950, she had had a prefrontal lobotomy and this meant that she, far more than I, needed the full- time attentions of a nurse to help her manage her diabetic routine and give her insulin shots. So at my father's request Mady stayed with us until my mother's death five years later."

When I saw those stigmatizing words on the page I wondered if I was brave enough to leave them there. Was it safe to tell the truth? I felt naked and exposed.

It surprises me now to read my other comments about Mady in 1981. Why was I so critical? Why did I focus on her strict economizing, her educational shortcomings, and her failure to keep me supplied with enough books because we never visited any public libraries? I remember wanting to read *The Wizard of Oz* and never finding it.

"Living with her in New York was like living next door to a giant toy store like F. A. O. Schwarz and not being allowed to window shop or buy anything," I wrote. "Popsicles, cotton candy, and Cracker Jacks tempted me, but I couldn't touch them."

Rereading my essay I felt bad that I was so harsh and unapprecia-tive. Had I forgotten Mady's delicious desserts? Floating island: little mounds of fluffy egg whites floating on a vanilla custard sauce. Thin Norwegian dessert pancakes (crêpes) filled with jam. Or her buttery mashed potatoes and Chicken à la King with rice and peas, which she cooked when a friend came over for lunch. And, above all, the birthday parties—with a chartered bus to take my class of eighteen noisy girls and me to the Ice Capades at the Roxy Theatre, and then a celebratory dinner at home.

Looking back, I know it's impossible to do an evaluation of a beloved person. Mady touched something so deep inside me that I hardly knew it was there. And losing her was the most painful experience of my life. But what I wrote in 1981 was a cool, detached appraisal, not an emotional eulogy or a deeply felt good-bye. Despite my determination to tell the truth, I was also trying to protect myself, to avoid mourning her. Then I could forget her laughter at a good joke, and the tears she wept noisily when her feelings were hurt. Every day she was true to herself. Her emotional honesty outweighed everything else, even her bleak Nordic moods, when she hinted that change is never for the better, or that our beach vacations together in Rhode Island might have been "too much of a good thing."

In the fall of 1981, the *Bulletin* was mailed out to the Farmington community. In addition to my essay, it included articles about a single mother juggling family and career and a three-generation family living under one roof. Stick-figure drawings of a traditional family, with the parents, a boy, a girl, and a brown dog, conveyed its theme on the cover. As I turned to the Table of Contents I saw that the editor, without consulting me, had chosen "My Other Mother" as the title of my essay. At first this sounded right. Later I decided it was misleading because it suggested that my two mothers were of equal importance. They were not: Mady was my primary mother. I was only at the beginning of the mysterious process of accepting her love and trying to integrate it into my sense of self. But with this publication I left the stigma closet, demonstrating a capacity for greater openness—in print at least—about my mother's illness and how it created the unusual family I had grown up in.

As soon as the *Bulletin* arrived in the mail I got a call from Whitney, one of my old school roommates.

"Sarnia!" she cried. "I never knew that about Mady and your mother! Why didn't you tell us?"

I didn't know what to say. Questions about Mady always led to my mother's mental illness—the subject I wanted to avoid. But now I had laid everything out for everyone to read. When I was younger

I didn't want to talk about Mady or my biological mother. Acknowledging my deep attachment to a woman who was an employee—a foreign, uneducated person—seemed impossible at a school full of the daughters of privilege. They would never understand. I wanted to be part of a normal family like Whitney's—one that looked like the drawing on the cover of the *Bulletin*. I wanted to claim my place in her world—meet some of the boys she talked about, visit the club where she had tennis lessons, and go home to a real mother as well as a father. Not a nanny. And because my mother had also been a daughter of privilege, it was easy to fantasize that one day my life would turn into something like Whitney's.

By the time the Farmington essay was published, a year after we left Florida, I had also made a change in my work life. In Florida I had worked as a freelance writer for *Miami Magazine* and the *Miami Herald*. Back in New York, I left the isolation of working at home and accepted an offer for a full-time job in public relations at the Cathedral of St. John the Divine, an iconic house of worship on Manhattan's Upper West Side. I took this position because I wanted the experience of working nine to five. I was also looking for solace, and what better place to find it, I thought, than in this Gothic landmark, with its choral music and the canon who walked down the long aisle swinging incense in a thurible every Sunday morning?

I needed comforting because our sons were growing up and leaving home—and me. In 1981 Ned started his freshman year at the University of Pennsylvania, and in 1982 Jonathan began his sophomore year at Phillips Andover, in Massachusetts. I also missed my Florida life and needed help adjusting to New York. Because my boss, Dean James Parks Morton, was a man of the church, I figured he might have empathy. After all, he was charged with delivering the message spelled out in Matthew 11:28: "Come unto me, all ye that labour and are heavy laden, and I will give you rest." That's what I wanted. Rest and peace of mind.

I was also interested in finding out how Dean Morton balanced his faith with the demands of a large congregation and his ambitions for a larger cathedral. At this time, 1981, the Cathedral was in one of its infrequent growth spurts. Under Jim Morton, a stoneyard had been established on the north side of the Close, at Amsterdam Avenue and 110th Street. There young people were trained in stonecutting so that the Cathedral could resume building the pair of towers on the western façade—and the stonecutters, most of them from low-income families, could learn a useful skill. A John Denver concert that year filled the vast nave to capacity, raising funds to help support the building program.

With several artists in residence—including Madeleine L'Engle, the writer, and Philippe Petit, the aerialist who had walked a wire between the twin towers at the World Trade Center in August 1974—the Cathedral bustled with activity. The Dean, a tall man with shaggy gray hair down to his fuchsia shirt and clerical collar, invited celebrities, U.N. representatives, and other speakers, like Jesse Jackson, to preach on Sundays. In January 1981, after the release of the Iran hostages, who had been held captive for 444 days, Dean Morton invited six of them, one after the other, to speak from the pulpit about "The Power of Powerlessness."

In this charged atmosphere, and under the loose supervision of Canon James Evans, I wrote press releases and developed contacts in the media. But I knew so little about television programs and personalities that I wasn't able to create large events to promote the Cathedral's activities the way Dean Morton could—and the way he wanted me to. When he told me that he had arranged for Philippe Petit to walk a wire suspended from the sixth floor of the apartment building across Amsterdam Avenue to the unfinished Cathedral tower, I was astounded. Nothing in my life prepared me to see anything but the deadly risks of gravity.

The Dean was elated.

"All the local TV stations are sending cameramen to record the event!"

"Well," I stammered, "I guess you're going to get lots of attention." How would his idea work out? I got my answer the next day when traffic jammed Amsterdam Avenue and enthusiastic crowds over-flowed the sidewalks and Cathedral steps. Philippe Petit walked the wire, and his image, with the Cathedral façade in the background, appeared on the evening news and on the following day's front page of *The New York Times*. The Dean was doing my job for me.

Canon Evans, my immediate supervisor, scratched his head and looked at me in wonder.

"I told you, didn't I, how I feel about all this?" he said.

"Tell me again."

"The Cathedral is the Dean's sandbox, and he can play in it."

It was hard to suppress a belly laugh. After almost a year of writing press releases I hated what I was doing. It was not the best way to escape my lonely writing life. I also disliked the tedium of working nine to five every day and sometimes on Sunday mornings. Clearly, I was in the wrong job.

After I quit the Cathedral, I felt euphoric. I was happy to return to freelancing. I wanted to write about the people and places I knew, do research and interviews, and send out queries to publications. I would continue looking for steady assignments from a newspaper or magazine. In this way I hoped I'd have stimulating work as well as the freedom to pursue other interests.

Soon after I left the Cathedral an old college friend introduced me to a short, stocky man with a big smile named Bernie Wohl. Trained as a psychiatric social worker, Bernie was the Executive Director of Goddard-Riverside Community Center, a private, nonprofit settle-ment house with outreach programs for children, teenagers, low-in-come adults, and seniors on Manhattan's Upper West Side. Bernie's friendly warmth and dedication to helping the most vulnerable people in that neighborhood, especially the mentally ill homeless, impressed me.

Under Bernie's leadership Goddard-Riverside Community Center had grown from a modest community agency into a huge organiza-tion. At that time the settlement house was expanding its mission to include permanent housing for the growing homeless population and college guidance for low-income high school students. Bernie needed more board members and volunteers and I agreed to join the board to help raise money.

After visits to other community programs I knew that I wanted to learn more about the professional skills that help troubled people make changes in their lives. After all, I thought, without family, financial security, and nursing care during the last seventeen years of her life my mother might have been homeless, too. This was the first time I'd ever considered her history in trying to decide what I wanted to do. I wondered if she had ever been as resistant to help as the homeless people I was seeing in the park.

It began to occur to me that if I got training in clinical social work I might also be able to figure out what had happened to my mother. In helping others I might also be able to help myself.

~

While I was volunteering at Goddard-Riverside, continuing to freelance, and trying to sort out my feelings about Mady and my mother, Ed was flourishing at J. P. Morgan. We were both enjoying our life in New York. The city seemed to have the best of everything—food, doctors, theater, concerts, shopping, and parks. And the interesting people. But because the bank regarded Ed as a global employee, there was always a chance they would relocate him. He was someone they could send anywhere.

In 1986 Ned was learning Arabic in Cairo and Jonathan was studying Mandarin in Taiwan. Ned had just graduated from the University of Pennsylvania that spring, and Jonathan had just completed his first year at Brown before transferring to Yale's China Program. Ed and I were planning to spend an August weekend in the country, and I was looking forward to having some time alone with him. We could take a hike in the forest and swim, and I could work on a couple of queries for a magazine. I drove upstate alone on Friday and as Ed arrived I was preparing dinner in the kitchen.

"I've got good news," Ed said as he put down his briefcase and pulled off his tie, giving me a hug. "The bank wants to send me to Amsterdam."

Amsterdam! I had been there once before. I remembered the Volendam women in their quaint white caps and wooden shoes and the wide streets crowded with bicycles and trams as well as cars and buses. But since then, in the early 1950s, I had been a French student. I was hoping any transfer would be to a French-speaking country. Paris was my goal.

Ed explained that he would become general manager of Morgan Bank Nederland, a wholly owned Dutch subsidiary of J. P. Morgan. He was confident that his management skills could make a difference, and that he could make the bank profitable.

"Amsterdam is at least three hours from Paris," I pointed out. I wasn't filled with enthusiasm at first. In following Ed's new assignment we would be moving closer to Ned, in Cairo, but farther away from Jonathan at Yale.

"Holland is right in the center of Europe," Ed said. "You can go anywhere from Amsterdam, by train or by car." When I studied a map I could see he was right. And so we started preparing for another move. I signed up for Dutch lessons at Berlitz and got in touch with several friends who had lived in Holland. They, in turn, gave me names of their contacts in The Hague and Amsterdam. They were all enthusiastic about their experience in Holland. And I comforted myself with the knowledge that once settled in Amsterdam I could continue to write, for it is natural, when immersed in another culture, to want to write about it.

I looked forward to life in the heart of Europe.

Chapter 16

Seven Years Abroad

Our new landlady sat on her large black leather chair as if she were enthroned. She was an elderly woman with short gray hair and the bulk of a Buddha. Her name was Grete Segall, but our Dutch real estate agent introduced her as "Mevrouw," the title for any woman in Holland, married or not.

"Nobody stands while I'm seated!" Mevrouw barked at Ed and me.

We took our places obediently at each end of the brown sofa in Mevrouw's home office, where the smell of coffee wafted in from the kitchen. We had come to sign the lease for the ground-floor apartment on the Apollolaan in Amsterdam. The apartment was located one flight of narrow stairs below the room where we sat. With her commanding voice Mevrouw made me so uncomfortable that even though the heat was turned on my hands felt cold and clammy and my breath came in short spurts. When Mevrouw's frog-like eyes met mine I felt small and powerless.

The apartment was perfect, Ed and I had agreed when we saw it the day before: a garage, a garden, an eat-in kitchen, and an easy walk from Ed's new office. All it needed was a shower stall in the second bathroom and a bookcase in my office. But I had noticed a little elevator, an umbilical connection between the front hall of the duplex apartment right above us, where Mevrouw Segall lived, and our new living room on the ground floor. The layout seemed odd in the part of Amsterdam the real estate agent had referred to as "the gold coast." What about our privacy? Would our landlady go up and down in that elevator, landing in our laps?

Sipping a cappuccino, I was filled with excitement, as well as anxiety, about moving to Europe. We were uprooting ourselves from our home in New York and taking our chances in a new country, in a new language, with Ed's new job in the bank. And now we were signing a three-year lease for an apartment owned by an imperious accountant—a woman who seemed anything but welcoming.

Ever since college I'd wanted to live in Europe. Although we had already lived in Boston, Bogotá, Miami, and New York, I was thrilled at the prospect of traveling to Rome, Paris, and London as well as to cities in Holland. As I packed up in New York I found tenants for our apartment and storage for our furniture.

But now there was the strange, tiny elevator that connected our landlady's apartment with ours.

"Don't worry," Ed said after we signed the contract. "She probably never uses that elevator. As soon as we start paying the rent there won't be any problems."

Ed was good at calming my fears, although, as I was to discover, he couldn't anticipate every difficulty.

When we finally moved to Amsterdam with our air freight, I plugged my American computer, with its transformer, into the outlet in my ground-floor office. Suddenly there was a loud pop and all the lights went out. I had tripped the circuit breaker, summoning Mevrouw and her trouble-shooting handyman, Mr. Snijders, to my office. He was a stout fellow in royal blue coveralls who smelled of cigars and left wet footprints on my area rugs whenever it rained, which was often.

"What are you doing?" Mevrouw shrieked. "Why can't you use a typewriter like everyone else?" Her frog eyes swallowed the whole room, with me in it.

Typewriter? Not a chance. I was happy to have a sleek new machine that made writing so much easier.

"That transformer could cause an explosion," Mevrouw scolded. "It could burn down the whole house."

I was more worried about what Mr. Snijders might do when he tried to fix the electrical problem. What would happen to my recent articles for the *Boston Globe*? He might delete everything I'd saved. But to my surprise he succeeded in solving the computer problem, using several transformers, and he didn't lose any of my documents. I was so pleased that I asked him to do other repairs. Soon he was coming and going at odd hours and I never knew where to find him in our apartment. I imagined myself emerging from a shower to find him staring before I could grab a towel.

One day he shook me awake from a cat nap because he thought I had died at my desk. Why couldn't he leave me in peace? And why was he dragging his feet about the repairs? Angry and frustrated, I climbed the steep stairs to confront Mevrouw.

"Well, my dear, what can I do for you?" she asked cheerfully. She sat in her favorite chair with a new portable phone on her large lap and thick reading glasses pushed back over a rebellious thatch of gray hair.

I took a deep, calming breath as I sat down.

"Our shipment has arrived and now we need help installing our washing machine," I said, smiling my way through this confrontation. "But Mr. Snijders is too slow with his work on the new shower. We need someone else to come in and help him stick to a schedule and get the job done. Can you help us find someone?"

Mevrouw raised her eyebrows. "Why did you bring an American washing machine when there are plenty of excellent European ones?" she asked. "Such foolishness. A waste of money." For a moment she reminded me of Mady, always looking for ways to economize, needling me about my spendthrift ways.

"But the Dutch ones are all small, front-loading machines," I said. "We need a larger one."

"You Americans!" Mevrouw grumbled. "It's always size that matters."

I could see we were getting nowhere and that she wasn't about to hire another workman. But I wasn't going to give up my washing machine so easily. I sat still and stared at her. I could be stubborn, too.

Mevrouw looked up at the ceiling and laughed. "Mr. Snijders had an Italian grandmother, so he has no sense of time. He's a creative artist. What's the big hurry?"

We had a good reason for hurrying. I wanted to get everything done so we could fly to Egypt to visit Ned, who was studying Arabic in Cairo. We hadn't seen him in months. So I considered my options. I could borrow an extra handyman from Ed's office. I could also change the locks so that Mr. Snijders couldn't enter our apartment. But I wanted peace, not an escalation, so I remained patient.

As I sat on Mevrouw's couch, her housekeeper placed a cappuccino and a pastry with whipped cream on the table in front of me. Mevrouw may have been stingy with her service, but she was more than generous with her sweets.

"You look tired and thin, Mevrouw Hoyt. You must have something to eat," she said in a honeyed voice I'd not heard before. "Enjoy it."

Moving across the ocean, unpacking, and organizing the house had worn me out. To make matters worse, Ed had flown off that morning for a two-day meeting in Paris, and instead of going with him to spend a few hours in the Louvre I stayed behind. I tried not to think about what I was missing. Besides, the pastry was delicious. I thanked Mevrouw and retreated downstairs, resigned to putting up with Mr. Snijders for a few more days.

A week later, when there was still no progress on the new shower, I telephoned Mevrouw. Before I could say anything, she had some questions of her own. How did I like the house? Did we have enough hot water? Enough heat? She wanted "friendship through the walls."

"Yes, the water is hot," I assured her. "It's scalding!"

What did she want now? I wondered. Was she trying to distract me by changing the subject? A new tactic in our power struggle?

"I still need the washing machine. The laundry is piling up," I said.

"Bring your laundry upstairs and my maid will take care of it until Mr. Snijders has completed the job."

But to me laundry is a personal matter—I didn't want her killing me with kindness and washing my socks as we were getting settled in our new Dutch home. Nevertheless, I gave in and took our laundry upstairs. From then on there were more cakes and cappuccinos. There was a stepladder and a vacuum cleaner whenever I needed them. Someone weeded our garden. When we went away for the weekend Mevrouw's maid fed our cat. Within a few weeks an orderly routine was established as Mr. Snijders finally finished the work I'd asked him to do.

Feeling more at home, I watched Mevrouw's comings and goings from my office window. By now, months after our arrival, I was becoming curious about her. Friends and clients of her accounting business picked her up for lunch dates. Smartly dressed businessmen held her arm as she walked slowly to their cars.

One day, Mevrouw emerged suddenly from the little elevator and seated herself at one end of my living room sofa. I sat down, as she suggested, at the other end

"I rent only to Americans," Mevrouw declared in a confiding tone of voice. "There are always German businessmen—sometimes even a Japanese family—who want to rent, but I won't talk to them. I would never get a good night's sleep."

Slowly my feelings about her changed. I stopped guarding our privacy so fiercely. I began looking the other way when Mevrouw used the elevator to sneak through our apartment to pick up her afternoon newspaper outside the front door.

One day she invited me upstairs for tea.

"Today we are going to speak Dutch," she announced. I was pleased to have a chance to practice. I told her a new story from my Dutch class, the one about the cow that wanted to be a horse, a metaphor for the recent sex-change operations in Holland. Did I realize, she asked on another day, that guilders earned in Rotterdam, invested in Amsterdam, are inevitably squandered in The Hague?

Our new friendship opened the door to a deluge of advice. I should read the Dutch newspapers, Mevrouw said, so that I could keep up with the news. Always park the car in the garage—there are vandals on the streets who steal radios. Avoid sick people and don't travel to unsanitary places. She told me which political columnists to read, where to stay on our weekend excursions, and which doctors to consult.

At times I felt like the daughter Mevrouw never had—the one to benefit from her experience and be impressed by her accomplishments.

"I speak seven languages," she told me proudly one day. "And when Carmen from Madrid first came to clean the house I realized I could make myself understood in an eighth—Spanish."

"May I borrow a couple of those languages?" I teased her. "I'll return them before we leave."

"Don't ever leave," she commanded.

Mevrouw's harshest words were reserved for American businesses. They were ruining the Dutch economy and Dutch companies. They were buying them out and firing loyal Dutch employees.

"The bank is planning to build a new headquarters here on the Apollolaan," Ed told her one day. "The old buildings in the center of town are charming but they feel like a rabbit warren. They don't work."

"What do you mean?" Mevrouw wanted to know. "They have worked for three hundred years!"

"Our New York bank—and other U.S. companies—want to affiliate with our Dutch partners."

"Huh!" she snorted. "'Affiliate' the way a wolf affiliates with a sheep! It will be more like a rape!"

"Look at Sara Lee, the giant food company..."

"Yes, I know—ten years ago they swallowed Douwe Egberts, our sweet little Dutch coffee company. In business since before the French Revolution. It's a disaster."

As it turned out, Mevrouw Segall was probably right about American businesses working in Holland. For by this time, only eighteen months into his job as general manager of Morgan Bank Nederland, Ed was miserable. He felt he had been set up for failure. I recognized the symptoms when he began exercising fanatically, jogging around the Vondel Park every night after getting home from the office, and then drinking Dutch gin before dinner instead of French wine.

I listened to Ed's complaints and tried to be empathic. His superiors in New York and Paris thought he wasn't trying hard enough to make the bank profitable, but he insisted it wasn't his fault. It was impossible to do business with the Dutch, he said. They were stubborn, and there was only one way to do things: their way. He was caught in a clash of business cultures.

It was widely known in the bank that the first of Ed's four predecessors in Amsterdam had bought the Dutch bank because he wanted a reason to travel there regularly. But it was a poor business decision. Once called Banque Labouchère and founded by Huguenots in the seventeenth century, Morgan Bank Nederland worked well on its own terms—leisurely banking for wealthy Dutch clients. Coffee and cakes were served to officers and their clients in a conference room before meetings started. There were generous employee benefits unheard of in America: a stressed-out employee could go *overspannend*, taking an indefinite leave of absence and returning to work when he felt like it. His job would always be waiting for him. With benefits like this, the bank could never deliver the profits New York was looking for.

Ed loved everything about Holland, except his job. He enjoyed the people we met as much as I did. But he couldn't continue to endure the unreasonable demands of his bosses in New York. As the primary breadwinner, with our health benefits tied to his salary, he wanted a graceful way to leave his role as general manager. He wanted to be reassigned within the bank, but he never said anything about this to his bosses in Paris and New York.

I too loved everything about Holland—the language, our new Dutch friends, the shops and fresh tulips on the Beethovenstraat, and the speedy train connection between Amsterdam and The Hague. Kroller Muller, the outdoor sculpture museum, was another favorite destination in mild weather. Even the wet gray skies, with clouds racing across the flat landscape, charmed me. I closed my eyes and ears to Ed's desperation because I didn't want to leave Holland.

~

Ed and I had lived in Amsterdam for almost two years when we flew back to America in June 1988, for a vacation with friends in Alaska. As usual, Mevrouw offered advice: We should pack half as many clothes and twice as much money.

Our KLM flight took us nonstop from Amsterdam to Vancouver. When Ed was paged on the loudspeaker at the Vancouver airport I was sitting next to him with our carry-on luggage. "Mr. Hoyt, passenger on Flight 21 Alaskan Airlines," the announcer said. "Please come to the ticket counter. You have a phone call from New York."

A chill ran through me.

"Who knows you're here?" I asked as Ed got up to walk to the ticket counter.

"I wasn't expecting any calls," Ed answered.

When he returned to the seating area he seemed flustered. "The office of the bank's president," he explained. "They want me to stop in New York on our way back to Amsterdam."

"They have no right to interrupt your vacation!" I could feel myself getting angry. "We made these reservations months ago."

"Calm down," he said. Ignoring my distress, he went back to the newspaper he'd been reading.

I didn't know what the call was about but intuition told me I wasn't going to like it. I felt caught in a plot to end our life in Amsterdam prematurely. I had only just arrived in Amsterdam in March of the year before—Ed had preceded me by several months. Hadn't the bank assured us that Holland was going to be a three-year assignment?

I was sure the phone call was about a job change. Would the bank's president call about anything else? Either they would bring Ed back to New York with a promotion or—and this is what worried me—they would send him somewhere else.

But where?

I managed to forget about the New York call as soon as we boarded the short Air Alaska flight to Wrangell. I told myself that Ed and I would be able to work things out, as we had in the past. We agreed to put any speculation about the job aside during this trip, not to inflict it on the other passengers, and to enjoy our first look at Alaska while we fished for salmon.

But by the time we had left Alaska a week later I had a lot of questions. As we settled into our seats on the flight to New York, I said to Ed, "No matter what, I hope we can stay in Amsterdam until the end of the year, and then go back to New York." We were both on edge.

"But jobs don't conform to personal whims," Ed reminded me. "Please understand."

"For God's sake," I said. "It's as though you're married to the bank. Or it's your mistress. The bank always comes first." I was almost yelling. "What about *me*? Don't I have something to say about this? After all, I'm the one who executes the moves."

"No. You're not part of the discussion. And you're being unreasonable." Ed turned away, ending the conversation.

I was getting anxious—and angry. Over more than twenty-five years of marriage I had learned that Ed sometimes had a short fuse before he exploded. Then he would apologize. But this time there was no resolution—just my resentment.

"I—unreasonable?" I was starting to shake.

"Yes! You have too many expectations."

I looked around at the other passengers, hoping no one had overheard our heated exchange—or noticed the tears that were beginning to flow down my cheeks. I moved to an empty seat several rows behind us.

When we arrived in New York, we checked into our room at the Westbury Hotel, and Ed continued downtown to Wall Street and his meeting with the bank's president. I tried to take my mind off our future by going around the corner to the Frick Museum to look at Dutch landscapes and French Impressionists. Maybe what one of the other Morgan wives had told me was true: I was nothing more than an appendage.

When Ed returned to the hotel in the late afternoon he seemed pleased and excited. He was smiling again. Maybe a meltdown had been avoided.

Indeed, there was no meltdown. Instead, Ed dropped a bombshell.

"They want me to go to Singapore and become the general manager of the branch there. Effective immediately. It's a good opportunity," he said. "If I don't take this job they will offer it to someone else. Soon."

My worst fears were coming true. "Why Singapore?" I wasn't smiling. I was stunned. I didn't want to move again, and certainly not so far away. But now, suddenly, we were running out of time.

My feet hurt from my afternoon at the Frick, and I'd kicked off my shoes. Now I stared at them as Ed began to talk. "You ask 'Why Singapore?'" he said. "Here's the reason. Looking ahead, they know that the Hong Kong office's future is uncertain with the 1997 takeover looming, and the Tokyo office has become too expensive. And they want to expand the currency-trading operation in Singapore, making it the bank's biggest branch in Asia."

"What?" I couldn't believe him. "This is impossible! We've only just gotten settled in Amsterdam."

"I don't care," he said. "You can stay or come with me—whatever you want. I can't do this Amsterdam job anymore and now, fortunately, they have given me a face-saving exit. I'm leaving Holland and going to Singapore."

His words frightened me. Maybe he was also saying that he was leaving me. It sounded like there could be no further discussion.

"But what about Ned and Jonathan?" I asked. "Jonathan still has one more year at Yale. Ned's in New York. We don't want to be so far away from them—especially not while they're making the transition from college into the real world. Doesn't that matter?"

"Oh, stop," he said. "The job in Amsterdam is impossible. I'm going to Singapore." He shot the words at me as if they were bullets.

I sat there, glued to the chair, furious. I'd never heard Ed sound so harsh. I felt bruised and hacked into little pieces.

That night I lay awake, wondering whether Ed meant to leave Holland and me, or just Holland. But then I thought maybe I should leave him. We could leave each other. Was this a prelude to divorce? Corporate life could split up couples and families in a heartbeat, and I was tired of arguing.

I believed him. He was fed up. Maybe I really was nothing more than a subordinate to the breadwinner, even though I could support myself and buy my own health insurance. But that didn't give Ed the right to be so cruel. He needed me even if he didn't know it. I'd have to save him from his own stupidity as long as he worked for the bank. I'd have to take care of our relationship. Soon enough Ed would be eligible for retirement, and we'd be free to make choices together. Or separately.

But now the bank was also putting impossible distance between us and our children. I could go along with Ed and try to make the best of our time in Singapore. Or I could find a small apartment in Amsterdam and continue studying Dutch. Or I could break the three-year lease with our tenants in New York and move back into that apartment, our family's home. Once I was living there I would be only two hours away from Jonathan in New Haven. And it looked like Ned would be working in New York, so I would see him regularly too. I could resume writing and join a writers' workshop.

The next day I went to my local library to look up Singapore. I remembered peninsular Malaya from fifth-grade geography, when it was still part of the British Empire, but I'd forgotten that since 1832 Singapore was the capital of the British Crown Colony known as the Straits Settlements, which included Penang and Malacca on the western coast of the peninsula. What I also didn't know was that while I was focused on European history in college Malaya had become Malaysia: It acquired independence in 1957, merging with North Borneo, Sarawak, and Singapore in 1963. Over the years Singapore had become a prosperous Asian tiger.

Prosperous or not, the thought of traveling to a place so unfamiliar, ten thousand miles away, and actually living there, filled me with an anxiety that was becoming familiar. What would life be like in Singapore? I didn't know anyone who had lived there, or even anyone who had been there. It would be an eighteen- or twenty-hour flight from New York, with a stop to refuel in Tokyo. And the time difference was twelve hours. The idea of moving there was daunting.

After we returned to Amsterdam from our 1988 summer vacation, the bank offered us an all-expenses-paid trip to Singapore so we could look around. We could visit a few condos, they said, and see the house reserved for the bank's general manager. Then we could decide where to live.

In early September I accompanied Ed on a brief business trip back to New York so I could meet with my old psychotherapist. I hadn't seen him in eleven years, since we moved out of New York the last time, to live in Florida. It was reassuring to hear his gentle voice on the phone when I called for an appointment. In his office, he looked at me intently as I told him the reason for my visit. "Talking through my dilemma with you will help," I said. He had a sense of humor—I hoped he could find a way to joke about it.

He chose not to. But he did offer encouragement. "It sounds as though you've gotten along pretty well since our last visit."

"Yes, I think so. But this is a curveball I wasn't expecting."

"Sure. So why don't you go along with Ed for a year? That's a reasonable amount of time. Then you'll know how you feel about living there."

A year in Singapore? In my fury I hadn't thought of a compromise. I figured it had to be all or nothing. I knew I could manage one year.

And even if I hated it I would have learned something about the region before I returned to New York. And by that time the three-year lease with our tenants in the New York apartment would be ending, so I could move back home.

When we returned to Holland from New York, I packed summer clothes for the six-day visit with Ed to Singapore. The KLM flight refueled at midnight in Dubai and then continued southeast toward Singapore. Just as dawn colored the Himalayas—jagged pink peaks stretching across the horizon—our breakfast trays arrived with cappuccinos, fresh orange juice, and warm croissants. Belted into my first-class seat I was suddenly swept up in a new sense of adventure. Living in Singapore for a while might be a good idea.

My new enthusiasm was quickly dampened when we arrived at Changi Airport and stepped outside in the equatorial afternoon. Just as a friend had warned, it felt like we had hit a wet flannel wall. And yet there was air conditioning everywhere, so we were living in two climates at the same time, one of them twenty degrees cooler and dryer than the other.

Still jet lagged, we checked into a tower suite at the Shangri-La Hotel. The king-size bed was turned down with crisp linen sheets under a jasmine garland. There were soft lights, music, fresh tropical fruits, and crimson orchids.

Two days later, while we were still enthralled with our new surroundings, the bank suddenly ended our Asian idyll. There were long distance phone calls and then Ed announced that he had to leave me alone at the hotel for a few days and visit the bank's office in Hong Kong.

"You have to abandon me, you mean," I groaned.

"I have to meet with my colleague there to discuss business policies going forward."

"Couldn't you wait a couple of days? We've only just arrived."

"I have to go."

Within an hour he had packed a clean shirt and some papers in his briefcase, had bought an airline ticket, and was out the door. Two more days alone at the Shangri-La Hotel wasn't what I was looking for, despite the luxurious setting. I wanted Ed to romance me into this adventure. Although I knew this was a business trip, I still wanted him to take the time to persuade me that he wanted—needed—me to join him in his new assignment. To help me know that I was an important part of this new venture. But he couldn't.

Looking back, I realize how bitter Ed was about his job in Holland, how angry he was that senior management couldn't understand that J. P. Morgan was expecting the impossible. Mevrouw was right: American companies really were ruining Dutch companies, trying to impose one business culture on another. Getting out of Holland was all Ed could think about. I would have to fend for myself.

Would there be anything satisfying for me in Singapore? In Amsterdam I had studied Dutch and written travel articles, and in Miami I'd worked as a journalist. What could I do in Singapore?

On my third day at the Shangri-La, while Ed was in Hong Kong, I got my answer. I took a shopping tour organized by the American Club. In the group I met an American editor and business writer who was working in Washington before she was recruited from *U.S. News and World Report* to edit *Singapore Business*, a monthly magazine owned by the Straits Times Company.

"I need writers," she said to me. "When you return and get settled, get in touch. I can use you." It didn't seem to matter that I wasn't a business writer. I looked forward to writing for the magazine and gaining new experience.

Back in Holland, we made preparations to leave. Bidding farewell to our new friends was hard, and hardest of all was saying goodbye to Mevrouw, who gave us more advice—this time warning Ed about the superstitious Chinese and their gambling habits. At our last luncheon Mevrouw turned to me and said in a choked voice, "I'm going to miss you. You've been darling tenants."

At the top of the staircase we said our good-byes. Instead of our usual handshake, I leaned down to give her a kiss, and I could feel the teary moisture on her cheek as mine touched hers.

"We'll always come to see you when we travel to Europe," I promised. "In the meantime, we will still be your darlings."

~

Ed and I flew from Amsterdam to New York, where we had Christmas with our sons, and another teary farewell. Then we flew to Singapore on December 31, 1988. We had decided to live in the bank's house, rather than a condo, and we spent a month at a hotel while workmen repaired and painted the house, wrapping it in bamboo scaffolding. After we unpacked and got settled, I called my new editor. When we met the next day for lunch she gave me several assignments.

Even before we moved in, it became obvious that we would need a staff to run this house. We were fortunate that there was already a Malay driver, Yusof, and a Tamil gardener, Suppiah, who had worked there for years, lovingly tending orchids in shaded pots.

A Filipina housekeeper came to work for us in February 1989. Marianita Fumar was a small, dark, and intelligent woman who smiled easily and addressed us as Sir and Ma'am. Having worked as a cook for many years in Singapore, she knew her way around and had many friends.

At first I didn't want to give up my usual kitchen routines. I enjoyed cooking. Ed and I had always prepared our meals together. We were not drawn to Singapore to become lotus eaters with servants. But gradually I began to appreciate Marianita's skills. She served delicious meals with pride and made an extra effort whenever we had dinner guests. I quickly became attached to her.

Ed also appreciated Yusof, the Malay chauffeur who drove the Mercedes sedan leaving Ed free to read the morning newspapers in the back seat, like a tycoon.

Toward the end of our first year in Singapore I saw a notice in the Singapore National Museum's monthly bulletin that an Oxford University Press editor was looking for writers to contribute to the company's "Old Asian Cities" series. I contacted the Oxford editor in

Kuala Lumpur. At her request, I wrote a sample first chapter for *Old Penang*. I knew nothing about Penang, but as a history major I was curious about the British colonial period and its writers, including Somerset Maugham and E. M. Forster. Following her approval of my chapter, I signed a contract to write the book and illustrate it with maps and prints.

From then on I was busy meeting people and learning about Asia. Ed, too, was busy—often flying once or twice a week to Kuala Lumpur. I used the library as an air-conditioned office on the ground floor of our house, and there I researched and wrote *Old Penang* (1991). Twice Ed and I traveled to the hilly island of Penang, which the British had used as a resort to escape the tropical heat. Two years later we drove to Malacca, in Malaysia, to talk with people and visit the places that, together with Singapore, had once been important centers in the spice trade under the Portuguese and the Dutch, as well as the British.

Happy as I was with our life in Singapore, I didn't like living so far from Ned and Jonathan. We tried to make up for our absence by spending vacations with them. We traveled to Australia during part of their summer vacation one year. When Ed and I saw Ned in Cairo in 1987, the three of us went on to Amman, Jordan, and visited the ancient city of Petra. Ned joined Ed on a trek to Ladakh, in the Himalayas, in 1992, and another year the four of us played golf at a Malaysian highlands resort.

Oxford University Press published *Old Malacca* in March 1993. I was pleased with the way my books had turned out. Ed could also look back on the five years in Singapore with satisfaction. The bank branch was growing, and he felt content with his job. We were more content with each other too. As we made preparations to move home from Singapore in October, I recalled how reluctant I'd been to move there, how anxious I'd felt about leaving Holland. Now, paradoxically, I was finding it hard to leave Singapore, where we had had such a full life. What was most difficult was another round of good-byes, this time to our Singapore friends.

I was devastated that we had to say good-bye to Marianita. Sorrow stabbed me in the chest, which I'd never expected. We had a business relationship—she was an employee. And yet she did things that mothers do—she took care of me. Wasn't that why I was crying so much as we hugged for the last time? Was I thinking about Mady? These farewell moments gave me the first inkling that all along Marianita had occupied a special place in my heart—a place I would always yearn to fill.

We returned to New York in the fall of 1993. Ed went back to J. P. Morgan's Wall Street headquarters. It was agreed that he would spend two years in the New York office before retiring in 1995.

As soon as he left the bank, Ed began to explore his options. I knew his endeavors would give him a sense of purpose, but my own path was not as clear. I couldn't figure out what direction to take. My mind had been opened to so many new places and ideas, as well as friends. I didn't know how I would use my experience to forge a new life. I felt stuck in a holding pattern and untethered to New York.

It wasn't just the noise and the traffic. I had never anticipated that living ten thousand miles away would upset my center of gravity. Where was home? Seven years abroad had made me wonder. I had trouble readjusting to American culture.

For a while we considered moving to a smaller city in the West where we had family and friends. Yet after another autumn—with the vibrant colors in Central Park and the pleasure of sleeping under blankets with the windows wide open—we realized the importance of the change of seasons. We decided that "home" really was New York, with its rich cultural life, our marital history, and the park.

Most important, our sons were in New York; Ned lived in Brooklyn and worked in Manhattan, and Jonathan was sharing a small apartment in the theater district with a friend. I assumed they would stay near us in the New York area. Yet what to me seemed like a perfectly sensible arrangement—all of us living in New York—couldn't last.

Both Ned and Jonathan were searching for partners: marriage was on their minds. In 1995, after moving to Mexico City, where he and a friend started Econergy, a clean-energy business, Ned met Anne

Wakefield, a Mexican journalist who worked as a news anchor and film critic for Televisa. They married in April,1996, and settled in Coyoacán, a Mexico City suburb. Following suit, Jonathan moved first to Washington, where he worked in the Department of Education, a job that recognized his efforts in the first Clinton presidential campaign. Then he went on to Stanford Business School and finally settled in San Francisco, where he met and married a Californian, Lisa Zahner, in 2000. She was working then in marketing technology.

I had cried about leaving Marianita. My tears had flowed when we left Holland and Singapore. Now I cried again as each of our newlywed sons moved away. To ease these separations, I organized a reunion for all the cousins in my mother's family, the Kidders and the Bulkleys. I hoped that our sons and my cousins of all ages could get to know each other.

Shortly after my mother's death, in 1958, I had become the custodian of family archives once stored in her bedroom closet. There was a scrapbook dating back to 1902 and several photo albums, including pictures of my grandmother's 1910 wedding trip to England with her new English husband. There were stacks of formal sepia prints and black-and-white portraits, and daguerreotypes dating from the Civil War. I labeled and dated them so that the whole family could see the memorabilia and order copies.

In October 1994, more than sixty cousins of all ages came to New York from Montana, Boston, Texas, New Jersey, Philadelphia, and Baltimore for a luncheon at the Cosmopolitan Club. On a side table I spread out the portraits, photo albums, and scrapbooks. Many cousins, eager to learn more about their ancestry, signed up for copies of the family photos and the calligraphic family tree.

For me, though, this was more than a social or genealogical gathering. I had an agenda. In my travels I'd been impressed by the families I'd met: They all had relatives who called, visited, helped, and stayed in touch. I hoped this reunion would strengthen ties within my loosely knit family.

But above all, I wanted the reunion to help me understand what had happened to my mother. I had reason to hope for this, because among my many cousins was Bo Kelly, the only son of my mother's first cousin, closest friend, and my godmother, the late Katharine Bulkley Kelly from Baltimore. With six married children and many grandchildren Bo was now the family patriarch. I had met him only once, long before marrying Ed. Might he have heard something from his mother about mine? I hoped he would have a clue to what might have caused her mental illness. Perhaps she had fallen and hit her head, causing irreversible damage—an accident that my father would not have known about because it occurred before his time.

Maybe Bo could share stories with me. I pinned my hopes on him.

Chapter 17

Social Work

$\mathcal{A}$ few months after our family reunion in New York, Ed and I drove to a Baltimore suburb to have lunch with my second cousins, Bo and Ellie Kelly. Since Bo's mother and mine had been close, I was hoping he would have information to share.

As we sat eating lunch on the Kellys' deck, I reminded Bo that I'd come to his mother's funeral in 1959. "And I remember meeting you both," I told him. "Ellie was wearing a black cotton dress. It was hot. And she was pregnant, I think."

"Oh, I was always pregnant!" Ellie laughed.

"Did your mother come, too?" Bo asked. "I don't remember—there were so many people."

His question surprised me. But with six children of his own, and many grandchildren, I could see Bo might have trouble remembering the people in his mother's generation.

"What happened to your mother?" he asked. "Sippy, they called her. What did she die of?"

"That's what I wanted to ask you," I said. I was pleased he knew her family nickname, but he was asking *me* the questions. It should have been the other way around. "There was so much mystery surrounding her. I thought you might have heard stories or overheard conversations."

"Not that I recall," Bo said. "But tell me about your mother. Was she sick a long time?"

How come he didn't know? I thought Bo knew more than I did. After all he was ten years older.

"She was mentally ill," I said, "and she was also diabetic. And when I was young she had a—she had a...." A chill ran through me as I paused at the embarrassing word. "She had a lobotomy. After that she seemed better."

Bo frowned as he listened. "No kidding," he said. "I didn't know that. That must have been tough for you. Sippy and my mother were so close at one time."

We didn't linger over the sadness—there was nothing more to say. "At one time" said it all; the cousins had drifted apart. We joked as we finished our dessert and coffee, and then Ed and I drove back to New York. I was happy to reconnect with the Kellys, yet it was clear that news about my mother's mental health had not circulated in her extended family. Secrecy prevailed. Everyone, it seemed, had forgotten her. But I was glad I had arranged the reunion, putting the spotlight on my mother the archivist who had preserved the family records. And my sons, who had never known their maternal grandparents, got a better picture of their own branch of the family tree. As Jonathan said, "The reunion gave me a new sense of connection and identity. I remember feeling proud to know more about my ancestral roots in New York, New Jersey, and New England."

～

Shortly after our marriage I noticed that my new Hoyt relatives were mostly male. Ed had a father, two brothers, four nephews, and ultimately we had two sons. Men outnumbered women more than two to one. Of course on the female side Ed also had his mother, her female partner, his stepmother, two nieces, and his two sisters-in-law.

But except for Diana they all lived in the west and didn't travel often to the east. Diana and I grew close over the years, and I was glad we were able to see her and Alfie and their children as often as we did. So when Alfie asked Diana for a divorce in the fall of 1984 Ed and I were shocked and saddened.

Diana was probably as surprised as we were. Ever since they graduated from college the twins, Ed and Alfie, had drifted apart. At one time they shared the same group of friends in Cambridge, but after completing their army duties they went off in different directions—Alfie into the printing business when he was marrying Diana and Ed into international economics as he and I were becoming engaged. It was only after our four sons were born within five years—Jonathan and his cousin Andrew arrived a day apart—that Diana and I started to spend time together bringing up our four boys. After Alfie left her, my sympathies stayed with Diana. She still loved Alfie, she told me.

Ed and I didn't understand the divorce. We had always thought they made a good couple. What caused the rift? we wondered. We speculated that as Andrew and Eliot progressed at school in Beverly, Massachusetts, Diana became more active as a drama coach, spending less time at home. Then Alfie's frequent absences for business travel in the Midwest must have also driven them further apart. Their divorce meant the end of our family gatherings during school holidays. Alfie moved to Milwaukee, leaving Diana in Ipswich, while Andrew and Eliot finished their undergraduate work at Harvard. For many years Ed and I didn't know much about Alfie's life.

After the divorce, Diana and her sons spent more time with her parents and siblings. We were no longer included in their trips to the cabin in Vermont. I missed her company—she was an excellent cook and we had had fun preparing meals and taking the children and the dog for long beach walks in Ipswich. Summers, we had joined her Adirondack hikes, and now they too had become memories.

Alfie also maintained his distance from us; he said he needed to live near the Milwaukee headquarters of the printing company where he worked. But Ed suspected he was having an affair with another employee. When we moved to Europe, in 1988, Alfie declined our invitation to visit Holland. "Too cold," he said. He preferred the tropics. True to his word, he visited us in Singapore with his elder son, Andrew. On that visit he confirmed Ed's suspicions—he was living with a woman he called Linda J., known as LJ. He came back to Singapore a year later and stayed with her at our house when we were traveling.

After that we didn't see Alfie and LJ for several years. In 1998 we traveled to Aspen for Alfie's younger son's wedding to Allyson. We saw Alfie and LJ then and also in 2001, at Andrew's wedding to Cecilia. But our family connection was never the same.

∽

In October 1993, Ed and I left Singapore and returned to the city where I had grown up. After seven years abroad, New York shocked me. My sensory filter—the mechanism that allowed me to enjoy the city's vitality without being bothered by its brashness—didn't work anymore. I was dismayed by confrontational behaviors. Pedestrians and drivers screamed four-letter words, cabbies gestured rudely in traffic jams, and horns honked on the streets, a sharp contrast to polite, soft-spoken Singapore.

When we left New York in 1986 I was no virgin expatriate. I had lived in South America and in two other American cities, and I'd always bounced back and resumed my New York life. But this time was different. I yearned for Singapore. It wasn't just the obvious pleasures I missed—spicy foods, sweet tropical fruits, street cooking smells of garlic, ginger, and shrimp paste. I missed Marianita, yoga practice at a friend's house, and our travels to India, Bali, Australia, Malaysia, and Indonesia. And then I'd had the good fortune to work with Azlina, my editor at Oxford University Press.

Living in Singapore had stretched my mind in new directions, challenging many of my cherished American beliefs. Prime Minister Lee Kuan Yew, admired by many Western leaders for his strategic global thinking, had a pragmatic approach to leading his island nation that made me reexamine old assumptions about good government. My liberal persona was born in my teens at the dinner table, where I argued with my Republican father about government handouts. Since then I knew I wanted to be part of a society that provides a safety net for the needy.

That's what I found in Singapore. Even with no natural resources other than the brainpower and work ethic of its people, the Singapore government houses the homeless, feeds the hungry, creates full employment, and eradicates poverty. A mandatory savings plan and the traditional extended family take care of retirement and the elderly. Abortion is legal. The country's astonishing success helped me overlook its harsh policies on drugs and weapons.

I couldn't live in Singapore for five years without noticing these contrasts. If Singapore's docile multiethnic population can thrive in a benevolent one-party dictatorship, I thought, why couldn't we in the United States, with our vast resources, take steps to accomplish similar social goals?

These thoughts made me feel like a traitor to American democracy, but I couldn't help following this mental thread. I questioned my American beliefs and my commitment to a system that often seemed corrupt, unjust, and too slow to change. Despite these political conundrums, I was sure I'd feel more at home as we moved back into the apartment and settled in. A heavy snowstorm early in January, a novelty after our long absence from chilling New York weather, thrilled us and sent us to the park on our cross-country skis.

Soon I started to contact old New York friends. One morning I had breakfast with three women who had become social workers and therapists. They were skeptical when I told them how much I liked Singapore.

"How can an American, a liberal Democrat at that, prefer the peace and security of a country ruled by a one-party authoritarian government?" the social worker wanted to know. "We hear it's a place where the censor cuts films and controls the sale of certain books and magazines. A place where political dissidents can be held without trial!"

"It's true." I nodded. "They even tried to silence me, a Western journalist, by withholding my work permit for almost a year. Vandals are caned and drug traffickers can get the death penalty. But it works. It's the right government for a small state with no natural resources in a vulnerable geographic position between Malaysia and Indonesia."

"Sounds awful." The social worker laughed.

"I doubt if most Americans would put up with fewer freedoms even if they had a squeaky-clean government and a thriving economy with full employment, like Singapore's," the therapist added.

Talk like this made my head spin. I wanted to find a way to reconnect with American life—and pull myself together—but I felt that during our uprooting I had left parts of myself scattered abroad and I feared I'd never feel at home again in America. Often, I felt like a spacecraft that had been orbiting the Earth and was trying to reenter Earth's atmosphere without a heat shield. And if I thought my old friends could help I'd have to think again, because most of them were busy with their careers, serving on boards, and doing good works. They had little free time.

I was in trouble. I knew I needed to reinvent myself and find new outlets for my energies. I had considered researching and writing a book about early American travelers to Asia—my English friend in Singapore had already done some preliminary research and he had good illustrations. I could carry the work further. But I didn't want a writer's isolation. Not yet. I wanted to work with people. I wanted to acquire new skills to make myself useful. I was already writing essays for the *Vassar Quarterly* about my experiences abroad, but I also wanted to help make a difference in people's lives.

Several of my old friends were social workers who had worked with immigrants and in mental health. They knew how to talk with people who had lost their way. I admired their expertise about family systems, homelessness, and addictions. As change agents they were also looking for ways to help our society become more equitable. In the back of my mind I thought that if I, too, worked in the mental health profession it might be easier to learn more about my mother's illness. Other social workers would take me seriously and I could learn from them.

A few days after breakfast with my friends I called the social worker and asked for advice about getting a degree. She recommended Hunter College's School of Social Work, located in our neighborhood. She agreed that in learning how to help others, either with concrete needs like entitlements, or with psychological problems, I would also help myself. I didn't know yet what kind of help I wanted to offer, but I knew I'd get more ideas when I went back to school. I was already familiar with the work of the helping professions at Goddard River-side Community Center on the West Side, where I had once served on the board. I planned to contact Bernie Wohl, its director, and ask him for a recommendation to Hunter.

I began to rethink the high price Singaporeans pay for their comforts, where people avoid political discussions at the dinner table and look the other way while their government silences political opposition. They have traded freedom for prosperity. Although they have a good government that produces access to high-quality education, housing, and employment, they have given up their right to challenge the distribution of political power.

In 1999 I applied to and was accepted at Hunter. There I chose the Casework track rather than Group Work or Research. My first internship as a student was at Gracie Square Hospital, a residential treatment center where mental patients come from other hospitals to be reevaluated. I sat with my young supervisor behind a glass partition, where we could speak and hear each other above the din on the floor. Beyond the partition patients sat on chairs and benches or paced the floor aimlessly. Many talked loudly to themselves. Others screamed. It could have been the ward in *One Flew Over the Cuckoo's Nest*. I became increasingly uncomfortable, and by the time the day was over I couldn't stop crying. At home that evening I felt so shaken that I knew I wouldn't be able to function at that hospital. The next day I went to Hunter's Field Studies office to request a different placement.

By the time I got my MSW and CSW degrees from Hunter, and my certification from New York State, in June 2002, I had had some valuable experience at the Henry Street Settlement on the Lower East Side and at an Employee Assistance Program at the Mount Sinai Hospital. I had also become a grandmother. With no daughters, I looked forward to getting to know both daughters-in-law, Annie and Lisa, and developing a close relationship with them. I watched them settle into their maternal roles, creating new growth in parallel branches of the family tree. I was thrilled with my growing family.

"Tell me your birth story," Lisa said one day when she and I were sitting in a Central Park playground watching three-year-old Owen play with a tractor. As the second daughter in a family of four children, Lisa was part of a large storytelling Swiss-Irish Catholic clan.

"I don't really know," I said. "I know my mother had a Caesarean and that she got a post-natal staph infection in the hospital."

"She didn't tell you about your first few weeks? Or what it was like the day they brought you home from the hospital? Or all the funny little things that might have happened during her pregnancy?"

I wanted to conjure up stories to share with Lisa but I had little to tell her. "No," I said. "She didn't remember much." There was silence while we pondered this odd fact.

"She probably didn't want to talk about intimate things," I said. "I believe she had a rather formal upbringing."

I had no answers to Annie's questions either. For her birthday one year I gave her a pin with an opal surrounded by diamonds that I had found among my mother's jewelry. But I couldn't tell her how or when my mother got it. Was it a gift? Or did she buy it on one of her trips abroad? My mother's jewelry had always been locked up in the safe, and I never saw her wear anything except the Art Deco emerald and diamond engagement ring my father bought her several years after they married, when he could finally afford it.

Jonathan had also given Lisa a piece of jewelry from my mother's safe, a dazzling diamond ring in an old-fashioned platinum filigree setting.

"Who wore this ring?" Lisa wanted to know. "It's beautiful!" She put it on her ring finger and admired its glitter in the sunshine.

I always assumed it came from my mother's mother or from Granddad Roberts, who doted on my mother, his step-daughter. Lisa accepted the idea that the ring came from the Bliss side of the family, and she adopted "Bliss" as a middle name for her first daughter, Sylvia.

I was pleased that Annie and Lisa wanted to know more about my family, and frustrated that I couldn't answer their questions. I was the only child of older parents, I told them, and there were no cousins my age. They were all older or younger than me. Lengthy separations from my mother had guaranteed my ignorance. And despite Mady's devotion, she couldn't provide any family history either. Meeting many of my cousins at the family reunion had satisfied some of my yearning for family connections while it whetted my appetite for more. I wanted answers not only about my mother's jewelry but also about her mental health. Why did she have a lobotomy? Now that I knew more about mental illness, I wanted to know what her diagnosis might have been.

~

After I graduated from Hunter I worked part-time at a nonprofit agency called Search and Care. Its mission was to help vulnerable seniors living alone to stay in their own homes as long as possible. The agency arranged Meals on Wheels and other services. I volunteered to match their clients with weekly visitors. Then I became a regular visitor to a woman in her eighties on East 96th Street. I tried to understand her stubborn refusal to leave her apartment and move closer to her son, her only child, in Maryland. But I could see that by helping her get necessary services, Search and Care empowered her with choice, which was important. I hoped that I would eventually become a permanent member of the small staff.

After a year at Search and Care, though, I decided to make another move. Ever since my own therapy in the 1970s and 1980s I had been interested in Freudian psychology, and I wanted to learn more about the unconscious. I was still trying to understand what had happened to my mother. So I enrolled at the Metropolitan Institute for Training in Psychoanalytic Psychotherapy (MITPP) on West Eighty-sixth Street. The program required evening coursework, therapy, group and individual supervision, and weekly appointments with several clinic patients who were taking psychoactive medications.

I realized that if I started this training in my mid-sixties I'd never finish it in time to set up my own clinical practice. But I didn't care. An important goal for me was to get the qualifying credentials so that when I approached professionals or institutions about my mother's psychosurgery—which I planned to do—they would take me seriously. I wanted to know if my mother's illness would be best understood psychoanalytically. I also wanted the experience of counseling patients with anxiety, depression, or addiction. I wanted to learn how to use myself and my knowledge to help others.

With my social work license and new training in psychoanalytic theory and practice, I felt I could better understand my mother's history. But there was a problem. I knew almost nothing about her surgery—where it had taken place and what exactly had been done. It could have been in Washington, D.C.; Hartford, Connecticut; New York; or New Haven, Connecticut.

In 1985, despite my discomfort using the word "lobotomy," I had written letters to New York Hospital (Payne Whitney Psychiatric Clinic) and elsewhere, trying to locate the right hospital. The Medical Records Department at each institution wrote back that "a thorough search had been made" but they couldn't locate any records indicating that my mother had been operated on there. Fourteen years later, in 1999, after several months of library research, I contacted a University of Michigan professor of psychology, Elliot S. Valenstein, author of *Great and Desperate Cures* (1986), a book about psychosurgery. He advised that even if the records could be located "it is highly unlikely that you will find anything useful in them." I became so discouraged that I gave up my search.

Ten years later, in 2009, I tried again. I wrote to New York Presbyterian Hospital, where my mother had died, asking for a copy of her medical records. Once again I was frustrated. "Medical records are retained for a period of ten years following the last patient care activity date for adults," the form letter said. My mother's death in 1958 meant that her records had probably been destroyed. I was too late.

I was not only looking for the records about my mother's mental illness. I often wondered about her experience as a Christian Scientist. Its rigid belief system began to be imposed on her when her mother sent her to Sunday School at age six. The legacy of a religion that rejects medical help, that advocates mind over matter, must have been confusing for her after she became diabetic; without insulin and medical interventions she would have died. No wonder she felt uncomfortable around doctors in her forties, long after she left the church in 1923, at the age of twenty-five.

~

By 2007 Ed and I were spending more time with our grandchildren. Whenever we went to Washington, D.C, we took Neddy's children, Didi and Alex, in their strollers to a local playground. And I loved being with Owen in Central Park among familiar landmarks—where I had once played under Mady's watchful eyes. I couldn't help thinking about other places I'd visited with her, places I hadn't seen for many years. So I decided to take Jonathan's daughter, Sylvia, on a short trip to Watch Hill, Rhode Island, where I had enjoyed so many happy days with Mady.

Chapter 18

Finding Mady

*I*n the summer of 1941, when the Germans occupied Norway, Mady couldn't return home to visit her family. I was almost three years old that year. To provide the vacation my parents felt she was entitled to, they sent Mady and me to a beach resort in Watch Hill, Rhode Island. She and I spent two weeks at the Misquamicut Inn, overlooking a tidal river, a place where slippery seaweed covered large, barnacle-crusted rocks along the shoreline. I loved to leap from rock to rock as Mady, always vigilant, beckoned me back to the safety of a grassy slope.

The Misquamicut Inn, Watch Hill, Rhode Island. This is where Mady and I stayed on our beach vacations in the 1940's and early 1950's.

Our beach vacation was a success and from then on, until my early teens, summer felt incomplete without a visit there with Mady. Every sunny morning we walked along the narrow paved lane lined with high hedges and weathered summer cottages, down the hill to the waterfront. Lugging towels and bathing suits, we headed toward the beach, where we spent a couple of hours wading in the shallow breakers and building dribble castles with moats and tunnels. Mady would also push me back and forth on the tall swings until I learned to pump myself into the sky. We loved our mornings, and by noon she knew I was ready for lunch and a nap.

On our walk back to the inn we always stopped to admire the bronze statue of Ninigret, chief of the Pequot tribe, which stood guard over boats tied up at the dock. But what interested me most were the tinny sounds from the merry-go-round and the vendors of cotton candy, popcorn, and salt water taffy. It would be several summers before I was free to explore these temptations on my own, because Mady didn't allow junk food or candy. Even peanut butter and jelly were forbidden. When I finally had a chance to indulge my cravings, the result was exactly what Mady predicted: I got sick to my stomach.

In those days children were not welcome at the beach in the afternoons, so after naptime the nannies who worked for the summer families organized Hide and Seek, Beckon, and other games at different cottages. They served ginger ale and gingersnaps, treats I didn't get at home. Running around outdoors with other children was a happy experience.

The sand, the rocks, and the salty smell of the sea live on in my memories. As an adult I was eager to recreate that experience. Beginning in 1996 Ed and I became summer visitors to an island off the coast of Maine. Many people judge Vinalhaven, with its pointed firs, lobster fishery, hidden coves, and high-bush blueberries, to be too far away, too cold, and too rocky. There are no sandy beaches on the island. Sometimes in midsummer there are days when the fourteen-foot tides, the frigid Maine water, and the southwest winds that come up in the afternoon make me yearn for that gentle beach in Watch Hill.

During the summer of 2008 the lure of warmer waters and softer breezes grew so strong that I reserved a room at the Misquamicut Inn in Watch Hill for Sylvia and me. I wanted to revisit my favorite old haunts and introduce them to her.

Sylvia, a city child, had reached the age of three and a half without damp salt air in her lungs, and the only sand in her sandals came from Central Park playgrounds. On the road with her parents and her brother, Owen, I began to wonder what our excursion to Watch Hill would be like. How had the decades changed this special place? Would it mean the same to Sylvia as it once did to me? I was sure the asphalt lane down to the water would seem shorter, and the cottages that once seemed gigantic would be less imposing. But most of all I wondered how long I could keep Sylvia happy so far from her own home, her big brother, and her parents. Would she like the beach? Would she delight in flying out over the sand as I pushed her on those tall swings?

On their way to visit friends in Boston with Owen, her parents dropped us off at the inn. At first, Sylvia was upset when they drove away without her. She ran sobbing after the car as it turned toward the main road, crying out for her mama. I thought my nostalgic visit was a mistake.

"Let's go down to the beach and look for some seashells," I said to her. "We can use them to decorate a box for Mom."

"Seashells?" Sylvia looked up at me. "I want to find a crab," she sniffed. "Yes. She sells seashells by the seashore," I crooned, hoping my silliness would distract her. There were other moments when I thought she would burst into tears, and I knew that if she did I'd have to try even harder to make up for her parents' absence. It made me think of the sadness I always felt when I had to leave Mady on my way to summer camp in Vermont. But Sylvia is resilient and she soon responded to my enthusiasm.

I took her small hand in mine as we set out to explore the quiet residential streets. It soon became clear that what was once a simple rustic resort, compared to the grandeur of Newport, had acquired the patina of wealth. European sports cars were parked on the carefully

raked gravel driveways. Landscaping crews stood on ladders, trimming high hedges. The simple cottages I remembered had expanded,
dwarfing their manicured lawns.

But apart from the new opulence, I could tell that Watch Hill was
going to be the same as before. Mildewed wooden furniture at the inn
smelled the same, and the screeching of the gulls as they patrolled the
waterfront or perched on tall poles still woke us early in the morning.
The air bladders on the dried seaweed popped when Sylvia squeezed
them and squealed with delight.

As we sat down for lunch at a local eatery, where they served Ritz
crackers with clam chowder, I imagined for a moment that I was a
child again, back in the dining room at the inn, my stomach growling
with hunger as I gulped my cranberry juice and smeared butter on my
crackers. I began to think that Sylvia was I and therefore, by simple
transposition, that I was Mady. In this familiar setting, with Sylvia, a
girl child like the one I had once been, my feeling grew much stronger,
just as it did for E. B. White in his essay "Once More to the Lake." I
would be busy cutting our toasted cheese, bacon, and tomato sandwiches in half or I would be saying something about how hungry she
must be, when suddenly it was Mady talking as she prepared our lunch.
It gave me a spooky feeling, as if Mady had suddenly come to life.

On Sylvia's and my first morning at the beach, the sun was so hot
that I had to cover her with sunscreen. And I bought her a sun hat
with a wide brim. She wriggled away from me, eager to run free on
the warm sand. It was Sylvia's objections to all this protection—"I
don't need a hat," she insisted—that made it seem that no years had
elapsed, that it was Mady shielding me from the sun and I protesting.
Walking back from the beach, Sylvia and I skipped over potholes in
the parking area, and one of her shoes came off, so that her foot got
scratched on the rough gravel. Her tearful outburst became mine as
I recalled the long walk from the beach back to the inn, when I was
tired and Mady had to hurry me so that we wouldn't miss lunch. And
suddenly I was inside Mady's head and heart, knowing, as I never had
before, what it must have been like for her to spend long days without

a Norwegian-speaking companion, entertaining me, someone else's child, an American child with few playmates.

I used to think it was easy to take care of an only child, especially a girl, but as I studied the hangdog look on Sylvia's face, which said, "You're a nice granny but I'd rather play with my big brother," I began to think that bringing her here alone wasn't fair. Nevertheless, I had invited her on this trip, so that I could be called back through the years to my own distant childhood. And this allowed me to relearn something time had caused me to forget: how much Mady loved me.

~

The trip to Watch Hill with Sylvia was a turning point. Finding information about Mady became an urgent matter for me. Somewhere—maybe on Ellis Island—I hoped to see her name on a list of passengers on the ship that had brought her from Norway to New York. But I didn't know which ship she had sailed on or even when she had arrived. In recent years I had become more aware of the gaps in my knowledge of Mady's story—who she was, when and why she came to America, and why she never married or had children of her own. My time with Sylvia prompted me to try to reconnect with Anne Kari, one of Mady's surviving grandnieces in Norway. Only Mady's family could answer my questions.

At first, Anne Kari and I exchanged Christmas cards; eventually we used e-mail. Our communications were limited, and I know now that this was deliberate. I was afraid to acknowledge my complicated feelings about Mady. But then suddenly I lost track of Anne Kari. After Christmas 2006, my card to her was returned, stamped with the Norwegian equivalent of "Addressee Unknown." At about the same time her e-mail address became invalid. I always expected to return to Norway one day, but I had made no plans. Now I was afraid that having postponed my visit for so long I had lost my only connection to Mady's family, and to Mady herself.

I was bereft. Why had I consigned this dear woman, who dedicated nineteen years of her life to me and my parents, to oblivion? How could I have severed my connection to her family and her beautiful country? I realized that only by continuing my search for information would I be able to probe more deeply into my feelings and find peace.

For more than a year after losing contact with Anne Kari I stared at a yellow Post-it on the edge of my computer screen. On it I had written "Petra C. Mortensen," a reminder to keep trying to find more information about her.

In December 2007, I mailed another Christmas card to Anne Kari. Once again I was disappointed when her card was returned with "Addressee Unknown." If I lost contact with Anne Kari, then I would have lost my only connection to Mady. I started to feel alarmed: Without realizing it, I had allowed my Norwegian roots to wither.

In June 2008, I decided to try again. In the Division of U.S. History, Local History, and Genealogy, at the main branch of the New York Public Library, I explained to a staff member that Mady had probably applied for American citizenship in the 1930s. With that clue I was able to locate her citizenship petition number on microfilm, with the filing date of February 1, 1937.

Then something remarkable happened. When the name Petra Charlotte Mortensen appeared on the computer screen, I began to tremble and my eyes watered. I was electrified with excitement. Surrounded by other researchers and staff librarians I had to step outside to the marble hall, catch my breath, and dry my tears. If her name was in the library's database, there had to be more information about her.

For almost thirty years—even longer if I counted the eleven years she lived in retirement in Norway—I had been privately holding the memory of Mady in my mind and heart. Now it was as if she were speaking to me and giving me a big hug. Her name—from the time I was very young I called her "Mady"—and the image of her face are always with me, but here, inside the vast New York Public Library, she was part of the historic record of immigration to the United States. My private reality was being validated and connected to the real world.

It had never occurred to me that an official document, displayed on a screen, could have the power to stir up so much love and longing.

That day in the library, I realized I was ready to acknowledge my Norwegian nanny as my real mother, the person who held me close against her soft, warm breast. She was the only one who dried my tears, sang me songs, and hovered over me when I was sick.

Grief started like a sprinkler system gone berserk, drenching my face and shirt. When Mady's name appeared on the computer screen, it shimmered and glowed. And then, as if on cue, more tears started to come—a well gushing forth from an ache deep inside me.

After this visit to the library, grief became my regular companion. It shadowed me on my long walks in the park, shared meals with Ed and me, and crawled under the bedcovers with me at night. I knew it would not leave my side until I was able to reconnect to Mady's family. As Mady's American daughter, I needed to make plans to visit her relatives in Norway.

I found comfort when I looked at the photographs of Mady taken in 1973 when she was in her eighties. There are the two of us seated in front of the Old People's Home, in Kristiansand. In a picture of her alone, she stares straight at me and smiles at the camera, even though by this time her vision is badly impaired and she can only see shadows. But it isn't just the photograph that keeps her close. The words I use to describe her on paper keep her safely rooted in my mind. Visiting grandchildren sleep in her old four-poster bed in the room next to Ed's and mine. When I tuck them in, I can see Mady at the desk, studying my fourth-grade speller and writing out new words—tricky ones like "benefited" and "receive."

~

On that day in the library, when I found Mady's citizenship petition number, I waited a while, taking deep breaths to compose myself, and then I spoke again with the librarian. She explained that if I took the petition number downtown to the Manhattan branch of the National

Archives and Records, on Varick Street, I could learn more about Mady's journey to America. At last my efforts were bearing fruit.

The next day I trembled as I took the subway down to Varick Street. There I obtained copies of several documents relating to Mady's journey and her decision to apply for American citizenship. The Certificate of Arrival, issued in March, 1931, stated that she arrived on the *Stavangerfjord* from Oslo on October 28, 1927, when she was thirty-four. Unlike some of the other Norwegian women on Mady's voyage, who planned to enter domestic service, Mady identified herself as a practical nurse.

I knew about her special training, but I was puzzled about why she came to this country to work when nurses could usually find work anywhere. Why hadn't she stayed in Norway or gone to another European destination? Mady's decision to immigrate to America must have had a lot to do with her family. It may even have had something to do with her love life, a mystery to me. I also didn't know anything about her parents, her father's work, how many siblings she had, or where she stood in the family birth order. I could only guess that her father was both a fisherman and a boat builder because the family lived by the sea. I knew nothing about her mother except that she died at age fifty-six, when Mady was twenty-three.

I decided to call the telephone number I still had for Anne Kari. It was possible that her phone number at a new address was the same as before. But when I heard a recording, in Norwegian, I didn't understand it. So I went to the Norwegian Consulate where I hoped to find a bilingual official who could translate what I had heard on the answering machine.

The cool blonde receptionist, her hair swept up in a bun, had boredom on her face. I smiled at her as I described my problem. "Can we telephone the most recent phone number that I have for Ms. Axelsen in Kristiansand?" I asked. "It has a recorded message on the line, but I don't understand Norwegian."

"We're short-handed," the receptionist said, without looking up. "It's vacation time and I'm alone here."

If she had looked at me she would have seen how anxious I was, but when I gave her Anne Kari's last address she couldn't find the Axelsens in her database.

"I can only do that if this is a family member," she said, with a hint of irritation. "That's the only way I can help."

Family. My face must have looked uncertain. "Yes, of course. Anne Kari is family," I told her. "Please. This is my only hope of finding her. I haven't seen her for years."

She looked at me with a sigh. "Why don't you just forget the past and move on?" she said.

I was panicked. If this woman stonewalled me, what was my next move? I had only a half day left to find some answers—the next morning I was planning to return to Ed at our summer house in Maine. Then I remembered that the Norwegian Seamen's Church of New York was just around the corner from the Norwegian Consulate. I called and got someone who suggested that I call back after noon when Hanne Engdal, the bilingual assistant, would be available. When I finally spoke with her, I was relieved to hear her say she could help.

Hanne entered Anne Kari's name and phone number into her computer system. Miraculously, Anne Kari's name, mobile phone numbers, and profession as a speech therapist popped up on the screen. It also showed a new address in Kristiansand. Hanne dialed Anne Kari's old phone number and listened to the recording. Anne Kari was away on vacation. When she dialed the number again, I left my message.

I thanked Hanne and left a contribution to the church. Back in Maine the following afternoon, I wrote to Anne Kari and told her that I wanted to come to Norway. I allowed enough time for the letter to reach her, and then I dialed one of the two mobile phone numbers.

"*Hallo,*" a voice said. "*Dette a Anne Kari hus.*"

"Hello. This is Sarnia, in America." My heart was pounding. I'd had so many disappointments—would this be one more? "I am your Tante Petra's girl from New York. Do you remember me?"

There was a pause.

"Of course, Sarnia! How are you? It's wonderful to hear from you!"

"I need to come to Norway," I told Anne Kari. "As soon as possible."

"Well, yes, come. We would love to see you again."

Her words brought grateful tears to my eyes. At last I was on my way back to Norway, and to Mady.

On another phone call, from Maine, Ed and I told Anne Kari about our plans to fly to Kristiansand from Copenhagen. On the phone, I was so overcome I could barely speak. I had to let Ed take over the call. I heard Anne Kari promise to meet our flight, but I wondered if we would recognize each other.

"Don't worry," she said. "You'll be the only Americans at the airport, and I remember exactly what you look like. I've seen so many of Tante Petra's pictures of you. She had your wedding picture on her bureau."

A new wave of tears filled my eyes.

"And you? I remember you had long hair."

"Not any more. I'm all gray, with short hair."

"So am I!" I laughed.

I was thrilled about our trip, and surprised by Ed's suggestion that we spend two nights at the Hotel d'Angleterre in Copenhagen.

"We'll get over jet lag faster if we stay in a nice hotel," he said.

I loved Ed's reasoning.

In the Danish capital we had two sunny fall days to wander around the old streets, and then we took an easy one-hour flight to Kristiansand. There, sure enough, as we entered the baggage claim area at Kjevik Airport, I saw a tall, heavy-set woman with short gray hair, thick eyebrows, and no makeup. Anne Kari waved to us as Ed wheeled our bags over to where she stood. There she and I embraced, a long warm hug.

Anne Kari invited us back to her apartment for tea and open-faced sandwiches before she dropped us off at the Caledonian Hotel, overlooking the container port.

"You said you liked sandwiches made the Scandinavian way."

"Oh, yes, the way Mady made them—with salmon, sliced egg, cucumber, and tomato. And lots of butter."

In the living room of Anne Kari's apartment I looked through the sliding glass door at a small balcony bursting with geraniums. Anne Kari opened the door, pointing to a large building on the hill below.

"There's the Old People's Home," she said. "Tante Petra's apartment was on the top floor, remember? The one with the best view of the harbor."

"I remember," I said. And then the tears returned, just as I knew they would whenever I saw people and places that had been part of Mady's life in Norway—the life I could never share. Anne Kari put her arm around me, as we both sobbed.

"She always said you were her daughter. A part of the family."

"I know," I said. "It's true." Anne Kari knew how much Mady loved me, how in Mady's heart I was a member of her family. But Mady could never share those feelings with me; she couldn't let my parents know how much we meant to each other. She protected them. At last I understood: Mady refused to become a plundering Viking.

"What did Mady do when she visited Norway on her summer vacation?" I asked.

"She talked," Anne Kari said.

"What about?"

"You! And your life."

Over the next few days, members of Mady's family—nieces and grandnieces—embraced me and urged us to return the following summer. Liv Simonsen, a young-looking blonde grandmother, and her husband, Sigurd, had created a genealogical chart, so that I could understand Mady's family. She explained that Mady had immigrated to America in order to help support the six young children of her widowed older sister, Anne Kristine. Liv and Sigurd also took me to the historic white church in Søgne where Mady's funeral had taken place. Finally, we drove to the little farmhouse where she grew up and where we saw the path she had followed when she cross-country skied to school. The red barn, the apple trees, the meadow, and the views of the water all reminded me of Maine. The next day Liv and Sigurd took me to the place in the graveyard where members of the Mortensen family were buried.

~

After our return from Norway I began to wonder again what had happened to my mother. For a long time something had been holding me back from looking for answers. The stigma of mental illness, probably. But in Norway I had begun to see that my attachment to Mady was so deep that it overshadowed any feelings I had about my biological mother. For Mady, always my protector, was my real mother, and Norway was the home in my heart. Norway and Mady's family helped to put my biological mother in the background, where she belonged. The emotional truth was setting me free.

Chapter 19

My Search for the Truth

On a brisk day in November 2008, I took the Washington, D.C., Metro downtown to the Gelman Library at George Washington University, where the Freeman and Watts Archives are housed. Beginning in the mid-1930s Dr. Walter Freeman and his colleague Dr. James Watts developed a technique for surgery on the frontal lobes of the brain. In this procedure, known as lobotomy, the patient's head is partially shaved, a local anesthetic is given, and a burr hole is drilled into each temple. Then the buttons of bone are removed so that part of the brain is exposed. Into each hole the surgeon inserts a blunt-edged scalpel and then sweeps it back and forth, severing the connections between the front portions of the brain and its deeper centers. Later, Freeman performed thousands of lobotomies using a modified household ice pick inserted through the eye socket into the frontal lobes.

Between 1936 and 1951 almost twenty thousand people underwent lobotomies in the United States. My mother was one of them.

Always controversial, lobotomy was a way of treating depression, mania, and various kinds of psychosis, including schizophrenia, in patients for whom no other remedy worked. Both Mady and Aunt Ethel had talked of my mother having had surgery, but I didn't know where it was done or why. For a long time I lived in ignorance about her surgery. And I had little hope of learning why my father had chosen such a drastic option. I wanted to believe he had made the right treatment choice, but I wasn't sure. It didn't help to hear the gasps from my friends whenever I mentioned the word "lobotomy."

On that day in November 2008, I spoke with the Gelman librarian, David Anderson, who promised to look for my mother's records and get in touch with me. After waiting for several weeks, and hearing nothing, I called him again.

"I'm sorry," he said. "I still have no information about your mother. Most hospitals don't keep records for more than seven years." They didn't have her records in Washington and they didn't know where her operation had been performed.

As I was waiting to hear from Anderson, I read a chapter in *Last Resort: Psychosurgery and the Limits of Medicine,* in which the author, the historian Jack D. Pressman, describes many positive results of psychosurgery on patients at McLean Hospital, a private affiliate of Harvard University Medical School, outside Boston. I was encouraged.

It was possible that my mother was operated on at McLean, but I recalled that she had also been hospitalized at Yale-New Haven Hospital—my father trusted famous institutions. I remembered that many nights during the winter of 1950–1951, when I was twelve, Mady and I ate supper without my father, because he wasn't expected home before my bedtime. It occurred to me that he might have been commuting to New Haven to see my mother.

In Maine, during the summer of 2009, I went to the Yale hospital website to resume my search. After so many false leads, I was discouraged. But to my surprise the website had a phone number for Medical Records and a person in charge of them. An administrative assistant named Nettie asked me to send copies of my parents' death certificates and to verify that I was their only child. A week after I sent her the material, she called to say that my mother's medical records had been located. They covered the period from August,1950, until May

1951. Soon a manila envelope arrived in Maine. It was almost two inches thick.

I was elated—my persistence had paid off. Still, I was terrified about what I would discover. It was strange to hold in my hands the information my father had withheld for so long. I had no idea what to expect, but I assumed there would be an explanation for the striking contrast between the flirtatious younger woman of the courtship letters of the 1930s and the embarrassing, uninhibited mother I remembered as a teenager in the 1950s.

For a couple of days I let the hospital papers sit on my desk. I feared they would be too disturbing to read. Finally, on the third day, I picked up the manila envelope and carried it to the dining table. Seated on the banquette, I stared out the window. I loved to watch the tall meadow ferns waving gently in the breeze in front of the birches down the hill. After breakfast I had seen Ed walking down the path through the meadow that leads to our dock, where the boats are tied up. I figured he was planning to bail them after yesterday's afternoon shower. It was going to be a beautiful day for swimming and canoeing, but I needed to begin reading. I needed to understand what had happened to my mother. And, as I had with my parents' correspondence, I wanted to share the information with Ed. I decided to wait until he finished bailing the boats.

For many years I had accepted the secrecy my father had imposed on our household. When Mady told me about my mother's operation I was so horrified that I suppressed the details, leaving myself with only the vaguest notions about her mental history. I knew that in 1945, when I was seven, she was a mental patient at Columbia Presbyterian Hospital, in the Westchester Division. I supposed she had other treatments—at that time patients were given electroshock—but any improvements were short term.

I waited for Ed to return to the house from bailing the boats, but it was taking longer than I expected. Staring at the Yale package, I got more impatient and anxious, as if it was going to bite me. I decided to open it. I would have plenty of time to discuss it with Ed later.

There were 270 pages, broken into several parts listed on a Contents page: Physical and Psychological Examinations, Doctors' Orders, Nurses' Observations, Metabolism Record, Social Service notes, and the History and Progress notes. Nurses recorded her meals, urine tests, and daily activities. There were thirty-one pages of single-spaced, typed notes of almost daily interviews with my mother, conducted by a Dr. Louis Micheels, the Dutch-born psychiatrist assigned to her case. These were followed by twenty-four single-spaced typed pages of Social Service notes from Marian Plant, the psychiatric social worker assigned to my father.

Buried in this chronicle of my mother's eight months at Yale were three pages titled Operative Record. They were signed by three doctors: Dr. German, the "operator" (what was an "operator"? I wondered), the anesthetist, and Dr. MacLean, the surgeon. Most important, there was a typewritten comment about the surgery itself, signed by Dr. MacLean. He described organic abnormalities that the lobotomy had revealed inside my mother's brain. Abnormalities? Did all lobotomy patients have abnormalities in their brains—is that what caused their emotional disturbances? And how did he discover abnormalities? Dr. MacLean's technical language didn't help. I would need to consult a neurologist to help me understand his findings. So I put those pages aside for later.

The Social Service notes, dated August 17, 1950, began with a sentence that astonished me. "The patient has become increasingly difficult for her husband to live with." Was my father's experience so terrible that he could barely stand to live with my mother? I knew nothing about that—I had always seen him as a kind and tolerant caregiver who carried his burden with grace. From time to time he lost his temper, but he was usually patient with her. Since 1941 she had a history of poorly managed diabetes; it was always difficult in those days to get an accurate reading of blood sugar. Her diet—portions of proteins, carbohydrates, and fats weighed on the gram scale in the kitchen—was also hard to follow because the portions had to be large enough to offset her insulin doses. And because she was so inactive, my mother wasn't hungry. No wonder she disliked mealtimes.

Looking at the Yale documents, I tried to reconstruct the history of my mother's illness and my father's struggle to help her. By 1950 something must have happened at home so that my father had to hospitalize her again. Maybe the electroshock therapy hadn't worked. He needed to find a place that could balance her diabetic diet with the insulin and try to understand her puzzling behaviors. Her hair looked uncombed, her dress was often partly unbuttoned, and most of the time she hid in her bedroom with the door closed. I wasn't allowed to enter—my friends and I had to play quietly in the living room. Marie Clark, my mother's Canadian nurse, known as "Clarkie," helped during the day while my father was at the office. But he needed help at night, too, when my mother snored, slept restlessly, or had sudden insulin reactions. Then he couldn't sleep—he worried she would slip into a coma, which would require urgent attention. My father always kept sugar cubes, a spoon, and orange juice handy for emergencies.

I turned back to the pile of papers on the table, thumbing through it as I waited for Ed to come back up the hill. On the first page of Dr. Micheels's Interview Notes, dated August 9, 1950, I read the following paragraph:

> At home she lived with her husband and a daughter who had been neglected considerably by the patient since birth. The daughter has been taken care of most of the time by the nurse of whom the patient apparently was quite jealous. She also mentioned the guilt she felt about her poor performance as a wife and mother. Since 1945, she has been frequently negativistic, retarded, and slowed down in motor activity, and would eat poorly. She would stay in her room and showed an urge to hoard money and food. Decayed food would be discovered in closets and drawers. . . . Her husband apparently has resisted for a long time her rehospitalization. He seemed to be at a "breaking point."

Neglect? Jealous? Guilt? This was the first time I'd seen these words applied to my mother. Mady, in her desire to protect me, would have kept me away from her. We would have been in Central Park or at the movies. Or I would have been playing at a friend's house. I simply had no relationship with my mother.

I looked down the hill again, wondering when Ed would finish bailing the canoe and the double-ended rowboat, the peapod. I wanted to share this information with him. I thought about the doctor and the clinical social worker who were assigned to my mother. It was hard to think of my parents as patients.

In the "Abstract," a summary of the family history, I read that my family was "loosely knit." I thought the psychiatrist was correct in that assessment.

Just at that moment, Ed walked in the door.

"The wind has died down and the water is smooth as glass," he said to me. "It's a perfect time to go for a row."

"But I'm hooked here," I said, shaking my head and pointing to the pile of papers. "I need to go on reading. This is fascinating. I'll go along later. Okay?"

Ed frowned and disappeared out the front door. I could hear him going down the steps to the basement and picking up two oars and a life jacket. I felt torn between wanting to go with Ed and needing to continue reading. Ultimately I knew he would understand.

Near the bottom of the third page I read the following:

> *After postponing her marriage several times because of "nervousness and frequent colds" it became a fact in 1934. Her husband is an extremely dependent, immature, almost childish man now in his late fifties. He worked himself through college and is now a partner in a stockbroker's firm. She characterizes him as "having made a great many mistakes, as we all do." He was opposed to hospitalization of his wife,*

feels very guilty, and asks for constant reassurance about her present hospitalization. The patient commented on her marriage. "I was not prepared and should never have done it."

I couldn't agree with the writer's judgment of my father. It was too harsh and unsympathetic. As I continued reading I became more and more immersed in the past. I could see my father in his straw hat and seersucker suit—I could even hear his voice and feel his scratchy moustache on my face. I could see my mother in her cotton wrapper and I could smell her foul breath. The hospital notes had transported me back to 11 East Sixty-eighth Street, where I would sit on a chair in the front hall and wait for my father to come home from the office so that we could do the word games in the afternoon newspaper. Childish? Dependent? I was unable to see him that way.

When my mother was admitted to Yale–New Haven Hospital in the summer of 1950, I was eleven, away at camp in Vermont. The hospital notes made it clear she didn't go to the hospital voluntarily. I could imagine the scene. My father and Clarkie opening the main door and pushing her into the building. My mother shouting, refusing to do what Clarkie asked, hitting them both with her shoulder bag, as if she was swatting flies. My mother was taller than Clarkie—about five feet, nine inches—and she wasn't easy to manage.

The intake nurse described my mother as "a thin, elderly woman with grayish hair and of average height." Elderly? My mother was fifty-two then. She was "uncooperative, depressed, jittery, and withdrawn." She had neglected her appearance so that her underwear was visible. All her movements were slowed down. Assigned to a private room, she wouldn't leave it without being urged, and she stood for long periods in a corner. There were roving movements with her eyes, frequent blinking, and evident difficulty in expressing any thought spontaneously. When asked a question, she would eventually respond, but the listener had to be patient. Sometimes, though, she would open her mouth and no sound would come out.

The details provided by Marian Plant, the social worker, and the doctor's descriptions made it easy for me to follow my father like a witness to his appointments with Miss Plant and the psychiatrist.

When Miss Plant entered her office on August 17, 1950, she saw my father sitting at one end of the sofa, his seersucker jacket folded on the cushion beside him. He stood up as soon as he saw her and they shook hands. I could easily picture their encounter.

"I'm sorry to have kept you waiting. I hope it wasn't long," Miss Plant said. She had already studied the file. A preliminary evaluation had noted some tension between my father and mother.

"I have to catch a train back to New York, but I can stay a little while," my father told the social worker.

She noticed he was fidgety, biting his nails and looking frequently at his watch.

"All I do is wait around hospitals," he said as his eyes swept around her office. "It really makes me mad."

Miss Plant looked at him carefully. He seemed depressed, the way he slumped in his seat. Deep worry lines spread across his forehead, and behind his rimless bifocals she saw his eyes blinking. Maybe it was tears; she couldn't be sure.

"I can certainly understand it would be very irritating to wait," she said. "I hope we can set up a definite time to meet when you come next week."

She stood up and opened the window. It was hot and stuffy in her office, even with the fan on.

"I don't know what information you want," said my father, Alex. "I don't know anything about psychology. And I don't know why certain questions are being asked."

Miss Plant leaned forward slightly. It was clear that my father was under a lot of pressure—he sounded defensive. She wanted, above all, to make him comfortable in this room so that he could get some support.

"My wife is a very gentle person," Alex began again. "She wouldn't hurt anyone. It's hard to see her here, where she's so confined. Just her bare room, the long narrow corridor, and the sun porch."

In the record Miss Plant acknowledged that for Alex to see his wife in the hospital would be difficult. It was always this way in the beginning with patients' families. The guilt. Wondering if they were to blame for the illness. Wondering if they had done the right thing.

"We understand that a hospitalization has many implications for the family," Miss Plant said. She wanted to sound empathic, so that he would know he wasn't alone in feeling guilty. But she wanted him to tell her specifically what it meant for him. This didn't always work. It would take time to build trust.

"I suppose I should have brought Margaret here a year ago," my father said. "But I guess it's silly to think now about what I should have done in the past."

"People always have questions in circumstances like this," Miss Plant said. Maybe he could begin to see it differently.

"All I know is that during the past couple of months I haven't been able to sleep, worrying about her."

Here it came. The man was at the end of his tether, ready to talk.

"She was driving me crazy," he went on, raising his voice in a sudden burst about his frustrations. "She wouldn't take her insulin. She wouldn't eat her meals. Whenever our daughter had a friend over to play she would retreat into her bedroom and sit on the edge of the bed for hours. All day long at the office I'd be thinking about her. And then there's our daughter. More than anything, I want her to have a normal upbringing."

This is good, Miss Plant thought. She would follow his lead. Focus on the family member who is not ill.

"Tell me about your daughter. How old is she now?"

"She's eleven. She's away at camp this summer. I'm going to drive up to Vermont and get her in another week. I'm looking forward to that."

"That will be nice for both of you," said Miss Plant.

Alex leaned forward slightly. She could see the sweat beads on his forehead.

"My wife's brother and his wife think I should keep Margaret at home. They want me to send Sarnia away, even though she's not even twelve yet, and fire the nanny! Home is the best place for someone like

I spent the summers of 1949 and 1950 at camp in Vermont.

Margaret, they insist. But I couldn't go on that way. I thought I was going to go to pieces myself."

Now Miss Plant knew she was getting somewhere. The brother. The sister-in-law. The child's nanny. It sounded like he was under a lot of strain dealing with the family, not just his wife.

"You are absolutely right," Miss Plant said slowly and emphatically. She wanted this to sink in. "I fully support your decision. The sick person should be removed. The healthy should not be disturbed."

She studied him. Even with his thinning hair he would be a handsome man if he ever had something to smile about. But now his fatigue, his upset—and the heat—made him look all wrung out.

Alex looked again at his watch. Abruptly he got up from his chair.

"I don't want to take too much of your time," he said. He cleared his throat and put on his seersucker jacket.

"But I want you to understand that this is your time, Mr. Hayes. This is time set aside for you."

"Thank you," he said. "I have to catch the next train. I'll come back in a couple of weeks. And I'll confirm the appointment in writing."

"All right, then. Good-bye," she said, shaking his hand.

∼

It was a Wednesday in September when Alex returned to the hospital for several appointments. The first one was with Marian Plant, and he was pleased to find her in her office.

"How are you, Mr. Hayes?" she asked, shaking his hand.

He looked at her carefully. She was wearing a gray woolen dress with a red velvet collar and a string of pearls. Just a kid—no more than thirty, he guessed. How could she possibly help him, or even understand what he was going through?

"The people at the office tell me I'm looking better—more rested," he said. He hated to admit how much easier it was at home now that Margaret was hospitalized. If she had stayed home much longer, he would have broken down; he knew that. While she was at Yale he didn't have to get up with her in the night or listen to her snoring when she finally got to sleep.

"You look better than the last time we met," Miss Plant said.

"Life feels more normal now," he went on. "I was getting so tense worrying about my wife and daughter. I always need to be a kind of buffer between them, protecting Sarnia from her mother. She doesn't like being with Margaret."

There was so much on his mind, he hardly knew where to begin. Yet Miss Plant seemed ready to hear about all his worries.

He noticed the way Miss Plant raised her shoulders as she spoke. It was a gesture that echoed his own helplessness. He had to admit it felt good to talk about these things but he wondered how Miss Plant could help. It was so embarrassing to have to admit that he, a man who knew how to take care of other people—who had done this all his life—was now in such a predicament, with so many problems in his own family. He wanted Miss Plant to know that he was used to taking on plenty of responsibility, that he wasn't avoiding it. But nothing was working out the way it was supposed to. Despite all his efforts Margaret was getting worse.

"I have plenty of troubles," he said. "And I wish someone could help me with them. But I've been on my own for a long time and I think I can take care of them myself."

Miss Plant leaned forward in her chair. "I can understand that you have a lot to think about now, but I want you to know that some of this responsibility can be shared. We want to ease the burdens in your mind."

He was silent for a moment, trying to think. "Well, I would like to place all the questions I have about my daughter's upbringing in your lap."

Miss Plant responded quickly. "I'd be happy to do whatever we can to help you with her. We know that a father depends on the mother for a lot of decisions about the children, especially the girls, but if the mother is unable to make them, we can think together about what would be best for your daughter."

"The main thing is I want her to develop normally. I want her to grow up in a normal environment."

Miss Plant looked up at him. "I gather from everything you've told me that there are positive signs. She's happy in school, she has friends and enjoys ice skating and piano lessons. And there's someone she's close to at home, isn't that right? The Swedish woman?"

"Yes, Miss Mortensen is Sarnia's nurse. She's Norwegian. And I think my wife is jealous of their relationship. Of course, I think it would be even worse for my wife if the nurse were younger and more attractive."

"Oh? Tell me about her."

He cleared his throat and looked at his watch. He thought he was taking too much of her time.

"Let's just say that she has never married and she's rather old-fashioned. She's not an unattractive person, but she's uneducated and she has her limits. Still, I know my daughter is very attached to her."

"It seems to me that in these circumstances your daughter would have some questions about her mother. Perhaps we can think about how best to approach this. Does she know why her mother is away from home?"

"She knows about her mother's diabetes but I've never mentioned the mental illness."

He looked again at his watch. He had an appointment with the doctor, and then he hoped to be able to see Margaret. He stood up and thanked Miss Plant. They agreed to speak further on the phone the following week.

Chapter 20

What Happened to My Mother

In November 2010, more than a year after I first looked at the Yale papers, I remembered the three separate single-spaced typed pages, two of which were headed, in small print, "Operative Record." The third page, also single-spaced, was dated February 22, 1951. Here were three more paragraphs about my mother's anticonvulsive medication. I had never heard about or seen her convulsions.

I had set these pages aside because the language was too technical. Right after Thanksgiving I called Dr. Linda Lewis, a neurologist at Columbia Presbyterian Hospital, and asked her to explain the reference to "an abnormality in the form of 'atrophy in the cerebral cortex'" of my mother's brain. What did they mean by "atrophy"? Dr. Lewis helped me get a more complete picture of my mother's illness and her significant loss of brain tissue. I began to see that my mother's diabetes complicated her mental functioning because low blood sugar can cause seizures, which in turn can cause bleeding into the brain. That would explain why I was never asked to help care for my mother. My father didn't want me to witness her convulsions. She was a lot sicker than I had thought.

The records explained that in the late fall of 1950 Dr. Micheels brought together my father and members of my mother's family to make a collective decision about the lobotomy. Most likely, Aunt Ethel, my mother's closest aunt, and Uncle Mansfield, her eldest brother, attended this meeting. The surgery was performed on December 20, 1950. I knew nothing about it.

Early in 1951, Dr. Micheels arranged to meet with my father after some additional tests were done on my mother. By that time, two months after the surgery, they would have more information, he said, and they would see just how far my mother's behaviors had evolved. Then he could help my father with discharge planning.

After spending almost two years living in Holland, I found it easy to imagine Dr. Louis Micheels as he talked with my father. Like most educated Dutch people, he spoke English fluently, with only a slight trace of a Dutch accent. I could see Dr. Micheels standing at the door of his office at the Yale Psychiatric Institute as my father approached, carrying his winter overcoat and a bouquet of red gladioli tied with a white ribbon. The doctor was a tall, dark-haired man, over six-feet-two, with broad shoulders. Wisps of prematurely graying hair made a fringe around his ears. As my father entered his office the doctor extended his arm to shake hands and motioned for my father to sit down on the other side of his desk.

"Nice to see you again, Mr. Hayes. I don't think it's too late now to wish you a Happy New Year. A Happier New Year, I should say. I know 1950 was an extremely difficult year for you."

My father acknowledged the greeting with a tepid smile that barely disguised his dread of the coming interview. He knew that Margaret didn't like Dr. Micheels; she thought he was too young. But there was much she didn't know about him, for he had not yet published the memoir about his experience as an Auschwitz survivor.

The doctor knew from earlier contacts with my parents how upset my father was. Being confronted with any kind of authority could set off my father's anger. But the doctor's training had given him confidence during family meetings, and he knew how to be empathic. He was satisfied they had done the right thing in performing the lobotomy, which had provided valuable information about my mother's brain.

He started off the interview with a neutral subject—a way to suggest his own frailty. "Would you care to join me in a cigarette?" Dr. Micheels asked, as he reached into a desk drawer and pulled out a package of Pall Malls. At least cigarettes, and the paraphernalia of smoking, could offer some distraction, he thought.

"No, thank you. I used to smoke Chesterfields. Now I just smoke a pipe, after dinner."

"A pipe is good," the doctor said. "But I can't seem to break the cigarette habit." He lit up with a lighter and took a few puffs. Immediately he felt more relaxed.

"Have you seen your wife today?" the doctor asked. "I assume those flowers are for her, not for me."

My father smiled at the joke. He hadn't been in this office for a couple of months and he noticed this time that one wall was covered with an antique map in black-and-white. "No. I plan to go upstairs to her room after this appointment."

Dr. Micheels put his cigarette down on the lip of a blue glass ashtray, reached for a manila folder, and pulled out a page of notes in pencil. He would start with the good news.

My father looked again at the map. "Amsterdam, 1645," it said inside the cartouche. It reminded him that the doctor was a foreigner—he would have preferred an American, someone closer to his own age.

"It's been two months since the surgery and Mrs. Hayes is making a good recovery. She has become more active—dressing and bathing without the help of nurses. She talks more freely. Before, she didn't want to leave her room but now she's eager to sit in the living room with the other patients. When I asked her yesterday if she was looking forward to your visit, and taking a short walk with you, she said she would like that very much. She wants to cooperate with the nurses. She even volunteered to help wash the dishes one day!"

"Well, that's a change." My father laughed. "She hasn't washed any dishes since we were first married!"

"Yes, considering her brain changes, it's amazing she has functioned as well as she has."

My father leaned forward in his chair.

"What do you mean, 'brain changes'?" he asked, frowning.

After taking another drag on his cigarette, the doctor got up from his chair and went over to the window and opened it. Maybe Mr. Hayes was bothered by the smoke.

Then he turned to my father. "I am under the impression that the surgeons, Dr. German and Dr. MacLean, reviewed the initial findings with you after the lobotomy."

My father shook his head.

"No?" The doctor looked my father straight in the eyes. Whatever the surgeons said, there was no point in beating around the bush. "What I mean is, this was not a normal brain."

My father crossed one leg over the other and scratched his nose. "What the surgeons have told me," he said, "is that ever since she started on Dilantin to suppress the convulsions there has been some improvement. There haven't been any violent seizures since then. I'm hoping to see even more improvements as we go along."

So the surgeons had informed the patient's husband about the good news, leaving out the hard truths. Now, Dr. Micheels saw, it was up to him.

"We also expect improvements," the doctor said. "But we have to face the fact that your wife was probably born with a malformation in her brain. This is not a normal brain," he repeated.

Dr. Micheels spun his chair around and took a three-dimensional model of the brain from a shelf. All its parts were labeled in black capital letters and colored in different pastels. "There is organic damage," the doctor went on. "We didn't know before we did the lobotomy just how affected her brain was. There has been significant loss of brain tissue, as seen in widened spaces between the folds of the brain. And normally, blood vessels–arteries—spread out over the surface of the brain, gradually getting smaller, like tiny capillaries. But what we found is that she has a nest of blood vessels, like a cluster of miniature grapes, in the frontal lobe area of the right hemisphere, and that nest shouldn't be there. It may have caused small leaks of blood into the brain—so that over time Mrs. Hayes's brain has been slowly destroying itself. This has been happening in the part of the brain responsible for decisions and executive functions, the part that solves problems and takes the initiative. This bleeding went undetected."

At first my father was silent. I could imagine that he had no idea what to say.

"I wonder if this was why she had so much difficulty making decisions," he said softly, almost to himself. Not hearing him, the doctor continued his explanation.

"Here, look at this model." He pointed to a place on the right-hand side of the front of the brain model. "This is where they found the nest of blood vessels. Then they cut the fibers in this area, here, which go to other parts of the brain. This disconnection reduces her personality symptoms, and relieves all the anxiety."

My father was still lost in a memory and didn't hear everything Dr. Micheels was saying. "Why did it take her so long to say yes when I asked her to marry me?" he murmured. "And even after we got engaged we waited more than a year while Margaret went back and forth in her mind about it."

Dr. Micheels listened. Soon he realized that my father had not absorbed what he was telling him about my mother's brain. The new information had just triggered a lot of my father's old questions about my mother's indecisiveness. The doctor knew he had to catch up and respond appropriately to help him understand her disability.

"More than a year. Really? That long?"

"Yes. There were times when I thought I'd lost her, when she talked about wanting to stay single. It never occurred to me that there might be other reasons for her dillydallying. I thought it was all to do with me. I thought it was her doubts about whether I'd be able to carry out my financial responsibilities. At that time, you know, we were just coming out of the Depression."

All along, Dr. Micheels had a hunch it would be difficult to communicate with my father, who was still in denial, unable to absorb the facts. He decided to talk about numbers. Mr. Hayes, like most men he knew, might understand the intangibles if he cited measurements. They might be more meaningful to someone who dealt with numbers all day, and would help him make an informed decision about my mother's future.

"We found something else when we did a brain-wave test. We do this to understand electrical activity in the brain—the charges that allow brain cells to communicate with each other. On the twenty-second of this month, we did some tests on your wife, and we recorded irregular, slow, low-voltage rhythmic frequencies, probably reflecting the motor retardation we are seeing. She measures four to seven cycles per second while a normal brain would register more than nine cycles per second."

Slumped in his chair, my father didn't say anything. He had been staring at the black-and-white map of Amsterdam with its orderly circles of canals. It was much easier to look at than the complex three-dimensional color model of the brain. He was fighting the urge to pick up the ashtray and throw it at the wall. His whole body had the look of defeat, as if he had just been whipped. Then suddenly he sat up straight, looked at Dr. Micheels, and raised his voice.

"I don't understand all this," my father said. "We come to a hospital to improve our health. Why has she worsened so much in the past ten years? She was fine during the first thirty years of her life. I met her in the 1920s and she was normal then. She was even well enough at forty to give birth. Why these problems, all of a sudden? Maybe I did the wrong thing, bringing her here!"

The doctor lit another cigarette and looked up at the ceiling for a moment. Then he went on, speaking softly.

"These changes—the malformation—they have been there all along. We just had no way of knowing they were there or what they were. Chronic severe mental illness can cause brain shrinkage and loss of brain tissue. Changes found during her surgery probably had many causes, including diabetes, the underlying psychiatric disease—I'm talking about the depression we saw when she first arrived at the hospital: the nest of abnormal blood vessels and the seizures. The seizures were likely secondary to the scars from the bleeding into the brain from the nest of blood vessels. And the electroshock therapy that she had during earlier hospitalizations may have affected all this. It was a perfect storm."

My father sat forward in his chair, legs wide apart, as if he were about to stand up. "You're giving me technical information I don't understand. Measurements of electricity in her brain, compared to other brains?"

He shrugged his shoulders. He had never thought about the brain as a source of electricity. "Why can't you tell me how this happened and what I can do to make her better? This is my WIFE! What is our life going to be like now? I'm sixty-one, Margaret is fifty-two. We still have some good years ahead of us. But all I can do with her now is take her out for a drive. Or a walk. Watch TV. Before, we used to do everything together. Golf, tennis, travel, go out to restaurants and a Broadway musical, play with our baby daughter. We had sexual relations. What's left for us?"

There was silence in the room. The doctor swiveled in his desk chair and put the brain model back on its shelf. Then he leaned forward on the desk, arms outstretched, with his hands in prayer position.

"Mr. Hayes, I know this is very difficult for you and your daughter. In psychiatry and neurology we don't have any good answers. But I think you'll see an improvement in managing the diabetes. She won't be so resistant to having her insulin injections or eating meals. She will be more compliant. Many things that used to cause her anxiety will not bother her. And that will be a relief."

My father reached for his overcoat, signaling that he wanted the meeting to be over. The doctor's office felt suffocating with all the smoke and the new information. He needed fresh air. Canadian air.

He stood and picked up the flowers and his coat. "Yes, I've already noticed that she doesn't fight back the way she used to. She does whatever I ask. I wonder if she is this easily influenced by everybody. She has even gotten mad at me recently—that means she's getting better."

Dr. Micheels smiled at the irony. He knew that the family takes the brunt of everything, even the positive developments. He opened the door, they shook hands, and my father left the doctor's office.

My mother was discharged from the Grace-New Haven Community Hospital on May 1, 1951. My father took her to the Hall-Brooke Sanitarium at Greens Farms, Connecticut, for further rehabilitation. I assume she went there for several weeks before my father transferred her to a small two-storey house in Tenafly, New Jersey. For two years she lived there with a full-time nurse—a hefty and cheerful woman name Marion Myer.

My father saw advantages to settling my mother in Tenafly, where he could play golf at his club. There she could continue her postoperative socialization during visits with her aunts, Ethel and Alma, and some of the friends she and my father had left behind when they moved into Manhattan in 1943.

But there were no advantages for me. On many weekends, in my early teens, I had to drive to Tenafly with my father to visit my mother. Mrs. Myer prepared a hot lunch for her and made me a roast beef sandwich. I ate, napped and did my homework, but without my school friends there wasn't much to do. I waited impatiently for Dad to finish his golf game so that he could drive me back to New York.

Shortly before I came home from my trip to Europe, in the summer of 1953, my father brought my mother home to the Manhattan apartment. Mrs. Myer, the nurse who had stayed with my mother in New Jersey, did not accompany her. My father had other plans for my mother's care. He assigned Mrs. Myer's job to Mady, making her my mother's full time nurse. And in doing so he left me in limbo.

By this time I was almost fifteen, old enough to enjoy more freedom both at home and at boarding school. I don't recall the moment when I heard about this shift in Mady's responsibilities. Did I even notice that her job had changed?

Arriving at Farmington, my father parked the car on scenic Main Street, in front of the historic colonial homes that had been converted into dormitories. Bright fall leaves already dotted the lawns and walks in front of the school buildings. I'm sure my father felt concerned about my mother during this outing, and he didn't want me to distract Mady from her new duties. Soon they would all wave goodbye and drive back to Manhattan, and I wouldn't see them again until Christmas.

As we walked to the dorm, Mady and my mother went ahead so that my mother could drink milk from the Thermos Mady had brought. As they passed out of view, my father turned to me and said, "You don't need a nanny any more."

I didn't ask him then where that left Mady, or what he really meant. Was he telling me to end our relationship? To stop loving her? I was excited and distracted by my new school and meeting my roommates. I wanted to like them and feel that they liked me. I didn't have time to think about Mady.

In one of her letters that fall, Mady expressed her feelings:

Dear Sarnia,

I shall not make excuses for not writing you sooner, but I really have been so busy getting everything out of the way for the painters, and now I am just as busy getting it back in place again.

Have you received the riding hat? I asked Saks to send it directly to Miss Porter's. Thank you for the card. I was hoping for a letter today but the mailman did not bring any. I know you have lots and lots of work to do, darling so I will not expect letters too *often. I do miss you, a great many times a day my thought goes to Farmington and you. I am so glad I saw your room because I can just picture you there around 9:30 when it is bedtime, and you use the flashlight.*

Bye bye for now, All my love to the sweetest girl.
Mady

I saved Mady's letters in a drawer. She was my confidante—the only person in the world who really knew how much I worried about my complexion or who could tease me about the boy I had met on the return voyage from Europe. I couldn't depend on my mother to mail me the things I needed—a polo coat, a bathrobe, jodhpurs and a cap for riding lessons—or to know about anything on my mind.

After we were settled in our crowded room on the second floor of the dorm, I noticed that each of my roommates had family pictures on her bureau. Mary Ann was the eldest of five, Whitney the eldest of four. Some of their pictures included dogs; others had boats in the background. There were framed studio portraits of their parents.

My bureau had no photographs. I wrote to my parents and asked them to send me some. Within a week they mailed me two old studio portraits—the one of my mother that had me seated on her lap when I was a few months old. In the family album there was only one photo of me with Mady.

Years later, before she returned to Norway in 1968, I often visited Mady in Weehawken. By then I was a mother of two boys, a wife with a busy husband, and the daughter of a father dying slowly of senile dementia, Parkinson's, and arteriosclerosis. Gratefully I accepted Mady's limited help with my sons. During my adult life I couldn't help noticing my father's discomfort in her presence. In his formal way he called her "Miss Mortensen." But for me she was a mother.

After my biological mother died, the mixture of relief and sadness erased any questions I might have asked. I wanted to forget her illness. From time to time I worried that the same thing, whatever it was, could happen to me. Confronted with my father's silence, I lived with mystery and confusion.

In time I began to feel differently. Becoming a grandmother in 2000 stimulated a new curiosity about my genetic makeup. After I became a social worker and a therapist-in-training, when the stigma of mental illness no longer had the same effect on me, I could speak about my mother's illness without shaking like a leaf in a stiff breeze. I could even say the word "lobotomy" out loud. I hoped that opening the historical record might yield some new insights. I knew it would help me to understand exactly what had gone wrong in my mother's brain. It would bring me closure. By 2008 I was ready to accept her story as part of my own. I no longer worried that I'd end up in a mental hospital ward like the grim place Ken Kesey immortalized in *One Flew Over the Cuckoo's Nest.*

Most important, I wanted to claim my deep connection to Mady— for her sake and mine. I had come to realize that my story was nothing like the family tales in *Mary Poppins* or *The Sound of Music,* in which the nanny helps raise the young children until they are about ten years old, and then leaves so that the biological parents can take over. Mady meant so much more to me. And yet my love for her made my father uncomfortable. It was hard for him to accept what the heart knows—that love plays by its own rules.

∾

My mother was buried in the Bliss family plot at Brookwood Cemetery in Englewood, New Jersey. She shares a grave with my father, who had made all the preliminary arrangements for her burial before his own death twelve years later. A prominent granite headstone, wide as the two caskets positioned side by side, marks their grave; giant oaks, maples, and rhododendrons shade their final resting place.

For many years I felt numb whenever I visited their grave. But now

I'm grateful to have tangible evidence that they lived and died, and that I played my role as a loving witness as well as I could. No one else knew more about their troubles than I did. I had searched for, and finally found, the truth. And that truth has given me compassion for my parents, and for myself.

Mady Comes Home

*W*hen Ed and I visited Norway in 2008, we hoped to see Mady's final resting place. I wanted to know she was at peace there. I expected that her white coffin—the one I'd seen in the photograph so many years ago—would be in the graveyard in front of the beautiful Sögne church, where other members of the Mortensen family are buried. I wanted to sit on the grass next to her headstone, have a few words with her, and pray.

But during that first visit, and on succeeding visits, I couldn't find her grave. Her nieces, Liv Simonsen and Anne Kari Axelsen, and Liv's husband, Sigurd, promised they would find her cemetery plot by the time we returned the following summer. They believed that she was buried in the unmarked grave occupied by her mother, Abel Pernilla, but that the record of her interment had been misplaced. They promised to make more inquiries to locate exactly where the coffin was buried.

I felt frustrated. Where did the church put Mady's body? In New York I had endowed a Central Park bench, with a plaque in her memory. Now I wanted to claim my connection to Mady in her homeland.

During the following summers—2009, 2010, and 2012—it was the same story. There was no grave. I thought about my parents' serene resting place in Englewood, and I wanted the same for Mady. I wanted a beautiful setting to honor her generous, loving spirit. Mady had no immediate heirs, but she had me. I was her survivor. Our connection was sacred, deep, and unique.

Finally, in 2013, I visited Kristiansand on May 17, the national holiday, and stayed with Anne Kari. A colorful parade brightened the damp, gray weather. The participants, dressed in their regional costumes, marched, sang, and waved Norwegian flags. The king spoke and an orchestra played the national anthem.

By this time Mady's relatives had still not found Mady's grave, but Sigurd, her niece's husband, had an idea, suggested by the groundskeeper at the church in Sögne. Together Sigurd and I went to the churchyard. With spade and trowel, and Sigurd's help, I dug up a kilo of Norwegian soil from the churchyard, packed it in a plastic bag, and smuggled it out of the country in my suitcase. The following August I brought that bag with me to our summer house in Vinalhaven, off the Maine coast. Like Mady's birthplace in Norway, Vinalhaven is made of granite and covered with pine trees and birches. Colorful wildflowers blanket parts of the landscape, together with ferns, bay bushes, grasses, and old apple trees.

Mady now has a final resting place in our garden. It is marked with a large, oval-shaped piece of rough granite, which Ed and I found on our property. Wildflowers and ferns are slowly taking root around it. Mady's name and dates are carved on the stone's flat surface. I consecrated this place, for to me it is holy ground.

On the 29th of August, 2015, I invited ten of our island friends to our house to help commemorate Mady's burial. I also invited Michelle Wiley, our pastor at Vinalhaven's Union Church, to offer prayers and a blessing as each person took a handful of Norwegian soil and sprinkled it around the stone. We stood in a half circle under the birches, and I explained why we were dedicating the piece of granite to Mady's memory. I told them about our unsuccessful search for her grave in Norway, and I told them about my love for her.

I stood near the stone and said to our friends: "I've asked you here today to join me in celebrating Mady, the woman who was my 'mother of choice,' not my birth mother. The time that has elapsed since her death—at least thirty-five years—has done nothing to diminish my deep affection for her. I sometimes wonder what would have happened to me if she hadn't been there. My gratitude for all that she did, not only for me but also for my parents, has grown exponentially as I watch my grandchildren grow. I mourn her passing. I think her final rest will be complete in this special place."

A piece of rough granite marks Mady's final resting place in Maine.

Then it was Michelle's turn. She spoke about Mady's grave as an altar. "She sacrificed her potential happiness as a mother so that she could provide a loving home for the children of others," Michelle said. It was true. I knew Mady could have left her job as a nanny at any time, and I also knew that she chose to stay with my family.

"What are you feeling now?" my friend Esther asked, when I finished speaking.

"Gratitude," I said. "I'm so thankful she stayed on. We loved each other. And I'm relieved that Ed and I have created this sacred place."

For years I had repressed my memories of Mady in an attempt to avoid experiencing grief about her death. Perhaps I was unable to face the fear about my own death. Now I was happy to create a beautiful reminder of her in a place where she could rest in peace.

"Love's favorite word is 'thanks,'" said Rosalie, another friend. "The language of love is gratitude."

I thanked everyone for sharing the occasion, helping to create a memorial to Mady. "This place will be a reminder about how much Mady loved me, and how much I owe her. She and her spirit have come home. Home to me."

After the Lord's Prayer and a blessing offered by Michelle, we adjourned for lunch. Then our friends left. The Gratwicks drove to their home in the village. Linnell went back to weeding her garden, Esther returned to her outdoor painting, and Mike boarded his boat to check his lobster traps. Our neighbors Katie and Burt agreed to join us as they paddled their canoe around the Cove. By this time we could see that the wind had picked up and we were going to have a hard row in our boat to Whitmore Pond.

Yet the summer wasn't over, and we knew there would be plenty of time for more excursions on serene waters, and to plant more shrubs around Mady's new grave in America.

About the Author

Sarnia Hayes Hoyt was born in Englewood, New Jersey, grew up in New York City and holds degrees from Vassar College and Hunter College School of Social Work. With her husband she travelled widely, lived on four continents, raised two sons, and worked as a teacher, publicist, and freelance writer. She is the author of *Old Penang* (1991) and *Old Malacca* (1993), both published by Oxford University Press. After living abroad for several years she returned to Manhattan to become a social worker and to solve an old family mystery. Why were there two mothers in her childhood home—one serving as a substitute for the other?